HORN OF
THE HUNTER

Books by Robert C. Ruark

HORN OF THE HUNTER

GRENADINE'S SPAWN

ONE FOR THE ROAD

I DIDN'T KNOW IT WAS LOADED

GRENADINE ETCHING

HORN OF
THE HUNTER

Robert C. Ruark

With 32 Drawings by the Author
and 32 Pages of Photographs

SAFARI PRESS INC.

Ruark, Robert

Safari Press Inc.

1996, Long Beach, California

ISBN 1-57157-023-3

Library of Congress Catalog Card Number: 2002104462

Readers wishing to receive the Safari Press catalog, featuring many fine books on big-game hunting, wingshooting, and sporting firearms, should write to Safari Press Inc., P.O. Box 3095, Long Beach, CA 90803, USA. Tel: (714)894-9080 or visit our Web site at www.safaripress.com.

DEDICATION

This book is for Harry Selby of Nanyuki, Kenya,
and for our good friends
Juma, Kidogo, Adam, Chabani, Chalo, Katunga, Ali, Karioki,
Chege, Mala, Gitau, Gathiru, Kaluku, and Kibiriti,
all good men of assorted tribes.

Author's Note

THIS is a book about Africa in which I have tried to avoid most of the foolishness, personal heroism, and general exaggeration which usually attend works of this sort. It is a book important only to the writer and has no sociological significance whatsoever.

HORN OF
THE HUNTER

Chapter 1

IT WAS very late the first day out of Nairobi when Harry
turned the jeep off the dim track he was following
through the high, dusty grass and veered her in toward
a black jaggedness of trees. The moon was rising high over a
forlorn hill and it had begun to turn nasty cold. The jeep
bumped and lurched and stalled once. She wasn't really a
jeep, but a kind of glorified jeep that the British call a Land
Rover. We had named her Jessica, figuring that to be a nice
name for a jeep, and Jessica, by temperament, seemed considerably more jeep than rover.

In the glare of Jessica's headlights the trees profiled more
clearly now. Harry flicked the searchlight upward and said:
"Lots of dead stuff. And water, too, down in that donga. I
expect we'd best camp here. *Memsaab* stiff and sore?"

The *memsaab* said with considerable feeling that she was
about as goddamned stiff and as goddamned sore as a girl
figured to get after riding from 8 A.M. over no roads in a goddamned jungle until past 9 P.M. Harry made a little depreca-
tory cluck and at the profanity suggested that he had a
priceless bottle of scotch someone in Nairobi had given him,
which would make a world of difference to anybody. He
turned to Chabani, the Wa-Kibuyu car boy.

"*Na kuja* lorry?" he asked.

"*Ndio,*" Chabani said.

"*Wapi pombe?*" Harry asked.

"*Hapa,*" Chabani said. "*Kariba.*"

The black boy handed Harry the bottle of scotch. "*Magi kwa bwana,*" he told the black boy, who crawled out of the jeep, and bled two cupfuls of water—now cold from condensation—from the tied canvas bags of water that were lashed to the steel uprights that supported Jessica's canvas top. The dust and little wiggly things settled in the water. The scotch burnt through the water going down. It stayed warm when it got down, lighting a tiny little furnace in the stomach.

"Painkiller," Harry said. "Cures everything. We'll make a nice *campi* here soon's the lorry comes up."

We could see the lorry, overloaded and grotesque with a dozen black boys making silhouettes from the tarpaulin-lashed top, lumbering and complaining and wallowing along. She had stuck herself like a contrary cow twice that day already. We watched her lights leave the track and turn in toward us. All of a sudden her lights pointed upward and her black shape lurched and stopped.

"Oh, Christ," Harry said. "Pig hole. You two wait here with the bottle and one of the water bags. I'll send Chabani back with some camp chairs and have him do up a fire while we wrestle the old girl out of her troubles."

He said something swiftly in Swahili to Chabani, who began to untie the dead Tommy ram from the spare tire on Jessica's bonnet, where it had been lashed down a couple of hours before when Harry shot it just at dusk. Chabani dumped it on the ground and took a *panga*, a big, curved, sawbacked knife, out of the back seat and dropped it on the ground by the dead Thomson gazelle. Then he tortured out the heavy, square green wooden chop box and put two canvas cushions from Jessica's hard front seat on it. He pointed to the chop box, smiled cheerlessly, and said: "Sit." Then he took the *panga* and disappeared into the grove of flat-topped thorn acacias. We could hear him breaking dried branches. Harry climbed back into the jeep and drove off to check on the lorry's sad condition.

Jinny looked at me with a very small, pinched face. She was wearing my trench coat and looked very small, although she is not small, and very miserable, although she does not have the face for misery. I poured her another drink into the gay red plastic cups and took one myself off the top of the bottle of Harry's whisky. It didn't taste any nastier.

I looked down at the dead Tommy, at the hole in his shoulder, centered exactly on the point and traversing all the way through him where Harry had shot him with the little Mannlicher. I was glad I had no license for Kenya and that it would be two more days before I would be allowed to shoot in Tanganyika. I wanted to see more of it first.

Harry had shot the Tommy ram swiftly and competently. We had not seen much game that day. Just on dusk we passed a few wildebeest and an odd zebra or two and began to see the Thomson gazelles in groups of a dozen. They were beautiful and dainty with their sharp, straight black horns curving a little at the tip, and the black bars on the gold hides just over the white stomach hair. We came along at dusk into a large herd of a hundred or more and Harry stopped the jeep suddenly.

"*Toa bundouki,* Chabani," he said. "*Kidogo.*" He turned half apologetically, like a schoolboy asking for permission to leave the room. "If you don't mind," he said, "I think I'll just nip out and shoot one of those Tommies for the boys' supper. They've been lying around town for a month and they're fair starved for red meat."

He got out and held the door open. "Care to come with me?"

I followed him, clumsily imitating the half crouch he used, and after half a hundred yards he stopped and held one hand downward, palm toward me. I stopped, and he crouched on his hams, both feet planted firmly in the short, crisp dry grass. The Tommies were moving off, not spooked but suspicious and shy, at least two hundred yards away. I could barely make out the flashes of buff against the Tommy-colored background. Only a little white blur caused by the flicking of their tails caught my city eyes. I wondered how a man could say definitely he was going to shoot anything and know to himself that he meant it and could produce it.

Harry was aiming swiftly at one of them—I couldn't tell which—and as soon as the gun came up to his left eye he seemed to fire. The little gun made an unconscionable amount of noise, and you could hear the bullet hit like a wet boxing glove on a sand bag.

"*Piga*," Selby said to himself. "*Kufa*." He turned to me. "He'll be dead just over there. I saw his tail stop when he took off. Always tell by the tail on Tommy. When it stops that circular motion, he's dead and just doesn't know it. Got this one through the shoulder."

We walked over to where the Tommies had been, and after about three hundred yards Harry pointed. "There," he said. I couldn't see anything.

"We'll just wait a bit until the lorry comes up. I usually have one of the Mohammedans in the Rover to make the religious thing, but Chabani is Ky-uke and no Moslem. We'll just let one of the boys leap off the lorry and do a *hallal*—cut its throat—so everything will be nice and legal."

The lorry came alongside, and one of the men, one with a white flat fez, leaped off and took a knife out of a sheath.

"*Pandi hi,*" Harry said, pointing. The boy raced off with long bounds and bent over something. He touched at it hesitantly with his knife, stood up straight, spread his hands, and made a little shrug.

"Too bad," Harry said. "It's too dead to be *hallaled.* They're not supposed to cut the throat unless it's a wee little bit alive, or the *hallal* doesn't count with Allah or Mohammed or whoever's watching. Pity. About half my boys are Mohammedans, especially the Wakambas. Moslemism is very popular with the Wakambas these days. Gives them great style. Not that they know what the hell the priest is saying half the time when they go to the *mousquetina.* Oh well. Let's go and collect the dinner. He ought to be tender. I chose a young buck."

The Tommy was lying dead. He looked clean and very fresh and sweet-smelling and seemed undisturbed by the small bullet, which had taken him on the shoulder and gone all the way through.

"He'll be fine," Harry said. "Pity about the Moslems, though. I shouldn't be at all surprised if there's not some finger-crossing and a few broken articles of faith tonight. Those boys get ravenous for meat when they're lying around town between safaris. When we get into real game country and start bringing in masses of meat they'll all have the belly-ache for a week. They eat up to twelve pounds of meat a day, you know. *Each.* All that rich meat is pure hell on the tummy after it's been used to a diet of nothing but mealie porridge. Here, Chabani," he said as the jeep drove up, Chabani proud and show-offish as he drove alongside the new Memsaab. "*Hapa.*" Chabani got out, produced a coil of rope off the bumper, and heaved the Tommy onto the hood, where he lashed it to the tire. It bled a little into the circle of the wheel. It was the first dead thing I had seen in Africa, and I began to wonder, with considerable nervousness, if I would be up to the task of feeding fifteen people who considered ten pounds of meat per diem, per each, a bare necessity of living. I knew what I could do with a shotgun. I did not know what I could do with all the fancy rifles I had, owing to never having shot any sort of rifle at anything but a target at the Campfire Club.

I was still wondering as we sat on the chop box, drinking whisky and water and waiting for Harry to come back with the lorry. Chabani had dropped an armload of dried, dead limbs and twigs a few feet away from the dead Tommy ram. He came over, asked me for a match, and then scuffed a handful of the dried grass from between his big flat feet in their tattered tan tennis shoes. He lit the handful of grass with a match, blowing on it carefully, and then started to feed it twigs, one by one, each no bigger than a kitchen match. His little blaze caught, and he fed it more twigs, gnarled ones this time, as big as a baby's wrist. The fire danced and reached up for more food. In a very few minutes he was feeding it logs as thick as his thigh, and in a very few more he was dragging logs so big he couldn't lift them but only snake them through the grasses. When he had manufactured a blaze as high as his head and as long as the lorry, he flourished a flat shovel from somewhere and robbed his blaze of a heaping shovelful of coals. These he took to a point fifty yards away and built himself a fresh fire from a heap of dead wood he had evidently gathered and left there. When it was crackling he came back, picked up the *panga,* and began to scythe about him in the clumps of high grasses that accented the trampled-down terrain. He grinned foolishly in the firelight.

Jinny and I had said nothing. She got up, shivered once, and picked up the tails of my trench coat, spreading her legs and subjecting the back of her stiff, shiny new khaki-panted bottom to the fire, as women have always done. She smiled for the first time since late afternoon.

"This is rather nice," she said. "I think I could use another drink, though." She held out her red cup and I dribbled a few more ounces of Harry's precious scotch into it. "I don't seem to miss the ice," she said, "which is possibly just as well. I wonder how long before they'll get that bloody truck out of the whateverkindof hole it's in."

"You've been three days in East Africa, Osa Johnson," I said. "If you've picked up 'bloody' already, you may as well say 'lorry' too. 'Bloody truck' sounds like an unpleasant physical disability."

"We've named this dirty little backbreaker, this jeep thing of ours, already," Jinny said. "If you call a jeep 'Jessica,' what do you think you should call a lorry who is going to live with you for the rest of your life?"

The scotch had achieved a definite command post in my stomach, and the fire was beautifully warm and crackly noisy by now.

"Well," I said, "if a ship is a she and a truck is a she, too, and if this ungainly slut is a lorry, there is only one name for her. Annie. Annie Lorry. Nice, what? Bonnie Annie Laurie, who is in the process of laying herself down to dee."

"Jesus," Jinny said. "Alone in the wilds of darkest whatever with a strange Englishman, fifteen blackamoors who possibly eat white ladies underdone, and a husband who makes Scotch-type puns, Annie Lorry, yet. I *like* it," she said with the charming consistency for which wives, the world around, are noted. "I wonder how fares it with Annie. She should have cancer of the differential."

"Not well," I said. "Here come the children of Israel bearing their chattels."

Harry was striding along at the head of his porters, carrying a rolled-up something, which proved later to be the toilet tent, on his back. The boys strung out behind him, loaded with other tents and odd, lumpy-looking packages and angular poles.

"Bloody thing's bedded down for the night," he said. "We'll dig her out after dinner. All the boys are starved, and I imagine you are. Also, they've all got dreadful hangovers, as have I. City life is not good for country boys, black *or* white. We'll set up the sleepers and turn old Ali loose at the cook fire for a little *chacula* and have a drink or so first to keep off the fevers and would the *Memsaab* like a bath?"

The *memsaab* muttered that as long as she was going to die anyhow, she would rather die drunk and dirty.

"She'll doubtless grow to love it," Harry said. "Well, cheers, chums. Wonderful stuff, isn't it? Tastes so nasty and feels so good."

One of the blacks came and took the dead Tommy away. Another set up a portable table and unflexed three camp chairs—canvas and comfortable. We set the bottle on the table. Harry excused himself and drifted away to supervise the erection of the tents. We weren't making an extensive camp—no mess tent, no tents for the boys, no tent for Harry. Just a tent for the *bwana wa safari,* which suddenly was me, and for the *memsaab wa safari,* which suddenly was Virginia. A hyena chittered across the donga. I didn't know it was a donga then—a dry river bed with just a trickle of water to one side. The hyena squealed, roared, growled, and then laughed in that maniac's mirthless hysteria which nobody has ever put down on paper correctly.

"My God," Jinny said, "what was that, a lion?"

"No," Harry said, sliding suddenly out of the darkness. "That was a hyena. The lion is over that way," with a sweep of his arm. "If you wait a second you can hear him. It's a cross between a cough and the first mutter of a summer thunderstorm. Now. Hear him? We call it *ngruma*, wonderful word for 'roar'—*ngruma*."

"No," Jinny said. "I don't hear him and I don't want to hear him."

There was a sudden crashing cacophony of assorted noises from the trees. It was a hoot and a squeal and a chuckle and a yell and a yip and a yap and a growl and a roar and a whistle and a clash of cymbals. We just looked at Harry.

"Birds," he said. "Baboons. Monkeys. Bugs. And away up the donga, one leopard. Also, there's lots of fairly fresh rhino sign down by the little river. Unpleasant beast, the rhino. Apt to come blundering into camp. Can't see very well. Knew a bloke once got up to go to the sanitary tent and when he stuck his head out to go back to bed there was this big rhino cow grazing between him and his sleeping tent. Stayed in the latrine all night. Most uncomfortable."

"My God," Jinny said.

"Looks about like time for a little *chacula*," Harry said. "You hungry?"

"Starved," I said.

"Famished," Jinny said.

"We'll be having a bit of the Tommy," Harry said. "A touch fresh for my taste, but if we don't get our bit tonight the boys'll have it gone by tomorrow. And it's a young one. Shouldn't be bad. Old Ali—he's the cook—is a ruddy wonder with game. Juma! Jum*aaaa!*" he yelled. "*Lette chacula!*"

"*Ndio, bwana,*" came back from the cook fire. A white-robed wraith in a white fez, followed by another banshee in white, writhed up from the smaller grove of acacias. They cleared the table of bottle and glasses and reset it rapidly with china plates and condiments. "*Soupi,*" the head boy,

Juma, said. I could recognize him now. He had a happy, evil sort of face, with a pencil-sized hole in his ear lobe that the fire shone through and an impudently cheerful look about him, owing undoubtedly to an Irish kind of snub nose. His color was very light, about gabardine. Juma was a Coast Swahili. He spoke and wrote Arabic and Swahili—Coastal Swahili, impeccably grammatic, and unlike the crude pidgin Swahili the Wakambas and Kikuyus and Nandis spoke.

"Very important fellow, old Juma," Harry said. "Got hell's own amount of influence with the boys. Priest of sorts. Threatens 'em with Allah's vengeance and lends 'em money at God knows what interest rate betimes. Between praying and usury he keeps 'em on the jump."

Juma and the other man fetched tureens of soup, undoubtedly Campbell's. The bread was toasted and hot. The butter in its green plastic dish was fresh and sweet. The Tommy chops came smoking from the fire, and they looked and smelled wonderful.

"Fancy a beer?" Harry asked. "We've got a couple of bottles in the water bag. Kaluku!" He spoke sharply to the other white-robe. "*Lette beer-i kwa bwana!*" Kaluku bobbed his head and swished his skirts off after the beer. It was barely cool and very pleasant, rather like Australian beer in its heavy body. It was beer that never saw a ball game.

"Local product," Harry said. "Called 'Tusker.' Bloody awful, I think. I love that Danish Pilsen they have at the Norfolk, myself. But this can taste awfully good—well, say a month hence."

"I ain't knockin' it now," I said. "Pass the Tommy."

Considering that this particular Thomson gazelle had been dancing on the village green about four hours ago, possibly contemplating matrimony, he was great. He was not so tough as tender, and he tasted unlike any game I had ever eaten.

No rankness, no gaminess, no stringiness. He was succulent and unfat and I had three helpings of him.

"Best of all, I think," Harry said. "Except maybe gerenuk that you get up in the N.F.D. Long-necked little beggars, but beautiful to eat. You'll really get to love Tommy over the long haul. He never gets tiresome on the tongue. This one's a touch fresh for my fancy, though. I like to hang it at least a day. I love meat," he said. "Give me cold meat and a hunk of bread and you can have all the rest."

We finished the meat, and I noticed that Virginia had not allowed her isolation in the midst of Africa to bother an appetite which always seemed to flourish best where night found her, whether at the Stork Club or some few miles out of Haddon Rig, the lost sheep station in New South Wales, Australia. She would leap slightly when a fresh, new hoot came out of the small, intimate jungle of trees, but as she leaped she chewed.

Juma, the head boy, came and swept away the dishes. He went back to the cook fire and returned with a smoking fry-pan.

"What's this?" Virginia asked.

"Dessert," Harry said. "*Crêpes suzette.* Old Ali always makes 'em first night out. Instills any amount of faith in the clients. Good?"

"Saints preserve us," Virginia said. "Wonderful. How does he do it on an open fire?"

"I don't know," Harry said. "I've had him for years. He can cook anything. Uses a biscuit tin for an oven. Tell me what you want and old Ali will produce it."

"If we eat like this on the first night out in a temporary camp," Virginia said, "God help my figure after two months of Ali's fine Swahilian hand with the skillet. I'm about to bust."

Juma and Kaluku came and cleared away the table. Juma fetched coffee, and I remembered a bottle of brandy I had stuck into the back of Jessica. We sat there facing the fire, listening to the night noises, the hyenas, the birds I did not know the name of, the leopard coughing somewhere up the creek, the bugs swooping and zooming but not biting. The moon had climbed steeply into the sky, and you could see the little hills plainly under it, like a long caravan of camels suddenly stopped and still to wait beside a well.

It was cold—not bitter, not quite frosty, but chilly-dew cold —and the fire was warm and wonderful. I was tired and I was full and the coffee was strong and black and the brandy slid down smoothly. I started to think about just how far I was from New York and newspaper syndicates and telephones and telegraphs and the 21 Club and income taxes and subways and elevators and then I sat up with a startled feeling inside. I am a hunter, I said to myself. I must be a hunter, or I wouldn't be here in the deep end of nowhere with a city-slicker wife and fifteen strange black boys and a young punk with no beard, practically, who says he is a white hunter. Looking at the fire and listening to the noises, I ran my mind back about what brought me here and wrote a little mental essay for myself as I sat and sipped the brandy.

The hunter's horn sounds early for some, I thought, later for others. For some unfortunates, prisoned by city sidewalks and sentenced to a cement jungle more horrifying than anything to be found in Tanganyika, the horn of the hunter never winds at all. But deep in the guts of most men is buried the involuntary response to the hunter's horn, a prickle of the nape hairs, an acceleration of the pulse, an atavistic memory of his fathers, who killed first with stone, and then with club, and then with spear, and then with bow, and then with gun, and finally with formulae. How meek the man is of no importance; somewhere in the pigeon chest of the clerk is still the vestigial remnant of the hunter's heart; somewhere in his nostrils the half-forgotten smell of blood. There is no man with such impoverishment of imagination that at some time he has not wondered how he would handle himself if a lion broke loose from a zoo and he were forced to face him without the protection of bars or handy, climbable trees.

This is a simple manifestation of ancient ego, almost as simple as the breeding instinct, simpler than the urge for shelter, because man the hunter lives basically in his belly. It is only when progress puts him in the business of killing other men that the bloodlust surges upward to his brain. And even war is still regarded by the individual as sport—the man himself against a larger and more dangerous lion.

Hunting is simple. Animals are simple. Man himself is simple inside himself. In this must lie some explanation for the fact that zoos are crowded on Sundays and museums which display mounted animals are thronged on weekdays as well as holidays. This must explain the popularity of moving pictures which deal with animals. This explains the lasting popularity of the exploits of Tarzan of the Apes, the half-animal figure created by Edgar Rice Burroughs.

Man is still a hunter, still a simple searcher after meat for his growling belly, still a provider for his helpless mate and cubs. Else why am I here? From the moment he wakes until the moment he closes his eyes, man's prime concern is the business of making a living for himself and his family. *Bringing home the bacon* is the modern equivalent of banging a curly mammoth over the head with a big sharp rock.

Man has found it exceedingly difficult lately to decipher the weird incantations and ceremonies which surround the provision of meat and shelter for his spawn. He is mystified by the cabalistic signs of the economist. He does not understand billions of dollars in relationship to him and his. Parity baffles him; the administration of ceilings and floors and controls and excises and supports does not satisfy his meat urge or his aesthetic response to the chase, when the hunter's horn of necessity rouses him. *These are pretty fine thoughts,* I thought. *I will think some more.*

But he can understand a lion, because a lion is life in its simplest form, beautiful, menacing, dangerous, and attractive to his ego. A lion has always been the symbol of challenge, the prototype of personal hazard. You get the lion or the lion gets you.

And he can understand a gun, because the gun is the symbol of man's brain and ingenuity, the device of difference between small weak man and big, brawny, cruel life. But I do not even know whether I can shoot a rifle yet.

And he can understand man, himself, puny ape with outsize brain and weak talons, short blunt teeth, and always ridden by consuming fear and uncertainty. And I am real scared at this moment.

And he can understand a star and a moon and the sun and grass and trees and uncontrived beauty, when modern art and physical formulae and aerodynamics and jet propulsion are cloaked in unreality.

A man and a gun and a star and a beast are still ponderable in a world of imponderables. The essence of the simple ponderable is man's potential ability to slay a lion. It is an opportunity that comes to few, but the urge is always present. Never forget that man is *not* a dehydrated nellie under his silly striped pants. He is a direct descendant of the hairy fellow who tore his meat raw from the pulsing flanks of just-slain beasts and who wiped his greasy fingers on his thighs if he bothered to wipe then at all. I wiped my greasy fingers on my thigh, for practice.

This is the only deeply rooted reason I can produce for the almost universal interest, either active or vicarious, in hunting. As time and civilization encroach more deeply on the individual, as man hunts his meat at the supermarket instead of in the swamps and forests, it is still interesting to note that in America some thirty-six million hunting and fishing licenses are sold annually, that the sale of outdoor magazines and books continues to boom, and that the firms which handle safaris in Africa are booked up four and five years in advance. Oddly, as the opportunity for direct participation dwindles, the interest in man versus animal continues to grow.

It seems to me I heard the hunter's horn earlier than most. I was raised in the country-small-town part of North Carolina. My grandfather was a hunter, and a serious one. So was my father, although he never shot anything larger than a five-ounce bobwhite quail in his life. When I was six years old they gave me an air gun, and I was physically sick from excitement when I killed my first sparrow. I was even sicker when I killed my first quail with the 20-gauge shotgun Santa brought me on my eighth milestone. Thereafter I hunted six days a week, and on the seventh I did not rest. I worked out the bird dogs on dry runs with no gun. We did not defile the Sabbath with gunfire in those days. I had few gods, however, that were not to be found in the fields and woods, and I early learned that you did not have to shoot it to enjoy it. Seeing it wild and happy more often was enough.

You might say that *Field and Stream* was my early Bible. I worshiped before the shrines of men like Archibald Rutledge, David Newell, and Ray Holland, a far piece ahead of Ernest Hemingway or Thomas Wolfe. I had good dogs as a kid, and a great many marvelous things happened to me in the woods. For a long time I had a small boy's dream of writing a story about my dogs and my quail—and of course, me—

and seeing it printed in a magazine with a cover by Lynn Bogue Hunt. This was the going-to-sleep dream. I never expected to achieve it, but dreams are not taxed for small boys, not even the wildest ones.

Somewhere along the way, when I was out after squirrels or creeping after ducks or following my old setter, Frank, after bobwhite, I got involved in an even more ambitious dream. I had early fallen under the spell of Mr. Burroughs and his *Tarzan*. Somewhat later came more realistic approaches to Africa—the Martin Johnsons, *Trader Horn*, *Sanders of the River*. I got involved with the travel tales of Somerset Maugham, and it seemed I would bust a gusset if I didn't get to see jungles and lions and cannibals someday.

I believe I planned to follow the Alger technique. I would return a lost wallet to a banker and get a job in his bank. Then I would marry his daughter, inherit his riches, and one day I would pack up and take a safari into Africa. I would see, and maybe shoot, old Numa, the lion, and Sabor, the lioness, and Tantor, the elephant. (Mr. Burroughs' nomen-

clature for Tarzan's playmates was even more colorful than Swahili.) *And then maybe, when I was rich and famous, I would write about Africa.*

The implementation of dreams rarely follows the script, but the endings sometimes turn out surprisingly well. I married no banker's daughter. I got into the seafaring business, and later into the writing trade, and then into the war business, and then again into the writing trade. I never got rich or famous, but I got action.

I saw Mr. Maugham's South Seas, and I had made six round trips to Africa. I wrote a lot of stuff for a lot of people—syndicated newspaper columns, and a raft of stories for a great many magazines, and several books. But I never stopped dreaming of lions.

For no real reason at all, save a boyish dream and a twenty-year itch, I suddenly rigged my own safari to Kenya and Tanganyika. It was *mine*. Nobody sent me. I was paying for it myself. Nobody goes along but my wife and the white hunter and a company of African "boys." I refused to share the trip with anybody else, even though I had offers of plenty of company.

There is not much personal adventure left in this world—not many boyhood dreams that lose nothing, but rather gain, by fulfillment. So I combined *two* dreams in one; I was on a safari and I was going to write about it.

The fire was beginning to shake into solid glowing coals now, and some of the night noises had stilled others, and new ones had commenced. The boys had finally succeeded in dragging Annie Lorry out of her sloven nest in the pig hole, and she was moored alongside the sleeping tent. Harry had stretched a length of canvas as a dew cloth from her topmost rigging to the jeep and had set up his cot under the canvas. I yawned. Virginia yawned. Harry yawned. Harry got up.

"Time for bed, I expect," he said. *"Nataka lala.* We'll up at dawn. Two more hard days' drive yet to come. Sleep well."

We walked to the tent, where a small carbide lamp blazed on a rickety little table and the two white tall cones of mosquito netting draped over cots with inflated rubber mattresses on them. I reflected that if it were possible for a man to be happy in this day and age I was a happy man. I didn't know precisely why, despite the fine talk, but I was a truly happy man.

Chapter 2

IT STARTED out to be a funny trip. It had to be funny, funny peculiar, that is, because the kind friend who had been giving all the good advice either through malice or stupidity completely misled me on the time to go: He said June was great. I was in Nairobi a little less than an hour before I found out that June was not great. June was ungreat. June was lousy. June was not the time to do anything, because of a simple truth. Rains make grass, and animals stay up in the hills where the grass is short and the carnivores can't hide in it, and when the miles and miles of bloody Africa are a bloody sea of six-foot grass, there are no bloody animals to shoot at or take pictures of or even to look at. They burn the grass in July to get it short again, and the decent hunting starts in August. My fine friend, the expert, sends me over in June, when the prairies are wet and all the game is either hidden out in the hills or still working on the water holes in the reserves. Some friend, my expert friend. Ten thousand bucks' worth of former acquaintance.

But we got it stuck together with all the guns and the cameras and the money and the tickets and the farewell lunch at the numerical place, as Eddie Condon calls the 21 Club. The lunch was reasonably Homeric.

It was a good lunch, unusual in that I had made a new will and we signed it with suitable flourishes. It was a *very* good lunch. At the airport the TWA pilot expressed some concern about the state of the *bwana's* exuberance. This was a sleeper plane, full of decorous people. The *bwana's* wife replied.

"Get into the plane," she said. "Take it off the ground. When you reach twenty thousand feet, open the window and stick out your hand. The old boy will be flying along right up there beside you."

There was rather a stiff-backed Lord Something-or-other aboard. I heard him asking the stewardess to lower his curtains and make his bunk immediately.

"I do not choose to look at those dreadful Americans for the next fifteen hours," said he. I cast about me for the dreadful Americans and realized with a sudden shock that he meant me. The hell with you, You Highship, I said to myself, and to prove that one American can lick a hundred limeys, I had my berth made, too, and slept all the way to Paris. That'll teach 'em, I said, because nobody sleeps when Buster snores. And Buster was in excellent form that evening.

We were just a touch heavy on the baggage allowance, owing to seventeen pieces of luggage, including a long-playing record machine which an itinerant piano player named Bushkin had forced into my fist at the airport.

"You may get lonesome out there with all the cannibals," said Bushkin. "You may yearn for civilization, and so here are some records by me and by Louis Armstrong and Lee Wiley to remind you of home."

(I sent Joe Bushkin a bitter wire sometime later from a place in Tanganyika called Lake Manyara. "Have finally found AC-type firefly," I cabled. "Have plugged in machine. Think you going little sour on left hand.")

(Mr. Bushkin's machine, plus a Remington .30-'06 rifle, a Winchester .375 magnum, a Winchester .220 Swift, a Churchill 12-gauge shotgun, a Sauer 16-gauge I borrowed from Bernie Baruch, an Ikoflex camera, a Rolleiflex camera, a Cine-Kodak movie camera, assorted film, thirty cartons of Chesterfields, and considerable ammunition, weighed slightly more than a fairy's wings. I recall we were 278 pounds over allowance. This puzzled a redheaded French customs employee.)

"*Seize bagage, monsieur?*" he said. "*Pour deux personnes seulement? Mon Dieu, seize bagage pour deux personnes, c'est affreux——*"

"But," I said in my cat's-in-the-garden-of-my-aunt French, "we go to hunt the lion in the *Afrique*. These *bagage* of which you speak are not so much *bagage* as guns and cameras and little teensy-weensy-type *pacquetages*, including contraband cigarettes to fool the British customs into believing they are household effects."

"*Ah, bon, bon,*" he said. "*A bas les Anglais.* You say you go to shoot in the *Afrique, hein?* I me myself once was in *Afrique* during a war and found fine sport there. Life was very *sportif.* We shot and we shot, and it was very *sportif.*"

"What were you shooting to make for yourself such a great sportiveness?" I asked.

"*Les Italiens*," he said simply, and flapped my *seize bagage* checks on the counter.

Cairo was unusual too. Everybody fell off camels at dawn in Cairo, including my ancient friend, Amin El Alaily Bey. Then we went to the zoo. I never did figure out why we went to the zoo, but the lions looked rather larger than life. So did the belly dancers in the night clubs. A man I know named Hassan, who was celebrating Ramadan, the holy month, took a sip of his seventieth lemonade that night and snickered slightly. I choked over the mouthpiece of my *narghile,* the water pipe that comes with the table in Egyptian night clubs, and asked him about the snicker.

"These two girls are the toast of Egypt," Hassan said. "We have just concluded a holy war with the Jews over the issue of Palestine. These two girls are the toast of Egypt, but they are Jewish. To me it does not make any sense that we applaud the girls and shoot their cousins." Then Hassan went to sleep.

Now in Kenya, a stone's toss across the border of Tanganyika, I woke up. A few mosquitoes buzzed dispiritedly about the net. Away off somewhere the lion coughed and complained. I contemplated the high cost of lions as I lay on an inflated chilly rubber mattress in a strange land. (The cost of lions is considerable.)

It had been such a swift transition from New York to a lion in your lap. Philip Wiley, I believe it was, once wrote that when you travel by plane you leave a little of your soul behind. I figured in my semi-sleep that a part of my soul was somewhere between Rome and Asmara, which is in Eritrea and which might stay right there in Eritrea for all of me. Or maybe it was just now trying to check into the second-worst hotel in Addis Ababa, since the Ras Hotel, naturally, would be off limits to souls that were traveling behind their corporeal headquarters. It is not lulling to think of souls when you are only half asleep in strange terrain.

A baboon barked somewhere down the donga and followed it with an outraged squawk. A little later the leopard which had outraged him sawed at the foot of the tree, from which the *nugu* undoubtedly was swaying from a limber branch. "Bastard," the baboon said. "Spotted, evil, ugly bastard." The leopard replied: "Just wait, *nugu*. I'll have indigestion over you yet."

(It sounded strangely like the first opening bark of a .20-millimeter Oerlikon machine gun, followed immediately by the chattering of the smaller AA stuff and accented by the hollow grunt of the bigger weapons. I recalled the same feeling of strangeness, some years before, when once again the workaday soul had not enjoyed an opportunity to track down its master.

(I was somewhere in the North Atlantic on an ammunition ship. I was wearing a scrubby beard. I had not washed for days. I had not slept for days. The convoy was under semiconstant attack by what the newspapers used to call a wolf-pack of submarines. I stank—chiefly from fear, secondarily from lack of opportunity to remove my long-handled drawers and bathe. The smell of fear was separate from the smell of dirty body. The fear smelled worse than the normal filthy smell.

(It had been seven days—seven days of other people's ships sinking, the nights lit up by the snowflake flares, the brief explosion of a sister ship, and sudden knowledge that there was one poker debt you were never going to collect. At least not in this world you weren't going to collect it.

(On the eighth day at 11 A.M. local time I decided that a man who had worn the same clothes for that many days and nights needed a bath.

(It was a gray day, just off the coast of Scotland, and we had had nothing to afflict us for the hours since general quarters. I took off the paper-lined arctic jumper and peeled off the sheep-lined coat and scraped off the long-handled drawers and unshipped the felt-lined shoes and tossed away the felt face-mask and lurched into the shower across the deck from my cabin. The steam of the shower removed the smell of fear and the smell of the dirty body and cleared some of the red from eyes which had not closed for seven days in a normal fashion in a bed. The ship rolled as only a gut-heavy Liberty can roll, and I fastened my fingers to one of the handles the geniuses who build modern ships attach to the sides of shower rooms. A great feeling of lassitude stroked me. And then there was a crash and a boom and a hoarse screaming of the ship's general alarm.

(I streaked out of the shower room, naked, soaking wet, scooped up a pistol and a helmet, and clambered topside to my gun station on the flying bridge. A ship in the convoy's center had copped it and was drifting back, sinking, smoking, dying. I looked around me. The AA guns were manned and ready. So were the bigger guns on the forecastle head and on the poop. So was I, too, I suppose. I had on a helmet and a pistol and a three weeks' beard. I screwed the battle phones to my helmet and checked in with fat old Donaldson aft on the five-inch fifty, and with Doughman forward on the three-inch fifty, and around me were Red and Plinsky and the Staley twins from San Francisco, all making technical noises like experienced warriors.

(And then I looked at me, naked as any jay bird, goose-pimpled out, wearing only a helmet and a pistol and a battle phone to cover my shame. And I thought that in the last few days I had lost a couple of friends and every day we burnt off the machine guns with a blowtorch to kill the ice and that stuff in my whiskers was solid frost and under my fanny were seven thousand tons of high explosives and that only yesterday I was the meek morning city editor of the Washington *Daily News*. A German submarine surfaced in the middle of the convoy and a half dozen ships blew him out of the water, making a god-awful noise about it. Depth charges plunked and thrummed and jostled against the bottom of my ancient bucket. It was cold up there with no clothes on.

(What, I said to myself, in the name of Holy Christ am I doing out here?

(The body was there but the soul was somewhere between the Fargo Building in Boston and the whorehouse in Gulfport, Mississippi—the cathouse being the only place that naval ensigns with wives could find to live while they were training to be heroes. You had to say that the whores were wonderful. They baby-sat for the naval wives and lent the incipient heroes a little money before the Navy's slatternly paydays, and they never, never made a pass at the boys in blue. They also looked most severe in the gambling rooms when the heroic husbands went up against the slot machines.

(At the time the ship sank that morning I figured my soul had left Biloxi and was headed by slow bus to New Orleans, there to go by Naval Air Transport to Jacksonville, Florida, in order to pick up a scabby old scow named the *Eli Whitney*, of which God had decided that I was to be gunnery officer. Transportation being what it was in the war days, I reckoned my soul was a good three weeks behind me, maybe more, because all I could recognize in this gray cold waste of water was a civilian's body. Certainly my curly civilian soul had no business there.

(Certainly if I were there in physical person my soul had too much sense to crowd into the act. I felt this considerably more strongly some months later, in Bari, Italy, when I was forced to be competently heroic while wearing a face full of lather and no helmet at all, on top of a sitting ship during an air raid. By heroic I mean I quit shaving and climbed up to the flying bridge. Apart from the nakedness, I shall always remember that my crew had been holding religious services that day, and the Protestant chaplain was trying to crawl under the portable organ. As I attempted to direct anti-aircraft fire—we never, *ever* hit anything—through a fluffy meringue of lather, I reflected idly that by now my soul had probably left London and was staggering aimlessly about Casablanca, a good six months behind me. I hoped my soul would check in at the Bar Nolly in Casa and inquire from Madame Gala if anybody named Ruark had been around looking soulless a few months ago.

(The lion coughed now, quite close. The birds and the insects and the baboons set up a new symphony. By dead reckoning I estimated that my soul was just getting off the Ethiopia plane in Nairobi, where Donald Ker, a professional hunter, was waiting to greet me.)

Mr. Ker had been quite British. He had been British much as the bloke who came aboard the old *Whitney* in Gibraltar in 1943 had been British. That one was a wavy-navy lieutenant with a beard.

("I say," the wavy-navy type had said as he climbed the jacob's ladder and shoved his beard over the rail. "Do you chaps have any cigarettes at all? Ah, wizard, wizard. I've got rather an interesting assignment for you. You're to have the honor of leading the first convoy up the Adriatic. Germans still about a bit, that way, and I understand the Ionian Sea is simply infested with mines. No, old boy, we don't have any charts. Just keep a sharp eye out for the mines, especially at night, and mind you well that the Jerries are still functioning across the street. Well, cheers, chaps.")

So we'd been met by Donald Ker at the Nairobi airport, and he had twinkled his chipmunk's cheerful grin at us and said something like:

"I say, I *am* dreadfully sorry that your man Selby—your hunter, you know—isn't here to greet you, but the Game Department just called and said a rogue rhino's raising vast amounts of trouble with the natives outside of town and so we've sent old Harry off to reprove it. Minds me of the early days when the department used to call me or Syd for us to come to the airport to shoot the wildebeest off it so the ruddy planes could land. We've cleared your bits now, so we might nip off to the Norfolk and have a spot of lunch before they close the dining room."

In retrospect I am a great admirer of Donald Ker, a small man who looks no more like a professional hunter than he looks like Blackbeard the Pirate. But Donald Ker killed his first elephant before his voice solved its adolescent squeak, and his first safari consisted of a can of beans, a gun, a bullet, and a blanket. He is one half of Ker and Downey Safaris, Ltd., and if you wish to book him you had better write a letter stating your plans some five years ahead of the moment.

"You know," Donald said over a martini on the Norfolk veranda, "there's a popular suspicion going the rounds that all professional hunters are nine feet high and drink petrol cocktails neat. I claim I disprove the point. I put myself through elementary school shooting elephants on holiday. I was smaller then than now. And that, chum, was never yesterday. Shall we push along to old Ahamed's and get you and the *memsaab* suitably clothed for tomorrow's exodus?"

"Jesus," said I, "tomorrow?"

"I rather like to get the safaris in and get them out," Donald said, twinkling his teeth. "And we do have to see to the boots and jackets and things. Also, the American consul wants you for dinner."

"This I need," I muttered. "This I need bad."

"Come along, come along," Donald said.

When your heart's in the highlands and your soul is lost, maybe still sequestered in the Nouvelle Eve in Paris, you go to the local Indian in Nairobi. He measures you. You go to the next local Indian—the bootmaking one—and *he* measures you, and of a sudden you have completed an outfitting that would take you six weeks to perform in the United States. In Nairobi no suit is so fancy it can't be delivered in a day. No boots are so special they can't be rendered unto the owner by tomorrow's noon. Under Donald's hand I was finished with the flannel pajamas, finished with the drill bush jackets, finished with the mosquito boots and the crepe-soled half boots before cocktail time, so we checked in at the little offices of Messrs Ker and M. Downey, Ltd. The phone rang as we entered. Donald accepted the call. He listened a moment and turned to me.

"The Game Department again," he said. "Some bloody leopard or other raising ned with the native chickens on the outskirts of town. Says if I've a client handy who wants to shoot it, he won't need a license and he may have the pelt. You?" He flicked an eyebrow.

"Not me, *bwana*," I said, "Just got here this morning, and my huntin' pants ain't been delivered yet. Let somebody else go shoot the leopard. I got to go to dinner with Angus Ward."

Ker shrugged and spoke into the receiver. I felt he was a touch disappointed at my lack of immediate spirit, but as I said, the soul must catch up with the body before you go into strange businesses, else the body is not competent to perform.

It is a long, long way, although short in miles, from the modern civilization of Nairobi's Norfolk Hotel to where we aimed in Tanganyika, because you have to go through little places named Narok and Loliondo and across a big plain named Serengeti. After you leave the Naivasha area there aren't any roads much, only tracks through grass and winding over and around mountains, and when you start across the Serengeti there is only a double-barreled peak to steer you sixty miles, and unless the day is clear you can't see the peak. You drive the hunting car by guess and by God. The weary old lorry labors behind you and now and again you pause to wait for her to catch up, the boys gray-faced with the dust and clinging to the tarpaulined top like a flock of baboons on a rocky *kopje*.

Much has been written about the profusion of game just outside Nairobi, and some sportsman once wrote a magazine piece called "They Hunt from Taxicabs in Nairobi," suggesting that it was simple if you desired to have your wife or daughter shoot a leopard. All you did was to nip into a car and go and collect it before cocktail time in the New Stanley Hotel. He was wrong on only one count: The Athi Plain outside Nairobi is a game preserve, and they hang you for shooting so much as a dik-dik in its confines. Africa is a large plot of land. In relatively few of its areas are you allowed to shoot anything. Achieving those areas is difficult and dusty. And the kidneys moan in anguish from the punishment they absorb from a bucking jeep called Jessica or any other name.

After rescuing that tin tragedy of a truck from the muddy misery of Tanganyika's trails a few dozen times; after Mama had surfeited herself with photographs of the odd Masai herdsmen we met; after a short call on the district officer in Loliondo, we pushed through a herd of spotted Masai cattle and rolled down a rocky hill and landed into the vast plain that is Serengeti. It is a plain now, sere dusty grass for as far as you can see. It was a lake once, a lake beneath the lip of mountains. It is sixty some miles straight across it and there is no road. There is no track. There is not much water and few trees and only a small, bitter alkali lake and a few damp patches of grass with treacherous soft cotton soil to stick you and, when it is dry, violent dust. And violent sun.

"This bloke I mention," Harry was saying, "was one of the few real crackpots I've been forced to entertain on safari. He was an Englishman, and he thought he was Tarzan of the Apes. He wanted to sleep in trees. He ran around naked all the time. I couldn't keep him from bathing in the streams, and the crocodiles were eying him appreciatively. He—— My aunt! Look yonder. What a lovely lion."

Apart from submarines boiling to the surface on a cold morning in the middle of a convoy, I do not believe there are many more impressive sights than a city man's first glimpse at a live maned lion loose on a plain in strange country, sinister and far from home. This old boy was a movie lion. He had a luxuriant mane and tufts on his elbows and he was right smack in the middle of a bare prairie. Him and his lady. She took off in a swinging lope. The old boy stopped cold and turned to inspect us with a cynical yellow eye. Harry swung Jessica past him at about three feet.

"*Jambo, Bwana Simba,*" he said. The lion grunted and scowled and began to move off. Jinny unlimbered the camera and stood up in the jeep. I placed both palms on her behind and braced her against the windscreen so she could take pictures. The lion, heavy-maned and very full in the paunch, swung off after his old lady. Then he stopped again, and Harry tooled the jeep to within six feet and halted it. The lion looked at us. We looked at the lion.

I know they will all tell you that so long as you stay in the car you are completely safe, but it is of small comfort on your first live lion. You keep wondering if maybe you won't meet an individualist who dislikes automobiles someday and suddenly find him in your lap. (I met a lady lion later who did not like jeeps, nor the people in them. She charged it three times, and the last time her jaws snapped a touch closer to my trousers than I like to remember. She remembered her hatred months later and charged another car. And then another month after that. She is going to surprise some camera tourist one of these days by removing his face from his Rolleiflex.)

A lion, loose, and six feet away, with no bars in front of him, is bigger than the lion you remembered from the zoo. His teeth are longer. He is scrubbier, perhaps, but loses no dignity and no ferocity. I was not displeased when he sauntered off. Neither was Jinny. She had not yawned back when the lion yawned at her. She was not bored.

"He's just off a kill," Harry said. "Look at his belly. Full of zebra. No trouble from this type. Let's herd him off after his bride and proceed. We'll see another dozen or so before dusk. Yah!" he said, and slapped the door of the Land Rover. "Shoo! Scat! Begone!"

The lion sneered, curling his lip and grunting. He got up and humped away, his shoulder blades moving angularly under the loose hide. Harry put on a burst of speed and we chased him a few hundred yards, the lion looking sarcastically over his shoulder as if to say, Christ, more tourists out to play. He stopped one more time, faced us, opened his mouth, and roared. It wasn't a very serious roar, but it seemed rather loud to me. Harry swerved the jeep and we bade him good-by.

"Lovely beasts, lions, you know," Harry said. "Live and let live. Not the king of the jungle, though. Never makes the effort. Elephant. He's the king. Buffalo the prince, and the leopard is the knave. The lion is a gentleman—a lazy old gentleman. Makes Mama do all the work. He stands upwind and lets his scent drift down to some poor *punda* or other and roars once in a while to amuse himself. The old lady, betimes, has sneaked around downwind from the zebras and they gradually work toward her. She makes two jumps and lands on the zebra's back. She hooks her hind feet into his stern and takes a mouth hold on his neck. Then she reaches around with her arm and grabs him by the nose, and crack! *Chacula.* Dinner. The old boy saunters up and they dine. Then they sleep. Then they dine again. Then they sleep some more. And then Mother bestirs·herself and goes to market once again. Be nice being a lion on a reserve. Nothing to do but eat and sleep and pose for pictures and fight with your sons when they've got big enough."

I will never, possibly, forget that first day on the Serengeti. We saw fourteen lions—one pride of five drinking peaceably and serenely at a water hole with half a hundred Grant and Thomson gazelles, only a few feet away from each other, and each animal serenely aware that nobody was going to eat anybody else. As we got off the plain and into bush we began to see giraffes and ostriches, and the antelopes thickened into herds of several hundred. The first stirrings of the semi-annual game migration was beginning, and the flocks of wildebeest, shaggy and high-humped like American bison, were beginning to move, along with their friends and companions, the zebras. We saw bands of five and ten thousand, and coursed them briefly in the car. At one cutoff we paused for a few unforgettable moments while some five thousand zebras thundered past our bow, their hoofs thunderous even on the grassy plain, and the dust boiling behind them like the wake of an armored column in North Africa. And now the grass was high, towering over the windshield of the jeep and pelting our faces with the sharp grains from the heavy seed heads. Hundreds of coveys of tiny quail sprayed up from under Jessica's hood. The seed heads got into her grille, and every so often we had to stop and clear them out of her front.

"Bloody Rover smells like a bloody bakeshop," Harry said. "Grass. Nine miles high everywhere. Too much rain this year. Too much water on the plains. Too much water in the hills. Game all massed in the reserves or up in the hills—anywhere the grass is short and the cats can't crawl unseen. I've high hopes, though, for where we're headed. It's freak country, a little strip about fifteen miles long by five wide, and the grass is never high there. I don't know why. Unless I'm off my reckoning, we'll find game in that area. We'll find the game in any area that's legal and isn't covered with a forest of this bloody grass. Let's stop for a bite of lunch and one of those delicious nutritious martinis you're always talking about."

We went down through a poison-green patch of grass that covered a wet spot, with Kidogo, the gunbearer, testing the terrain with his horny feet ahead of us, and trundled up to a high knoll where a patch of mangy acacias gave a grudging shade. Harry's curly black hair was whitened and stiffened by dust. Jinny's blond crop under the bandanna and the Stetson was blonder. There was dust in my whiskers and dust in my mouth and dust in the water bag and dust in the plastic glasses and dust in the gin, which made a very nice hot martini if you like them hot. I like them hot.

Chabani and Kidogo got the chop box out of Jessica's back seat and spread the front-seat cushions around under the

trees. We had a couple martinis apiece and then we had a bottle of Tusker lager and some remnants of the cold Tommy and a can of cold spaghetti and bread and butter and pickles. The tsetses fed on us sparingly as we ate. A few hundred yards away a herd of wildebeest stared stupidly at us. The sun filtered through the acacia tops and we sweated and the insects' bites itched and our eyes were red and I still decided that I was a happy man, with two months ahead of me and nothing to do except look at the game and maybe shoot a little of it and not answer any telephones.

"When we get off this bloody reserve we'll have to shoot

a big piece of meat pretty quick," Harry said. "It's been a hard three days for the boys, and they'll be ravenous and eat too much and I'll have to dose them all for the bellyache. Sooner we get them fed up and over being sick, the better. I hope we can shoot something big like an eland. They love the fresh meat and the fat and they make biltong out of what's left and they make shoulder straps for their wives out of the hide."

"What sort of shoulder straps?" Jinny asked. "What do they use them for?"

"Oh, for carrying wood," Harry said. "The wives, I mean. They can carry more wood for their husbands with good comfortable shoulder straps. The wives are very happy when their husbands bring them the eland shoulder straps. Shows the men are thinking of their happiness and welfare."

"Men," Jinny said, finishing her beer. "Where is the ladies' room?"

"Try over there behind that tree," Harry said. "Mind the snakes."

Virginia walked off, and I had to laugh a little. She was wearing dust-stained khaki pants and ankle boots, a belted bush jacket with empty cartridge loops in the front, and a saucy double-brimmed terai over a gypsy bandanna. What she wore couldn't have cost twenty bucks, if you forget the Abercrombie and Fitch boots, and this was the girl who used to play the Stork-21 Club circuit in New York. If she had her mink with her in those days she was worth twenty thousand bucks on the hoof, and she wouldn't have thought of walking three blocks if there was a doorman handy and a taxicab to hail. She always needed a quarter to go to the little girls' room, and now here is a raw stranger, Harry, directing her to the nearest bush and telling her to mind the snakes. This, the girl who wore a Hattie Carnegie frock and a rhinestone hat to ride a camel after a slightly wet evening on the town in Cairo . . .

"What are you snickering about?" Harry asked.

"Nothing much," I said. "I was just thinking about a dame who is afraid to walk the dogs in Central Park, who is afraid to spend the night alone in a Fifth Avenue penthouse, who spends God knows how much money on girl lunches and at the hairdresser and on her clothes, who would rather be naked than unminked, who wouldn't ride a bus or a subway to save her life, all of a sudden lost out in the African bush with twenty bucks' worth of Indian-made shoddy on her back, fifteen strange cannibals and a strange East African guide, riding in a jeep, looking at lions at close range, weighing a good ten pounds more from dust alone, drinking a hot martini, and going to the john behind a tree while a rank stranger tells her to mind no snakes take a chunk out of her. That is what I am laughing at—Osa Johnson Ruark, girl adventuress."

"I was serious about the snakes," Harry said. "Touch more beer in the bottle. Have it? Knew a girl once was bit on the bottom. Hell's own trouble trying to decide where to put the tourniquet."

"Not so much farther to go now?"

"Ought to make the permanent camp on the Grummetti sometime after dark," Harry said. "Must stop off and see the Game Department bloke. Nice lad name of Thomas. Sign the register and that sort of thing. He'll buy us a drink. Then I want to stop in the village—the Wa-Ikoma *manyatta*—and pick up old Kibiriti. He's wired for lion, and I've a hunch we'll need what he knows. Maned ones, shootable ones, getting tougher and tougher to come by. Here's the *mem*. Let's be about."

"Who's Kibiriti?" Jinny asked as she got into the jeep and straddled the gearbox.

"Bit of a sorcerer," Harry said. "I expect his mother was a lion. He thinks exactly like a lion. He can find lions when other lions can't find lions. I don't know how he does it. One time I was in great trial and trouble with a couple of sports, must-have-lion-or-the-safari's-off type of blokes. I looked high and low. I put out kills and I said prayers. I consulted witch doctors and learned how to talk lionese. No lions. Nobody speaking in camp, just sitting there being surly over the gin-and-lime. Boys all unhappy. What's called lionitis out here. Whole *campi* upset. So I send out a hurry call to Kibiriti. He arrives, complete with three wives. God-awful ugly except the young one.

" '*Simba,*' I say. '*Mbile. Simbambile.* Got to have two, in a hurry. *Pese pese* hurry. *Suria* hurry.' *Suria's* a bad word. Old Kibiriti looks around and sees his wives are happy with their new friends—shocking morals, these people have—and scratches his head. 'The Douma,' he says. 'We go there for the lions.'

" 'You been there lately, you heard anything about lions in the Douma, you know for sure?' I say to Kibiriti. 'No, Bwana Haraka,' he says to me, 'but I feel like there are two large black-maned lions in the Douma. We go to the Douma.'

"So," Harry said, "we break the camp and we go to the Douma. First night we shoot one fine *simba.* The next day we shoot another fine *simba.* Don't ask me how he does it, but you'll have a chance to watch him work. We'll pick him up in the village as we go through. He's having a little trouble with three wives and will be glad to take the trip. That last wife of his is awfully young and pretty and she's claiming most of his time. Others raising hell."

Bwana Thomas, the Game Department type, wasn't in his compound, being out after some poachers. The *askari* took our names and looked at the licenses and allowed us to fill the vehicles and the water bags with some of Bwana Thomas' nice fresh rain water, and we pushed off. We headed on a nebulous trail for Ikoma, a village of some half thousand, in God's back yard of Tanganyika. This was a lion-hunting village. Its young men all had their personally killed manes of big *doumi* lions, each killed with arrow or spear, of course, and illegal, of course, as illegal as the marabou stork plumage they wear when they dance, as illegal as the colobus monkey fur they wear when they dance.

The drums had been ahead of us. Kibiriti—which means "matches"—was expecting us. He made a big thing of seeing his patron saint, Bwana Haraka, once again, and was most hospitable about the premises of his newest wife's compound. They are impeccably considerate about wifely rights in Tanganyika. Each wife has her own hut, her own goats to tend, her own water to draw, her own mealie corn to tend, her own wood to fetch, and her own babies to have. She brews her own brand of beer for her man, who, in order to show no favoritism, stays only a week with each wife unless he is cheating, and Kibiriti was cheating at the time.

It was coming on for dark when we took Kibiriti away from his mud-wattle hut and his new baby and his euphorbia cactus *boma* and his pretty, shy new wife. He perched atop the lorry, his red fez cocked rakishly, as full of importance as Winston Churchill coming over for a new loan. I wished later we had kept him, for in the eighteen miles that separated us from our first permanent camp site Mr. Harry Selby, the infallible white hunter, to whom I had entrusted my life and that of my wife, got lost. Hopelessly lost. Bitterness was added to the brew when that ungainly slut, Annie Lorry, the faller-in-pig-holes and sticker-in-mudholes, that slab-sided, over-loaded, weak-axled travesty of a truck, had to come and find us.

"This," said Mrs. Virginia Ruark, "is one hell of a way to start a safari. I am lost in Tanganyika with a child who does not know his own way, and a fool—meaning you—who was better off loaded at lunch at Toots's. Pass the last of the scotch. If the lions eat me tonight they will not eat me sober."

"I'm most awfully, dreadfully sorry," Harry said. "But the bush has changed since I've been here, and what with the high grass and all, I seem to have missed the little avenue I must use to get from here to there. Let's swing back again and see if I can't pick it up again. Meantime, I think I'll have a bite at that bottle myself. Been a long day to get lost at the end of it."

It was an eerie evening. The sky was dusted with stars against the incredible furry velvet blue of the African night. The bush bulked black against the horizon, making strange animal forms, like a fancifully trimmed yew hedge on an English estate. The vast plain of grass—shorter now—was silver in the night and glimmered like a field of wheat. A slim, graceful crescent of moon made the grass sparkle as we sped over it fruitlessly, seeking the harbor entrance to the camp we knew was over a long, low-bulking hill. Little bat-eared foxes scampered ahead of us and grimaced at Jessica's headlamps. Night jars whooshed and got up ghostily ahead of us, fluttering off like startled spirits. My knees ached. My back ached. My knees cramped. My eyes were full of dust and my beard itched. My irreverent wife began to sing a song to the tune of "How High the Moon."

"How tall the trees," she sang. "How green the grass. How skinned my knees. How tired my—— Pass the spirits, Buster," she said. "And where is Jack Armstrong, the all-East African boy, aiming to take us now?"

"Home to Campi Abahati," Harry said. "I see Annie Lorry's headlamps. She's waiting for us around that corner and just past that hill, damn her eyes. She found it first, and I shall never forgive myself."

"What does Abahati mean?" Jinny said. "Bugs in bed or rhinos in the john or what?"

"It means Happy Camp, Lucky Camp," Harry said, and pressed the gas. The jeep leaped and bounded at fifty miles an hour over the plain, occasionally loosening teeth as Harry struck a stone or a hole or a stick.

"Happy Camp, yet," Virginia said. "Lost in the jungle with two idiots and they call it Happy Camp. Ah well, a girl learns to put up with anything if she's married to a writer. Lead on, MacSelby, and tell the hyenas they got new food for thought, meaning me."

We couldn't make much out of Campi Abahati at midnight, except that seven hyenas, three lions, and an assortment of baboons and leopards seemed to be eagerly awaiting us. It looked pretty dreary.

"This doesn't seem like the happiest *campi* I ever *campi-ed* in," the *memsaab* said as we crawled under the mosquito nets and a lion voiced a certain amount of displeasure fifty yards away.

When we left it ten days later she cried. And not from relief.

Chapter 3

I WOKE UP in an Old Testament, or possibly Koranic, paradise. To estimate a paradise today you have to call it a place that God was happy to make, had not erred in the making, with the original creatures in it and not even man behaving very badly. The Happy Camp, the Lucky Camp, was on a grassy knoll overlooking the Grummetti River. We pitched the tents beneath big thorn acacias. Up the river a leopard sawed. Over the hill a lion spoke. The baboons came to call to see that we were doing everything right. Halfway between the camp and Harry's favorite leopard trees was a big anthill twelve feet high. Somewhere along the marsh there would be a couple of juvenile twin rhinos, especial friends of Harry's, and one old buffalo bull with a crumpled right horn.

"One of these days I shall have to kill that ancient character," Harry said at breakfast. "I have wasted more time stalking him than I have time to waste. I get up to him at last every time and he looks at me and leers. He knows that I won't permit the client to shoot him, with that ugly, stupid, worn-down horn. He wastes my time, but he is a friend of mine, and I've never had the heart to settle his troubles for him."

I am always amazed when I think of how much living can be compressed into a tent settlement. We had four major tents, not counting the toilet one. We had a big double-fly job for the *memsaab* and the *bwana*. Selby slept in a single double-fly. There was a big open-faced dining tent in which all the boxes of food were stacked. There was a tiny cook tent, and some of the boys had shelter-halves. It takes fifty minutes to set it all up, and the next day it bears the earmarks of a thriving city. Somehow it suddenly becomes logical to go to the john in a canvas cell and to wash your dirty body in a canvas coffin, in water full of living things, and to sleep soundly with the hyenas tripping over the tent ropes.

The sounds become wonderfully important. There is a dove that sounds like a goosed schoolgirl. He says: "Oooh. Oooh! *OOOHH!*" The bush babies cry. The colobus monkeys snort like lions, except it does not carry the implied threat. At first it is hard to tell the baboons from the leopards when they curse each other in a series of guttural grunts. A hyena can roar like a lion. A lion mostly mutters with an asthmatic catch in his throat. The bugs are tumultuous. A well-situated jungle camp is not quiet. But the noise makes itself into a pattern which is soothing except when the hyenas start to giggle. A hyena's giggle is date night in the female ward of a madhouse.

"You will find yourself growing fond of old Fisi," Harry said. "He's a noisy nuisance and a cheeky brute, but if you took him out of Africa it wouldn't be Africa any more. He's a tidy one too. Cleans up everything for you."

We slept late that morning, bone-sore from the three-day drive, and along about elevenish Harry said we'd best go and sight the guns in. We left Mama in the camp to repair the ravages to her beauty and drove out along the plain. The grass was short. The grass was trampled. And all the animals in the world were busy trampling it.

Our camp was cuddled in the crook of a low mountain's arm, but behind was plain, a brilliant yellow plain dotted with blue-and-white primrosy sorts of flowers. Wherever you looked there was life. Five thousand wildebeest there. Five thousand zebras yonder. Two hundred impala here. A thousand Tommies there. Five hundred Grant gazelles there. A herd of buffalo on the river. Harry's twin baby rhinos. A shaggy-necked, elky-looking waterbuck with his harem in the green reeds. If you grew grass on Times Square and cleaned up the air and made it suddenly quiet and filled it with animals instead of people you might approach some likely approximation of what I saw that morning, with the sky blue and the hills green and the plain yellow and blue and white.

The animals looked at us casually and with little curiosity. We stopped the jeep beneath a thornbush and Harry motioned to Kidogo. Kidogo, wearing his floppy shorts on his skinny bowed legs and his big cheerful grin on a face like an Abyssinian king, picked up the *panga* and walked a hundred yards away to another tree and chopped a big blaze off it with the *panga*. Harry took a couple of cushions out of the Land Rover and laid them on its bonnet. He spraddled his short thick legs, leaned the .375 against the cushions, and fired. Kidogo tapped a point of the blaze with his *panga*.

"High and left," Harry said. "We'll just rearrange these graticules." He did something to the scope and then rapped on it with a big .416 cartridge to see that the new setting was solid. He fired again, and this time the big Winchester was dead on.

"Good gun, that," he said. "Just remains to see if you can hold it as steadily as it'll shoot straight for you if you give it the chance."

We—he—sighted all the guns, the .375, the .30-'06, the .220, and the big ugly .470 double. I shot them all afterward. They all seemed to kick. The big .470 had a push, but it pushed you back two feet. I was beginning to feel nervous, having never shot anything more serious than a shooting-gallery duck with a rifle. These guns seemed to make a god-awful amount of noise.

"Tell you what," Harry said. "We'd best break you in easy and get you used to the light and the guns. On the way back to camp we'll let you shoot a zebra for the boys to eat and a Tommy for us to eat and a Grant and a wart hog for a leopard bait. I've a very fine tree just down from the camp. Always seem to haul a leopard out of it. Harriet Maytag shot an eight-foot tom out of it three months ago, and the *manamouki* —the tabby—had a new boy friend in it the next night. A lot of blokes fancy just hogs for leopard kills, but I've had any amount of luck with Grants. To play the percentage evenly I generally use both a Grant and a pig. Been awfully lucky so far."

We climbed into Jessica and aimed for the camp and lunch. A herd of Grants looked at us and ambled slowly away, walking gingerly on seemingly sore feet.

"See the old boy, the last one, just over there?" Harry said. "He's an old ram and about ready for the hyenas. He'd be tougher than whitleather and his liver is full of worms and his meat is measly, but the leopards won't care. Get out and wallop him. *Toa* .30-'06," he snapped over his shoulder to Kidogo. The Nandi gunbearer slid the bolt of the little Remington and handed it to me. I slid out of the car and crawled to an anthill. The jeep went away. One does not shoot from cars in Africa, nor until the vehicle is a good five hundred yards away. The Game Department aesthetically deplores car shooters and also puts them in jail.

I have shot at submarines and I have shot at airplanes and I didn't shake, but now I shook. The sight of the rifle was revolving like a Catherine wheel. It seemed to me my breath had ceased forever, and I was panting like a sprint horse extended out of class in a distance race. My eyes blurred. I aimed at the gazelle's shoulder, waited until the rifle stopped leaping, snatched at the trigger, and heard the bullet whunk. I aimed at the shoulder and I hit him in the hind left ankle. Great beginning, boy, I said. Steady rest on 135 pounds of standing animal and you hit him in the foot. I shot five more times, carefully. The last time I shot he jumped into the bullet which broke his neck. He went over on his horns, and the jeep drove up to get me.

"Nice shooting," Harry said.

"*Piga. Kufa. M'zuri sana,*" the boys said.

"Nuts," I said. "It looks like I am a shotgun man."

"You broke his neck," Harry said.

"I was aiming at his behind," I said.

"It's like that for everybody at first," Harry said. "The light, you know. Everybody misses at first."

"Look, the light hasn't got anything to do with my shakes," I said. "The light doesn't make the gun wiggle like a cooch dancer. I got no guts. I shake and I can't control my breath. I aim at the shoulder and hit it in the foot. I am sighted in on his can and I break his neck. This we can't blame on the light. This we can't blame on the gun."

"Take it easy, take it easy," Harry said. "It happens to everybody. Even Hemingway. It even happened to Theodore Roosevelt."

"Bwana Haraka," Adam, the Wakamba gunbearer, said. "*Pandi hio. Ngiri.*"

"Nice wart hog," Harry said. "We need him to go with the Grant. *Toa* .220, Kidogo. You can shoot this one from the car," he said to me. "It's vermin and legal and you can get a steady rest on the windscreen. Wallop him up the rear. Bullet ranges forward, and if it doesn't break his back it'll work into his chest cavity."

The pig was trotting, his antenna-tail straight up. I held the little hopped-up .22 on his buxom backside and it felt steady. I squeezed and peeled a ham off his right hip. He let out a squeal and went into the bush, leaving blood behind him. We tracked him and we never found him and I looked sadly at the .220 Swift and sadly at the boys and sadly at Selby.

"You can blame the gun on this one," Harry said. "The bullet broke up on the outside of the pig. Didn't penetrate. I have read a lot about these speedy little guns, but it seems to me they wreck the little stuff and just savage the bigger stuff. Let's try it once again on the hyena over there. This is the only hyena you get. I don't like to shoot them, even if they are miserable creatures. Except on the farm. When you see one of your dairy herd come in with her udder ripped off, or if you watch old Fisi standing by a calving cow so he can snatch the calf when she drops it, or when you wake up one night to find one looking at you as if you were a mutton chop, you shoot hyenas. Wallop this one. He's got an especially evil look on his face."

The hyena was watching us as we drove up, his big dog's face mean and sullen, his lion's ears pricked, scabby hide ugly in the sun. As we approached he gallumped slowly away, the hindquarters that God crippled sloping down from his bear's body, a dog's head with a lion's ears on a bear's body with the hind legs of a crippled beggar. Fisi, spotted and stinking and no friend to anyone. I shot him. I shot him nine times with the .220 Swift. I hit him every time, and every time the bullet splattered on his outside. One time I hit him in the face and took away his lower jaw and still he didn't die. He just bled and began to snap fruitlessly with half a face at his own dragging guts. I spoke my first command in Swahili.

"*Toa bundouki m'kubwa,*" I said. 'The big one. Gimme the .470." The gunbearer snapped the barrels onto the elephant gun and slipped a couple of cigar-sized shells into it. I held it on the gory hyena and took his head off.

"They say it's a good woodchuck gun, the .220," Harry said. "I'm inclined to believe they may be right. But for pigs and hyenas and such it ain't much gun, is it?"

"I just fired it for the last time," I said. "I wouldn't even use it on a woodchuck. Or a skunk. Or anything else I had any respect for. Give it to the deserving poor."

"I am beginning to like you a little bit," Harry said. "I am completely caught up with clients who want to go out and slay a bull rhino with one of these silly little freak guns with an ounce of lead and a lot of speed. I am strictly a heavy-bullet man myself. I cannot abide wounding things that could be simply killed if you used enough gun. But you'd be surprised how vain some of these sportsmen are. It gets us professionals killed. Some sporty type wants to do it all himself, wounds it, doesn't want us to collaborate, it goes off into the bush, and then I wind up having to go after it."

"Pal, you are not hunting with a vain man," I said. "Anything I shoot that needs extra shooting you are invited. Be my guest. Collaborate, when and as necessary, and do not pause to check with your client. Shoot it first and I will argue with you later."

We shaped back to camp again and put up another hog, a biggish boar accompanied by the sow and six piglets.

"You'll kill this one well," Harry said. "Mind what I say. Use the .30-'06."

The boar was running diagonally across and ahead of us. The Remington felt comfortable in my hands. I swung it ahead of the boar's shoulder and squeezed her off. The pig did a forward flip and stayed still. One of the gunbearers exhaled sharply.

"*Kufa,*" he said. "*M'zuri sana. Piga m'zuri.*"

"Old Bwana Firecracker," Harry said, grinning. "The toast of the Muthaiga Club. You have now passed your apprenticeship. That is a very dead pig and a very nice shot and we will hang the pig in the tree next to the Grant and we will shoot us a very nice leopard, and now for Christ sake quit worrying about your shooting."

Just before we got back to camp we remembered that I was supposed to shoot a Tommy for our table. There was a likely-looking one standing and switching his tail. I got out of the jeep with the Remington and shot at him. I shot at him fourteen times. My wife killed him three days later. He had horns good enough for space in Rowland Ward's records.

I did not speak much during lunch.

I don't think I ate any, as a matter of fact. All I could think of was the fact that the guy who couldn't hit a Tommy was supposed to shoot a lion.

We left the *mem* in camp again to do whatever it is that women have to do, and we went down by the reeds. We had Kidogo and Adam and Kibiriti along as ballast. We drove slowly along the wet edge of the high green reeds and we flushed a herd of waterbuck, but the bull wasn't much and you can't eat them anyhow, so we pushed on and then Kibiriti rapped Harry on the shoulder. A ripple showed through the reeds.

"*Kita,*" Kibiriti said.

It was a hunting cheetah, and you could see his small round head plowing through the reeds, and he looked over his shoulder once and then took off like a shot.

"*Hapana,*" Kibiriti said.

"He's right," Harry said. "This one we will not see again. When they go they *go,* and you have had him. Let's go shoot a zebra for the blacks to eat."

Kibiriti said something rapidly in Swahili. It was about a paragraphful of Swahili.

"The old boy's come down with one of his hunches," Harry

said. "He's feeling liony. He says that, the way the moon is and what with the rains and all and the state of grass and economics amongst lions in general, he feels like a lion ought to be about three miles from here, contemplating his navel under a tree hard by a rocky hill. To my certain knowledge Kibiriti has not been here for a year. But if he feels liony we'd best go and take a *dekko* at his hill. Don't let the fez fool you. This is a true savage, and he is finer with a bow or spear than anybody I ever met, and he *feels* lions. Are you up to shooting one today, your first day?"

"Christ preserve us," I said. "Let's hope this lion fancier is wrong. Today I would hate to go up against a bull butterfly."

"You'll change your tune when you see your first shootable *simba*," Harry said. "You'll be awfully brave. You'll probably be so scared that you will mistake fear for bravery and do everything right."

"That's nice to know, Mowgli," I said.

"What's this Mowgli business?" Harry asked.

"He's a fictional figure," I said. "Kipling dreamed him up. He lived among the beasts of the field and seemed to like it. His mother was a wolf."

"Did he have fleas?" Harry asked politely, and swung the jeep toward Kibiriti's hunch, his lion-tenanted rocky hillside.

And it was that simple. We traveled the three miles. There was a rocky hill alongside the marsh. There was a clump of thorn, and under it there was a lion, catching a nap in the afternoon sun which slanted under the umbrella tops of the trees and struck some golden sparks from his blackish-yellow hide.

"*Simba*," Kibiriti said. "*M'kubwa. Doumi*," as a man might remark that if you go east far enough on Fifty-fourth Street you will find the East River.

"I'm damned if I understand it," Harry said reverently.

"This silly bastard is infallible. I *know* he hasn't been here in a year. I also know that three days ago there couldn't have been a lion in the neighborhood because the game is just starting to come in. But here we are. Your first shooting day in Africa and now you've got to shoot a lion. His mane is a little short on top and he's a little past prime. But he's the biggest blighter I've ever seen, and today a lion is a lion. I think you'd best collect this bloke, and maybe we can better him later."

I looked at Kibiriti's broad black face and saw the sun shining through the holes in his pierced lobes. I looked at his red fez and disliked him extremely.

"Why doesn't this idiot mind his business and stay home with his wives, they should cuckold him constantly?" I said bitterly. "Why has the son of a bitch got to go around finding lions on my first day when I can't hit a Tommy in fourteen tries and mammock up a wart hog and shoot Grants in the feet? I don't know anything about shooting lions. I couldn't hit myself in my own foot if I was a conscientious objector. I don't even know if I *want* to shoot a lion. Tell that grinning bastard to quit living my life for me and find his lions on his own time."

"Everybody wants to shoot a lion," Harry said. "That's why safaris cost so much. Even Aly Khan wants to shoot a lion. It's the high cost of lions that's ruining our economy. You can't mean you'd pass up a bargain lion your first day? Harriet Maytag shot one her first——"

"God *damn* Harriet Maytag, whoever she be," I said. "All I hear is Harriet Maytag. Harriet's leopard. Harriet's lion. So all right. Call me Harriet. Let's go shoot the damn thing and then I will be sick."

Harry grinned. Selby is an extraordinarily handsome young man, with the kind of curly black hair and dark eyes that bring out the mother in women. He also has wrists as thick as ordinary men's ankles, and a hard mouth that turns down at the corners. In town he looks like what the fagot writers call a "pretty boy." Take him into the bush, among the blacks and beasts, and he is called *m'zee* by natives. *M'zee* means old man. It means respected, ancient sir. It means wisdom and courage and experience. At that particular moment I decided that I had met few people with so much to admire and so little to worry about. He swerved the jeep away from the lion and we stopped her on the side of a hill, five thousand yards away. I lit a cigarette and passed it to Selby. I lit one for myself. Looking at the hands, I noticed that they were not shaking.

"What do you know?" I said wonderingly. "Check old Francis Macomber here. All I need now is Virginia to shoot me in the back of the neck."

Harry unbuttoned the left door from the jeep. He tossed it onto the grass. He said something to Kidogo, the bowlegged gunbearer. It sounded like *wapi hapa iko simba lio pandi hi m'kubwa bandouki bwana piga bloody nugu*. I didn't really listen. I was sending my soul away again. I hoped it was at Toots Shor's having a drink with friends.

"We will collect this *simba* like this," Harry said sternly, like an over-young professor lecturing the class. "Kidogo drives Jessica here. I sit in the middle. You sit on the outside. We will drive as close as we can without annoying this creature overmuch and taking care to observe the government's rule about five hundred yards away, et cetera. When I nudge you, fall out of the jeep. Fall flat and lie still and then we will crawl as close to this *simba* as we can, and when I tell you to shoot him you shoot him. The idea is to get close as you can— less danger of wounding him that way. You wound this chap, old boy, and he gets into those reeds, and we will all have a very nasty time. I'd *not* wound him if I were you. When you've shot him once, shoot him again, and then shoot him once more for insurance. Very sound rule. Old Phil Percival taught it me. All set?"

I couldn't say anything but yes. Kidogo had taken the telescopic sights off the .375. I slid back the bolt and caught the comforting glint of the bullets in the magazine. There was one in the chamber. Good-by, Mother, I said to myself. Et up by a lion in the bloom of youth.

"Well, let's go shoot him," I said. "What are we waiting for?"

"That's the spirit," Harry said. "*Pese pese. Suria. Kwenda.*"

The jeep began to roll, Kidogo obeying motions of Harry's hands. We approached the lion deviously. We seemed always to be going away from him but actually were growing closer. Kidogo took his foot off the gas. Harry hit me in the ribs with his elbow. I fell out of the jeep. I remembered to fall with the gun protected and pointing away. Harry tumbled out behind me. He had a dirty, rusty-looking .416 Rigby bolt-action rifle in his hand. He had told me once that it could not hit anything but lions.

I was on my belly in the stiff, coarse yellow grass, and the lion was looking enormous now, staring in that oddly stuffed-shirt profile way they do, like bankers contemplating the future. A lion's hide is not tawny. It is yellowish-black. This one flexed the muscles of his forelegs, hooking his claws, and flicked his back hide to express annoyance at the camel flies that buzzed around him. I was humping along on my elbows, with the gun pushing out ahead of me. I seemed to have done this before.

I had done this before. I had done it in an Italian town a long time ago, when a shot spurted at me from out of an alley along the Corso, and I had fallen to the cobbles, clutching and cocking a Walther P-38 which I had bought for a carton of cigarettes from a Scots paratrooper who had killed a German paratroop lieutenant at Termoli and who had liberated his sidearm. Some more shots spurted from the alley and I shot back at the shots, moving the P-38 gently from left to right and shooting out the full magazine. No more shots came from the alley. There was nothing in the alley but a dead co-belligerent with a lot of new navels. We used to lose a lot of allies in those days, before we disarmed the co-belligerents.

I was feeling now like the lion was a co-belligerent in an alley, and the feeling flooded over me like it is when you come in from a long day in the snow, and the fire and the whisky both start working on you at once. The Winchester was as light as a Walther P-38 liberated from a dead German *leutnant* at Termoli.

We were close to the lion now. I could count flies on him. Harry reached back and touched me, pressing me down behind a hummock. The lion turned his head and looked straight at us. He *was* a little scruffy on top, but he had a fine dark mane below. His feet were as big as Satchel Paige's feet. His head was as big as a bale of hay. He yawned and I saw he had his right canine tooth broken off. He was huge.

"Wallop him," Selby whispered.

I got up on one knee and went for just behind his ear. He flopped over like a big dog, kicked once, roared once, and stretched out. I never did hear my gun go off and felt no concussion, although a .375 magnum is not as kickless as, say, a P-38 Walther pistol.

"This is the biggest lion I ever saw in my life," Harry said. "Also the deadest. But I should slip another one into him just behind that shoulder blade if I were you. I keep telling you, these dead animals are the ones that get up and kill you. Bust him again."

I busted him again. You could tell he was dead from the sound of the bullet hitting him and his bodily reaction to the bullet hitting him.

"*Kufa*," Harry said. "My Christ, he's huge. An old boy to boot. Shouldn't be surprised if he isn't the type that citizen in Ikoma was calling a cattle killer. He'd be about ready for cattle now and mauling the odd native now and then. He's about ten years old. I might say you shot him rather well, chum."

"I always shoot lions in the ear," I said. "Like I always shoot Grant gazelles in the foot. I was probably aiming at this one's can too."

"No bloody fear," Harry said. "I was watching you. Old Bwana Simba. Old Bwana Lisasi Moja. One-Bullet Bob. The toast of the Muthaiga Club. Here come the worshiping throng. They want your autograph. Kill a lion, make friends, influence natives. Nice going, chum."

The boys knew the script well. They all gave me the special handshake, grasping the thumb, roaring asthmatically, and telling me that I was the one-shot *bwana*, the mighty *simba* slayer, the protector of the poor. I agreed readily and then went over behind a bush and vomited just a little bit. This was because of something I had eaten disagreeing with me. Then I went to look at my lion. He looked awfully rumpled. A dead lion has no dignity. All the majesty leaks out of him with the blood. He looks like a moth-bit rug, and after a while his mane drops off.

"This is a hell of a lion," I said. "He looks like Russell Nype. I have just slain the only crew-cut *simba* in Tanganyika."

"Who's Russell Nype?" Harry asked.

"He's a society-type singer wears horn-rims and goes out socially with the Duchess of Windsor," I said. "He made the crew cut what it is today. Friend of the Donahues."

I looked at my lion. The top of his brainpan was off. We walked off his measurements and he was ten foot six. That is a lot of lion. His paws were as big as pumpkins. It suddenly occurred to me that I had crawled up on this thing as close as I had to get and when I had to shoot him I shot him and didn't wound him and of a sudden the boys were admiring me and Harry was kidding me and I felt real good. I hadn't spooked. I hadn't butched it. I hadn't looked bad in front of the boys.

I am a hell of a fellow, I said to myself. I am a slayer of Simba, Lord of the Jungle. And anyhow, I didn't run or fire into the air. Whisky is indicated.

We wrestled the corpse into the back of the jeep, on a matting of rushes so he wouldn't bleed up the Rover. I talked a great deal on the drive back to camp and accepted congratulations freely. One of the camel flies bit me painfully, and I didn't care. I was suddenly free of a great many inhibitions. Every man has to brace a lion at least once in his life, and whether the lion is a woman or a boss or the prospect of death by disease makes no difference. I had met mine and killed him fairly and saved him from the hyenas which would have had him in a year or so if one of his sons didn't assassinate him first.

When we hit the camp the boys knew. They surged over the jeep and me and mauled us all and told us *m'zuri sana, bwana,* and waited for the money tip to the whole camp. They did a sedate lion dance and ran me for alderman of metropolitan Ikoma.

I went down to the tent to collect the hero's bride. She was taking a nap. She bubbled gently as she snored.

"Get up, you lazy slut," I said. "While you are sleeping your life away I have been out slaying lions and protecting

the honest poor. Come and see what Father done done with
his gun. And bring your camera."

Virginia came with the camera. We posed the defunct
simba suitably, his chin arrogantly on a rock. The blacks told
me again that I was one hell of a *bwana*. Then the lion's eyes
opened. Then his ears twitched. Then he uttered a grunt.
Then I found myself alone with a lion and Mr. Selby. The
admirers had achieved trees. I am not ashamed to say I shot
my *simba* once more in the back of the neck. Like Harry says,
it's the dead ones get up and kill you.

Chapter 4

THE night we got lost coming into the camp I looked at this brawny child who was going to run my life for me with a slightly new interest. I had lived in the same car, the same camp, with him for three days. We had had some drinks in the Queens' bar in Nairobi and lunch together at the Traveller's Club and I liked the way he tackled the check, like a man used to reaching for it. He had no impediment in his reach, I thought, and snickered at the pun. I would have liked it better if it had been *my* pun.

I had seen him shoot the little Tommy, and I had heard a lot of tall tales about Selby. They told me how he could tie two rocks to strings and start them swinging, like counter-pendulums, and then dash off to fifty yards away and wheel and shoot the two twines as they passed in their pendulum swing. They told me how he took a Rigby .450 No. 2 and shot the two swooping kites, the swiftly sliding scavengers, with a right and a left. A man who shoots flying birds with an elephant gun shoots pretty good. They told me about the last buffalo too. The one that Bob Maytag shot and they thought it was dead. It got up and Harry hit it over one eye and Maytag hit it under the other eye and it still kept coming. So Harry shot it through the *pupil*. I presume he wasn't aiming elsewhere.

He seemed the kind of kid girls might like to marry or mothers might want to raise. He was polite to excess, extremely courteous to Virginia, and he always offered a cigarette when he smoked one himself. He blushed rather easily, and when he swore it was self-conscious. Virginia after three days was just a little bit in love with him already. With the tumbled curly hair and the deep eyes and the self-confidence and the reputation behind him for being all man, and clean man, you would wonder how the women left him single that long. And shy, too. And modest.

He was a long way from the fictional idea of the professional. The popular conception of a white hunter, built largely in the American mind on film portrayals by Gregory Peck and Stewart Granger, is almost as erroneous as the movie and popular magazine accounts of African safaris. According to what you may have seen or read, the basic idea of a professional hunter is roughly this:

He stands about six foot five, sports a full beard, and is drunk (off his client's liquor) most of the time. He always makes a play for the client's beautiful wife and/or sister, and always scores. He shoots lions with pistols and wrestles with snakes and buffalo for fun. When he is not out on safari he hangs around bars in Nairobi, ogling the girls and thumbing the big cartridges he wears in the loops of his jacket. He does all the shooting for the client, while the client sits comfortably in the shooting car. He is always taciturn in a me-Tarzan-you-Jane manner. He has a secret sorrow which drove him to a life among the wild beasts. His business is regarded as butchery, and it takes a superhuman man to be a competent butcher.

This is about as accurate as the average movie presentation of high life in New York, or the general supposition that all Englishmen have no chins and sport monocles. In some respects the white or professional big-game hunter, African variety, is the toughest man in the world, and in others he is as gentle as a dead dove and as unsophisticated as Huck Finn. He is competent at his job, which is why he is alive, but you will see more rugged types on the dance floor at El Morocco. And he is the last of a breed of men who have such a genuine love for the wilds and such a basic hatred of civilization that they are willing literally to kill themselves with backbreaking work and daily danger, on a nine-months-per-year basis, for less pay than a good waiter in New York draws. They forswear matrimony, generally, because no wife lasts long when the old man is off twisting the tails of leopards for most of the calendar year. They save only a little money, for the upkeep on their hunting cars largely outweighs their income, and they blow the rest in Nairobi between safaris or in the rainy seasons when hunting is impossible. They are referred to as a vanishing breed because there are somewhat less than thirty practicing top pros in British East Africa today, and in a very short time there will be little big stuff left to practice on. It is thought by most of the smart ones that the next three or four years will see the last of safari in the old sense, when a man went out to kill a lion, a leopard, an elephant, and the more elusive big antelopes with some feeling of certainty.

Harry Selby is possibly the best of the current bunch—certainly there's no better about, and his popularity is such that he is booked up five years ahead. He was not yet twenty-seven at the time I write but has been an able pro since he was twenty. He was born and raised in East Africa, on a cattle farm in Nanyuki, Kenya Colony, and had killed his first elephant before he was fifteen. He looks like a public-school boy and speaks an impeccable British English in such a gentle voice that even an occasional "damn" sounds very wicked.

Tony Henley, whom I had met, was raised on the slopes of Mount Kenya and was an old pro at twenty-three. He is a blond youngster who looks like a substitute end on a high school football team. Tony Dyer, at twenty-six, looks like the valedictorian in a junior-college graduation exercise. Donald Ker, a partner in the firm of Ker and Downey, is a small, thin, mild-seeming man in his forties, who put himself through school shooting elephants for ivory when he was a 110-pound stripling. His partner, Syd Downey, looks like an ordinary businessman, is pushing fifty, and still is rated one of the best in the business. Andrew Holmberg, the expert on mountain game, is a strapping, rosy-cheeked six-footer who might very well be a junior advertising executive. And the now-retired dean of the bunch, Philip Percival, who raised Harry, is a plump old gentleman with stubby legs, who looks about as fierce as Colonel Blimp.

Yet all these men have made a business of mingling daily with lions, leopards, and the most dangerous trio—buffalo, elephants, and rhinos—and have managed to stay alive, although nearly all have horn wounds and claw scars, and all have considered death as a daily diet. They have a tremendous respect for dangerous animals. When they are hurt, ninety-nine times out of a hundred they are injured trying to protect a client who has just shown arrant cowardice or com-

plete stupidity. Yet no client is ever publicly branded a coward. No client is ever tagged as a kill-crazy meat hog. No
lady ever misses her lion—not for the record, anyhow. The
code says that the hunters don't talk, once the safari is over.
That is ridiculous, of course. They talk plenty, mostly among
themselves, but occasionally to customers they have come to
know and respect.

The function of a professional hunter on safari is almost
godlike. He is responsible for the safety of the whole shebang
—you, himself, and the black boys who make up your *shauri*.
He is the guide over trackless wastes. He is the expert on
finding game and seeing that his dude is in the best possible
position to shoot it.

If you ask him, he will shoot it for you, but he will quietly
despise you as a man, and the contempt he feels will be
mirrored in the black faces.

If you wound an animal, it is the hunter's responsibility
to go into the bush and finish it off, both out of humanitarian-
ism and caution, since a wounded lion or buffalo is bound to
kill the first unlucky local who crosses his path. At all times
he is the servant of the Game Department, whose laws are
strict and in whose employ are many spies.

The hunter stands at your side to backstop you on dangerous game. His idea of the pleasant safari is one in which
he is not forced to fire a gun once. But if the going gets nasty,
his big double is your insurance.

"I don't care a damn about these people who can split a
pea at three hundred yards," old Phil Percival once remarked.
"What I want to know about a man is how good he is on a
charging buffalo at six feet."

My man Selby, to that specification, seems excellent. I
asked him about the last buffalo he was *forced* to shoot. The
buff had gone down, and it appeared his back was broken.

As Selby and the client approached cautiously, the buff got up and charged at about fifteen yards. The client let him have one in the chest and one in the face.

"The first bullet hit him here," Selby said, "just under the right eye. He kept coming. At about ten feet I hit him just here, over the left eye. He continued to progress."

"What did you do then?" I asked him.

"Well," Harry said, "at about four feet I shot him again. I shot him through the *pupil.*" He rummaged through some photos and showed me the dead buffalo. There was a hole under one eye, a hole over the other, and where the left eye belonged was a hole as big as an egg. The buff had died and fallen on Selby's feet.

The heavy work for a hunter is not so much the location of game and the supervision of the final kill as the camp routine. He supervises a tiny portable city—administers loading and unloading in exactly the right order, ordains the pitching of camp, selecting camp, looks after the water supply, supervises the skinners and trackers and gunbearers and porters and cooks and body servants. He must be an expert mechanic —he must be able to rebuild a motorcar from the spare parts he carries and improvise those parts he has not.

The hunter is responsible for correct victualing of an expedition that may be out from town three or four months, so that he needs a dietitian's knowledge of supplementary canned goods and a balanced menu. He is directly responsible for providing an average of ten pounds a day, per man, of fresh meat. In most cases the ordinary day's killing will keep sufficient meat in camp.

As the head of a safari, the hunter finally combines the duties of a sea captain, a bodyguard, a chauffeur, a tracker, a skinner, a headwaiter, a tourist guide, a photographer, a mechanic, a stevedore, an interpreter, a game expert, a gin-rummy partner, drinking companion, social equal, technical superior, boss, employee, and handy man. The difficulty of his position is magnified in that he lives in the pockets of his one or two clients for long weeks, and unless he is a master of tact, nobody is speaking to anyone else when the safari pays off in Nairobi. The old-timers had a phrase to describe a safari gone sour.

"I'm still drinking their whisky," the hunter would say, meaning that all social intercourse had ceased and the safari was operating on a basis of frigid politeness, with the hunter keeping himself to himself except during shooting hours.

More dangerous than an angry cow elephant with a young calf, Harry had said, is the woman on safari. She is generally rich and spoiled, old and full of complaints, or young and apt to fall a little bit in love with the hunter. In a tent community, this puts rather a strain on the young man who is accepting the husband's pay to hunt animals instead of wives. Living à trois can be a difficult operation in the midst of Tanganyika when the memsaab has a tendency to cast goo-goo eyes at the professional and invent ways to catch him alone. "Even the best of the sporting ladies," Harry said, "even the most rugged of the female hunters, has a tendency to woof at the monotony of the food, the lack of toilet facilities, and the prevalence of bugs, snakes, and scorpions. Africa is dusty, and Africa is wet and hot and cold, and a tent is not the Norfolk, nor is a canvas tub a Grecian bath. Warm martinis can irk on a delicately reared lady. A girl gets tired of hearing incessant conversation of guns and game and grass. I know of no hunter who is delighted at the prospect of setting out with a lady who may turn out to be either shrew or nymphomaniac."

Some of the ladies can be fun, though, he said. Selby was out once on a more or less photographic safari with the Duchess of Grafton.

"We were taking some snaps of impala, or something tame," Selby said, "when we spooked an old gentleman rhino who was very cross at being woken from his nap. As we'd no license for rhino, I didn't like to shoot it, so I said to the Duchess: 'Your Grace, you'd best make for yonder tree.' The old girl took off at the speed of knots and went up the tree like a squirrel, camera and all. Then I entered into a delaying action."

Back in Nairobi, however, the Duchess told the press a different story.

"I was safely ensconced on my limb," the Duchess said, "when I heard a small, polite voice below me. It was Mr. Selby, who was running round and round the tree, with the rhino's horn just behind him. The small voice said: 'If you please, Your Grace, would you mind moving up another branch? I may need the one you're sitting on.'"

Selby denied this. He says it would never have occurred to him to address her as "Your Grace" under such trying circumstances.

Harry was talking on as he shoved the jeep along. "The sense of humor of these men is rather amazing. We have an old-timer, Murray Smith, who once dived into the bush with his client after a wounded rhino. The old rhino boiled out from behind a thorn tree, and as old Murray squared away to face it, he went tail over tip into a pig hole and sprawled flat. The *faro* came at him, and all Smith could do was seize its horn with both hands and hang on for dear life, with the *faro* bouncing him up and down. The client, I expect, wasn't a coward, ran up and stuck his gun in the rhino's ear, and saved old Murray from a very sticky finish. Later somebody asked him what he thought of when the rhino had him down.

"'All I could think of,' Murray said, 'was that now I had

hold of it, the horn seemed *longer* than I thought it was when I told the client to shoot.' "

Harry was saying that there are clients who are too brave, who insist on shooting everything themselves, and who also insist that the hunter not shoot under any circumstances. These are the people who generally get the hunters maimed, since they are prone to shoot too fast and from too great a distance, wounding the game and making it necessary for the professional to go and collect it from the thornbush.

There are the too timid, who shoot wildly, run away, drop their guns, and generally foul up the detail. They refuse to take advantage of the old safety axiom: "Get as close as you can, and then get ten feet closer." They bang away from afar and gut-shoot the lion or merely annoy the buffalo, and the poor old pro has to make amends in the name of the Game Department.

There is the complete phony, who gets out of the city limits and says: "Look, you shoot it all, but don't tell anybody." This is a fairly simple type to handle, since a competent pro can round up the fraud's complete bag, on reasonably mediocre animals, and send the fellow back to brag in his club in no time at all. But a hunter spits when he mentions a client of this sort.

From the hunter's standpoint the ideal customer is a man who is scared enough to be cautious but brave enough to control his fear. He follows instructions, knows and is frank about his own limitations on stamina, and quits when he has had enough of mountains and swamps and dust and bumps for one day. He shoots his own game but is not averse to a little help when a buffalo or something else large and fierce needs some extra killing. I learned about this one later.

"You know," Harry said, "there's hell's own amount of

clients who carry on frightfully if the hunter collaborates. They won't even accept the animal, won't even let the boys skin out the head. Lot of bloody nonsense, of course, but there you are. They're the chaps who get us killed."

The true professional hunter has something of the bull-fighter's philosophy, in that he has no guarantee he will see the bright lights and pretty girls of Nairobi ever again. In the final analysis he has to stand and fight. Each man I came to know has had a dozen slim squeaks, mostly from elephants and buffalo. When the crisis occurs, there is no place to run, no tree to climb as a rule, because the wounded animal usually starts his charge in thick bush, from a few feet, and he nearly always sees you before you see him. Some remarkable escapes from certain death have occurred.

Frank Bowman, an Australian and a very fine hunter who is now retired, once sat on the ground with a twisted ankle and no bullets for his gun while a wounded buffalo got up and staggered, sick but still furious, toward him. Bowman screamed for a gunbearer to fetch more bullets, waited until the bearer had run to the car to get them, slapped two fresh bullets in his double, and shot the buff at a range of about one foot. It fell in his lap. The time between no bullets and two bullets must have been the longest recorded wait in the history of hunting, at least from Bowman's angle.

"This gunbearer, Adam," Harry said, "was elevated to the aristocracy in the following manner: Old Phil Percival, with an empty gun, was being chased round and round the hunting car by a wounded buffalo, and all the natives in the back—save Adam—panicked and went over the side. Adam was a porter then. He sorted through the dozen different varieties of cartridges in the back of the car until he found a couple of slugs that fitted old Phil's gun. He handed them to the old boy as he went round the car for the umpteenth time. Percival loaded his weapon in full flight. He settled the animal. As of then Adam was promoted."

Percival, Harry told me, in his later days as a hunter, had still another narrow squeak. Three rhinos charged him and Tommy Shevlin, an American sportsman and a fine shot, penning them in a narrow avenue cut through the thorn. Shevlin's killing shot dropped the nearest rhino across old Philip's legs.

Anyone who hunts elephants, rhinos, or buffalo is a candidate for catastrophe. It is occasionally necessary, in a buffalo stampede in high grass, to whack the nearest animal and *climb up on him,* so that the other great beasts can swerve aside and pass around you. Both elephants and rhinos will charge, unwounded and unpredictably.

The point is that what is one client's rare thrill is routine for the pros. I imagine Murray Smith has been hurt three or four times. Selby has already had six or seven scrapes with buffalo, several with elephants, and a couple of do's with lions and leopards. Syd Downey has been tossed twice by buffalo and has contracted sleeping sickness from tsetse-fly bites. Nearly all East African hunters have a chronic malaria that reduces them to bone-breaking agony and pitiful shakes several times a year. Their lungs are abrased from constant inhalation of lava dust, and their eyes are permanently bloodshot from dust and glare.

Their average day starts at 4:30 A.M., and they rarely bed down before 11 P.M. During the course of a day they will drive a hunting car an average of 125 miles over trackless, tough terrain. They will walk an average of ten over mountains and through swamps, and they will crawl from one to five miles on their bellies. If you are hunting elephants you will walk from twenty to thirty miles a day over dry river beds that suck your shoes into the sliding softness and make every step a mighty effort. The sun smites like hammers all day long, and the nights, in most parts of huntable Africa, are bitter cold. After a full day's work they are still supposed to supervise the constant necessary repair of the hunting vehicles, see that the camp is in good order, solve the problems of from one to two dozen natives, tend the sick, and still be jovial drinking, talking, and card-playing companions to the paying guests. Added to the general chores is the task of explaining the same things, over and over, to a succession of clients who want to know (and rightly) what is that tree, what kind of bird is that, why do we camp here instead of there, and what were the boys saying in Swahili? The hunter also must listen to all the alibis, again and again, as to why the shooter missed the topi at twenty-five yards from a steady rest, and must soothe the injured pride of the man who is paying a hundred dollars a day to do something he would really rather not do, such as crawling through thorns after a sick and angry leopard.

The question, then, must be: *What do they get out of it?* They don't shoot unless they have to, and mostly they take no delight in killing, but rather regard it regretfully as the logical end point of an exciting adventure. They are the greatest of game conservationists—the strictest abiders by the rules. They'll average five or six hundred bucks a month, plus free food and whisky, but they'll spend three or four hundred fixing up the cars they wreck in their mad dashes over rocky hills and pig-hole-riddled fields. They put up with boors and bores and bitches and cowards and braggarts and creeps and occasional homosexuals who have the eye more on the hunter than on the game. They work harder than any of the blacks in their retinue. They have no home life—they don't even share the canvas latrine tent which is set up for the client. They consider death as calmly as life, even when it applies

to themselves. They drink too much, like sailors off a long cruise, when they are in town, and they mostly throw away their money. There is no real future in professional hunting— when you get older you get too cautious for your own safety, and your slowed reflexes make you a liability to yourself and to your party. You cannot bet on yourself as a husband, for what wife will hold still for a husband who is away nine months of the year?

I believe I already knew what they get out of it. There is a simple love of outdoors and of creatures, as against a hatred

for the contrived living of cities, for the claustrophobic con-
nivances of civilization, that drives a man to the vastnesses of
Africa to fulfill some need of basic simplicity in himself. My
friend Selby, hopelessly lost in the jungles of so small a town
as Nairobi, is Moses leading his flock when all he can see is
horizons and a lion or two. The complete love and trust of his
blacks are testament to this.

He is happy in the dawn and in the tiny-gleaming fires of
the camp, and secure in his knowledge of domination of his
element. He worships a buffalo or a lion or an elephant because he knows it can kill him painfully if he is not very careful. He builds his own bridges, makes his own roads. He still
has the thrill of providing his own food and the food of his
friends. He recognizes the inevitability of death as an adjunct
to life.

There are no more jealous people in the world than hunters.
They have an intense pride in their work. A good white
hunter will work himself into a breakdown to scare up a
record bag for a man he despises. Hunters criticize each other
constantly, and each man has his secret ground, a territory
he endeavors, as long as possible, to keep from shooting the
easy animal—what he wants is "heads."

"You are not shooting an elephant," Selby told me. "You
are shooting the symbol of his tusks. You are not shooting to
kill. You are shooting to make immortal the thing you shoot.
To kill just anything is a sin. To kill something that will be
dead soon, but is so fine as to give you pleasure for years, is
wonderful. Everything dies. You only hasten the process.
When you shoot a lion you are actually shooting its mane,
something that will make you proud. You are shooting for
yourself, not shooting just to kill."

These few surviving men are largely Jasons in search of the
Golden Fleece, and they do not care who brings it down, so

long as they are present at the chase. Selby and his companions will actually work harder for a man they loathe than for
a man they like and admire, because the ultimate end is noble
in the mind.

I was beginning to be impressed with this boy, even though
he got us lost, after just a few days. I hoped he was going to
like me. I hoped I wasn't going to embarrass him. I hoped I
wasn't going to shame myself in front of the blacks or run at
the wrong time. I hoped I wasn't going to drink too much. I
didn't want my new young friend to worry about the steadi-
ness of my shooting hand. About that time Harry clapped his
hands.

"Boy," he said. "*Lette gin-i.*"

The boy brought the gin. It was warm but palatable.

Chapter 5

THERE WAS something enchanted and enchanting about the little lucky camp on the Lower Grummetti, eighteen miles from the shambling village of Ikoma in Tanganyika. We lived later in lovelier camps, scenically—the jungle camp at Mto-Wa-Mbu, at the fundament of the Ngoro-Ngoro crater, was more Tarzany and more majestic. The temporary camp on the Little Ruaha River was the most beautiful spot I have ever seen. What Virginia later called "Hippo Haven" on the fringe of Kiteti Swamp, on the high plain away up from Mto-Wa-Mbu, was breath-taking, with its cool canopy of huge wild figs and acacias, their trunks yellow-mottled like a leopard's hide. But the little lucky camp—Campi Abahati—grabbed and hung onto my heart. Maybe it was because it was my first one, my first permanent one.

We had come round the elbow of the little mountain and pitched the tents on a grassy slope fifty yards away from the river greenery. It was always cool without being creeper-jungly and bug-infested there. Coming up to it in a car was like a ride through South Carolina savanna land, with its clumps of dwarf oak and second-growth scrub pine. The grass looked like the broom grass of familiar quail country. The trees around the little river looked like the trees around the edges of the Green Swamp, where I shot my first deer as a youngster. Outside the flower-decked yellow plains looked like land I'd seen before—rimmed here by a patch of wood, squared off there by a strip of green reed by a wet spot, regimented by a green hill, and dappled by little isolated groves of thorn that looked like seedy orchards on Maryland hillsides. The fantastic thing about the high East Africa country is that it always looks like some place you've loved—the country around Monfalcone in Italy, a slice of Spain, a piece of English countryside.

Nobody but us was shooting here since the rains, and the game was thick and very tame. The lions had just come in, following the migration off the Serengeti. The second night in camp a pride of five strolled through the middle and relieved us of two Grant gazelles we had hanging back by the cook tent. There were three leopards, at least, within half a mile. We could hear them hunting up and down the river at night. We could hear the leopard's racking cough and the curses of the baboons—friends who soon developed a steady habit of checking by the camp at exactly 4 P.M. to see what the visiting baboons were doing. They were especially intrigued by Virginia. They had seen so few baboons with white hair.

"I never shoot them, even though they *are* a pest," Harry said the first day out. "It's too much like murdering a relative. There is one trick to getting rid of them. You run down a small one on the plain and paint him with luminous paint and turn

him loose at night. The whole troupe takes off for parts un-
known. I suppose they believe in ghosts."

We didn't shoot around the camp, and the beasts seemed
to appreciate it. A herd of impala was always frolicking, showing their heels and pawing at the ground like puppies, a few
rods away. The guinea and the spur fowl and the doves kept
a fearful clamor going all around us. The baboons and the
bush babies and the colobus monkeys and God knows what
array of noisy insects kept the place in a clamor, but it was a
peaceful clamor. The hyena symphony at night was superb,
like calliopes gone mad. The lions grunted as they hunted,
and one old boy about six miles away was complaining bitterly about his rheumatism on every cold night.

The boys were very happy to be back at the Happy Camp
after six months. Each man knew his own place, where he
was, where to pitch his shelter-half, where to put the cook
tent, where the best dry firewood was, where to get the water.
There was an awful lot of singing out behind us, mostly by
Katunga, the mad Wakamba skinner, who squatted happily
on his stringy thighs and chanted what seemed to be highly
humorous and very dirty songs in Wakamba. Katunga wore
a pair of ragged shorts and an old police sweater which
sagged down past his knees. He wore a jaunty Australian
military hat, pinned up on one side, with a brilliant blue spray
of vulturine guinea-fowl feathers in the band. He hoped we
would kill soon, and frequently. When he was not skinning he
was supposed to gather firewood, and Katunga's contention
was that anybody who was called "Bwana" Katunga and who
shared his snuff with the best hunter in Africa, his Bwana
Haraka, was too dignified to gather firewood. So Katunga
sang, and Katunga skulked, whenever Juma, the head boy,
acquired one of those why-don't-you looks in his eyes.

We knew what we wanted here. There was a deep reservoir

of common game—the plains antelope, the waterside animals, and a sprinkling of the bigger stuff, lions, leopards, buffalo, rhinos.

"We should get you a decent Tommy, a good Grant, a decent buff, a fair shot at a leopard, and possibly a rhino," Harry said on the second day. "The tough part is over. There'll be no lionitis in this camp, because you've already got old Scruffy. We'll do what we can and then push on back across the Serengeti and over Ngoro-Ngoro and down to Lake Manyara. It's stiff with rhinos there by the lake. Then we'll go on up to this new country of Frank Bowman's and see about those monster kudu. Then if we've time we'll whiz back to Nairobi and go on up to the N.F.D. for a look-round at elephants and stuff."

The ordered simplicity of the day was what struck me after so long a period of overcomplication. At five in the morning either Gathiru or Kaluku would bring the tea into the tent and shake me awake. They aroused Mama more pointedly. They let the air fizz out of her mattress. Then they would unhook her mosquito netting, and there wasn't much she could do but get up. During the night your boots had been dubbined and left by the bed. Your fresh bush jacket and pants and heavy socks had been laid neatly on the canvas flooring of the big double-fly tent. There was hot water in the basin at the wash table out front. The fire in front of the mess tent had been revived. The morning was cold and gray and dewy, and the birds were just beginning to speak. Juma would have the table set in the mess tent, with its clean checkered cloth and its green plastic dishes. There was no New York *Times* by each plate.

Selby was usually up, sitting morosely on a non-burning log by the fire, wearing a ratty old turtle-neck sweater under his green bush jacket. And wearing the look of a man who has had malaria all his life and who is never really comfortable until the sun breaks.

"Good morning, Bob," he would say. "Good morning, Virginia." He always gave "Virginia" the formal four-syllable pronunciation. We would say: "Good morning, Harry." Then nobody would say anything. We would eat cold plums or cold pears, their syrup chill from the night, and we would drink two cups of tea and eat a slice of crumbly toast with marmalade and then Harry would say, "*Kwenda,*" and the boys would drive up Jessica, the jeep. Kidogo and Adam and Chabani, wearing the same miserable look of recently awakened malarials on a cold morning, would be standing silently in the back of Jessica, clinging to the hold-on bar over which the canvas top was stretched when we were not hunting. We would drive a mile through the frosty woods in the half-light and then turn out into the plain. Then we would hunt—Harry driving, Virginia in the middle, me on the outside, the boys standing up and peering from the back.

It is a relatively new kind of hunting, certainly a radical change from the old foot-safari days, and even a change from the heavy hunting-car days, when you had to pay some respects to terrain. Nearly anywhere an animal could go, the little British Land Rover named Jessica could go. In a day's hunt we would cover thirty square miles, putting 150 miles on the speedometer.

When we saw likely-looking game one of the boys would point. Harry would stop the car, get out the glasses, stare long, and speak for the first time since breakfast. "Nice impala ram over there," he would say. "Let's go and look at him more closely. Lovely rack on him."

He would drive off in a curiously circuitous fashion, always seeming to go away from the animal, and always approaching more closely. Selby, like most of the able professionals, can see animals with a naked eye at four miles and judge their horns accurately within a quarter inch before the visitor can tell what species he is looking at.

"Hmm," he would say, "*toa* .30-'06, Kidogo," and turn to me. "This is the best I've seen lately," he'd say. "I'll drive you past that anthill over there, and you fall out. After I've driven away, you stalk up to just behind that thornbush and take him from there."

When you are out in the bush for any considerable length of time you do not remember days by date or week or weather. You reach backward to the day of the buffalo or the day of the lion or the day the lorry busted her axle. The day of the waterbuck was quite a day. It got to be more of a day as it went along. It was a hazy day, made more hazy by what Virginia called the "thousand-dollar pills," some sort of modern scientific confection which was guaranteed to cure anything from clap to constipation. I was using it for a chronic sore throat and a burning itch in the middle ear, a couple of little symptoms which had ripened last spring into a beautiful streptococcus invasion of my skull.

We headed out of camp with the dew still bright on the grasses, looking for nothing. It is a gorgeous way to hunt, looking for nothing. You spin along in the jeep and just look. The breakfast is still warm inside you and the second cigarette is tasting almost as good as the first. The sun is just beginning to take a touch of chill off your face, and the woods and plain are alive, vibrant with tentatively stirring animals. The birds, just wakened, are starting to scratch and fly and complain. You drive along by the wood or the river or out along the veldt and you almost hope you will see nothing worth working for that day because it is more fun to watch it than to chase it or shoot it.

"I think we'll check down by the river and see about that waterbuck," Harry said, driving around a herd of impala that seemed trying to set a record for altitude in their leaps. "The ones we have seen have been fairish, but I seem to remember an old gentleman from the last trip who's got more horns than he needs. They must be making his head ache. He used to live over here," Harry said, driving through some reeds and coming out of the reeds to draw up to a small grassy hill with trees and shrubs that looked considerably more like woodcock country than waterbuck country. As we drove up to the summit of the little hill a herd of perhaps a dozen waterbuck broke from the rushes and loped leisurely up the hill and across a small pastury-looking field and stopped just short of a wood.

"That's the gentleman I had in mind," Harry said. "I believe he's the best I've ever seen, but I've never yet had a good close look at those horns. Suppose we walk a bit and investigate this fellow."

We climbed out of Jessica. Kidogo handed me the Remington, and Harry started a stalk in that half crouch which looks so easy at first and then forcibly reminds you of age and girth as it continues. I was puffing when Harry held his hand, palm down and pushing backward, in the stop sign. We were in a small copse of trees and thick lianas as big as your wrist, with the dew still heavy on the grass underfoot and on the leaves that brushed your face. Harry reached around, grabbed my gun arm, and pointed with my arm. The herd of buck was in the pasture, feeding straight at us. You could feel the fresh brisk wind blowing directly into your face, curling back your eyelashes and causing a constant rustle in the trees—which is always fortunate if you are the kind of man who steps on dry sticks and goes through bush like a bull buffalo in a hurry.

They were beautiful. A little suspicious at the extra rustle I made, maybe, but with no scent of our presence and no real worry about the snapping and crackling in the clump of trees. The bull was looking straight at me.

Waterbuck are awful to eat, since they are tough and carry an insect repellent in their hides, a greasy ointment that comes off on your hands and smells like hell. Their fat is made so that it congeals swiftly in the cooking and winds up in hard balls, stuck in your teeth. But there is no more ruggedly handsome animal in Africa.

The bull will weigh nearly as much as an elk. He is not so rangy, nor does he stand so high, but he has a thick, tufted elk's neck, a noble face, a compact, heavily furred body. He will weigh around seven hundred pounds. He is beautifully marked in black and white and grayish-fawn, and his horns are slim parentheses that are heavily gnarled at the base and finish off in four inches of clean ivory point. Perhaps a kudu is more beautiful, but he does not own the compact, rugged, swell-necked masculinity of a mature waterbuck.

My boy was walking steadily toward me. My breath had come back a little. The Remington was braced in the crotch of a small scrubby tree. The gun was shaking again, and the limber limb was moving gently to match my shakes. The buck kept coming. I put the post of the telescopic sight on his chest, sucked in my breath, and started what I hoped would be a squeeze.

The squeeze was two-thirds complete when Harry's hand came back and closed over my trigger hand.

"Watch," he said. "Wait."

The magnificent bull separated into two animals. What I had been aiming at suddenly became a cow, who sidled off to the left. My bull had been standing so directly behind one of his wives that his horns had appeared to be growing from her head. In a hundredth of a second I would have shot the cow. When they separated, it was exactly like watching two images merge and move apart in the sighting machinery of a Leica. The cow sidled off. The bull looked me straight in the eye at thirty yards and snorted irritably. His horns appeared to be the size and length of two evenly warped baseball bats.

Harry's hand came away from my gun hand. The post went back to the old gentleman's chest, and the unseen force which fires guns operated. There was a whunk like a boxer hitting the heavy bag. The waterbuck went straight up in the air and turned at the top of his leap. He must have gone a good six feet off the ground. The herd of cows and yearlings went off with a snort and a crash. There was nothing to be seen.

"I hit him," I said to Selby. "I hit him where I was holding.

I was holding just to the right of his breastbone. If this boy ain't dead I am going back to Nairobi. This is the first time since I've been here that I felt confident about anything."

"You hit him all right," Harry said. "I heard the bullet smack. But where you hit him remains to be seen. Christ, wasn't he something to see standing there with that head thrown back? Let's go see what happened to him."

Kidogo and Adam had come up. They looked at Selby.

"*Piga,*" Selby said. "*Kufa*—maybe. But he was a big one. A real *m'kubwa sana.*"

"*Ehhh,*" the boys said without much enthusiasm. Kidogo, stopping, tracking, walked over to where the animal had been when I shot him. You could see the deep scars his feet had made in the turf when he jumped. Fifteen yards away Kidogo stooped and picked up a stalk of yellow grass. It was brilliant scarlet for three inches at its tip.

"*Damu,*" Kidogo said. "*Piga m'uzuri.*"

"That's heart blood," Harry said. "Not lung blood or belly blood. The lung blood's clottier and pinker. The belly blood's got more yellow to it. You got this bugger in the engine room, I think."

Everybody tracking now, including me, we followed the bright slashes of blood for fifty yards or so, turned a sharp L around the patch of bush, and almost stumbled over my fellow. He was completely dead. I had taken him through the heart squarely as he stood with his head up and his chest thrown out. Harry took one look at him and let out a yell like a Masai *moran* on the warpath. He threw himself at the animal, seized it around the neck with both arms, and kissed it in the face. Both gunbearers fell on their knees. Kidogo picked up the great noble head by the ears, and he kissed the buck. Adam ran his fingers up and down the chestnut-colored horns, rubbing his fingers over the ivory tips. He said a short prayer in Wakamba. Selby hit me a punch in the chest that nearly floored me, and both boys grabbed me by the arms and danced me around the waterbuck.

"I don't suppose you know what you've got here, old boy," Harry said. "Unless I am mad or drunk, you have just walloped the best waterbuck that anybody ever brought out of Tanganyika. If this one isn't thirty-four inches I will carry him back to camp on my back. This one you can hang on your wall, chum, and Mr. Rowland Ward's records will be very pleased to include him at the top of the heap. Very nice shooting, *bwana*. For one dreadful split second I thought you were going to loose off at that bloody cow. I would have sworn she was the bull. Those horns of his were sticking right out over her ears, and it wasn't until she moved just a fraction of an inch that I realized she was standing square in front of the *doumi*. If she hadn't moved you'd have shot her, the bull would've spooked and would have been halfway across the Serengeti by now. You're a lucky lad."

This was quite a creature, this buck. You couldn't close your hands around his horns at the base. They were serrated and very clean, and they curved inward at each other in a nearly perfect ellipse. His big bull's neck was thick and shaggy with a chest mane. He had a big deer's face, although he was an antelope, and his hairy hide was gray-fawn like a good tweed suit. He was very heavy. It was all the four of us could handle to heft him into the back of the jeep. He smelled like hell, with his insecticide coming out of his special glands and making sweat splotches on his hide.

"We'll take this baby back whole," Harry said. "I want better pictures of him than we can get here. We'll go back to camp and let the *memsaab* do her stuff with the color box." Harry patted the buck on his poll. "You beauty," he said. "You lovely, lovely hunk of horn."

He wheeled Jessica around and we headed back to camp. We were driving slowly across the blue-and-white-flowered plain, full of self-congratulation and the yearning for a celebration drink, an afternoon off to gloat, an afternoon free of hunting, for no man likes to cheapen his achievement by doing something competitively else that same day. A miss on a good head can spoil the hit on the other. This waterbuck was all I wanted from that day or that week, for that matter. I was a little drunk already with the wine of the fine fresh morning and the first real good shot that I had actually made on purpose. I was warmed by the sun and by excitement and by the approval of the boys. They grinned when I turned my head and offered cigarettes. Like Charlie MacArthur when he offered Helen Hayes a bag of peanuts, I was sorry at the time that my cigarettes were not emeralds.

The plain was like a great wheat field, and Jessica went smoothly along in it, her windscreen down, and the grass seeds hitting you in the face as she plowed like a ship through the sea of grass. Tiny quail buzzed out from under her bonnet. Cloudlike flocks of weaver birds swarmed in masses, dipping and twisting like a miniature tornado. Kidogo braced his bowed Nandi legs around the waterbuck's horns and leaned over to seize me on the shoulder.

"*Simba*," he said. "*Kishoto kidogo, Bwana Haraka.*" Harry swung Jessica left a little, and there the *simba* was. My neck hair was lifting again. There is no other word in Swahili that carries the electrifying impact of *simba*. Away off, making a gentle ripple in the sea of yellow grass, two rounded ears were flattened to a yellow skull as a lady *simba* stalked a herd of zebra. Her ears looked like a Portuguese man-o'-war sailing along on a quiet ocean. You couldn't see her slither as she moved, belly flat-pressed to the ground, and just her nose and ears showing.

"Let's go and have a look-see," Harry said, wheeling the Rover. "The old girl's stalking a kill. You very seldom see a solo lioness. The old boy has got to be around somewhere, probably upwind from her, letting his scent float down to distract the zebra while she sneaks in for the kill. Very sensible arrangement. Make the wife do the work, what?"

We drove in narrowing circles through the grass and came up on the lioness. The zebras spooked and took off. The lioness looked annoyed. She curled a disdainful lip and made a half pass at a charge and then bounded away into some scrubby thorn acacia. We circled the bush. On the other side of the prickly island we turned up three more lionesses. And four unsteady, spotted, clumsy cubs. The first lioness growled and started toward the car.

"Mama *simba*," Harry said. "Old boy's bound to be about somewhere. Wouldn't find four *manamouki* and young *mtotos* together without the big fellow, unless he's just been killed, and nobody can've hunted here since before the last rains. Must be the fellow we've heard roaring 'cross the river at night. Nice one, I'll promise you, by the sound of him."

We widened the turning circles, and suddenly Kidogo tapped shoulders again. "*Doumi*," he said. "*M'kubwa sana. M'uzuri sana.*"

He was, too. He was *m'kubwa*. He was real *m'uzuri*. He was male, all right, and he was very big, and he was awful good. His ginger mane sparkled in the climbing sun, and his gray-tawny hide glistened. He looked very burly and handsome against a backdrop of green bush, the yellowing grass just matching his hide. He looked at us and yawned as we drove slowly toward him, with all the bored disdain that a prime lion can muster. He spun on his heel and sauntered into the bush.

"Beauty," Selby said. "Much better than the one you've got.

Let's go and have a spot of lunch, pick up the *memsaab,* and after we've eaten we'll come back and collect him."

I said nothing. I had been out long enough to know that Harry thought like an animal, and while I didn't know how he expected to find the lion in the same spot, or how he figured to get him out of the bush, or just how we'd shoot him, or how we'd cope with the others, I shut up. Anyhow, that waterbuck was enough achievement for one day.

We drove the bumpy eight miles back to camp, took black and color pictures of the buck, knocked off a pink gin or so, and ate.

"Come on, Mama," Selby said to Virginia. "We are now going out to collect a lovely lion"—in the same tone as a man who says he is going to walk down to the corner for the papers.

"Yes, master," Virginia said. She had quit asking questions, too, some time back. "Just so long as it's a *lovely* lion."

We drove away. Two miles from where we'd seen the lions Selby stopped the car. A big bull topi was standing sleepily under a tree.

"Get out and shoot him," Harry said. "We need him in our business." I got out and shot the topi. We opened up his belly. One of the gunbearers hitched a rope around his crooked-ended horns, and we headed for the lions, the topi bumping along behind the car.

"Hors d'oeuvres," Selby said. "The lions must be hungry, otherwise the lady wouldn't have been out after those *punda.* Can't have killed lately. We will ask our friends to tea. Fetch'm out of the bush for the party."

We drove up and saw all the lionesses and the cubs where we'd left them. Mama lion snarled.

"Unpleasant sort," Selby said. "Got an ugly face for a lion. Disagreeable. Oho," he said, "look there."

Here was Papa, all right, and he was about twice as big, twice as massively maned, and twice as fine as the other we'd seen that morning. He raised his heavy head, looked at us a very short second, and leaped into the bush. His mane was bright cherry-red.

"Shy type," Selby said. "Wants coaxing. We'll coax him." We drove back and forth in front of the bush.

"Smell it, chum," Selby said. "Smell it good. Smells nice, what? Pray do come and dine with us."

He drove then to a broad, clear, grassy oasis in the bush and dropped the topi. It was at least a couple of hundred yards from the nearest thorn. Then we drove a couple of thousand yards away and killed the motor under a mimosa. Harry got out the binoculars.

"All we need now is a few fine vultures or a noble hyena or so," Harry said. "If just one vulture drops, or old Fisi comes bouncing out to feed off that kill, you'll see more lions boiling out of that bush than you'll know what to do with. They just can't stand to see anything else chewing up that nice, fresh topi. They're greedy, just like people."

The vultures came and circled slowly and warily in the clear blue sky. The sun was boiling down now, and everyone was sweating—me especially. The executioner's job was mine. I'd killed my first lion ten minutes after I'd spotted him and hadn't really had time to think about him before I was tumbling out of the jeep with a gun in my hand and crawling toward him. But now it was past three o'clock and I'd been thinking about this fellow for four hours.

"Damn birds," Selby said. "They know the lions are there. You can't depend on vultures. If they work for you they're fine. If they don't they can bugger up the whole bloody issue."

Finally, after half an hour, one bird dropped his flaps and volplaned down to approach the kill warily. We beamed him in on a prayer. He sank his beak into the topi's belly.

"The rest'll come now," Selby said, "and then the parade'll start. Consider that we have a dead lion. Watch, now."

A half dozen, then a dozen vultures skidded down. Now the sky was blackened with birds.

"Thank you, *ndege*," Selby said. "*Asante sana*. Here comes the parade."

Four lionesses came out of the bush, finally followed by the big male. The younger male did not appear. They went quickly to the kill and commenced to feed.

"Young one's lying doggo, licking his wounds," Harry said. "He and the big boy had a fight after we left, or else he'd be out there feeding with the rest of the pride. If he's not dead he's awfully discouraged. Shouldn't wonder if we find this one marked up a touch when we collect him.

"Hmmmm," Harry said. "Old boy's got his head stuck all the way into that topi's paunch. Guess we'd best go and terminate his troubles for him. Mind, I'd really *not* wound this un if I were you. Any lion's troublesome enough in thick bush when he's hurt, and if this bloke gets into that thorn we'll have *two* wounded lions, a mother with cubs, and three more lionesses to deal with. That's a lot of lions. Let's go."

We took the door off the jeep, and Harry gave the wheel to the car boy, Chabani. Kidogo was carrying the big .450 No. 2 Harry checked his .416, and I slid a second look into the bolt of my .375. The bullets were there, all right.

We passed fairly close aboard the five lions, who never raised their heads. Chabani swung the car round behind some bush, and Harry and Kidogo and I fell out of the open door. The car took off, and we commenced to crawl. We crawled to within forty yards and crouched behind a small tussock. The lions never raised their heads. These were hungry, disdainful lions.

"End of the line," Selby whispered. "Wallop him."

I got up on one knee and set the sights on the back of Gorgeous George's neck and squeezed off. He turned over with a roar and began to flop. Three lionesses let out for the bush. The nasty lioness inaugurated a charge toward us and then halted. Gorgeous George got up on his front feet and began to shake the earth with noise.

"Clobber him again," Selby said.

I had to stand now, and as I stood, the lioness charged. I was not uninterested in a charge of a lady lion, but the papa was galloping around, roaring and carrying on, and I was having a hard time getting the gun on him. He held still for a second, finally, and I socked him again, this time directly behind the ear. He flopped over with a grunt, and I was free to use both eyes on the lioness.

She had come to us, was still coming at twenty feet, and came again another five. I switched my gun toward her and noticed Selby still casually on one knee, his scarred old .416 held rather carelessly to his cheek. At about twelve feet she put on brakes, stopped but her tail was still waving and she had a mighty big mouth. Selby got up. He advanced toward her, and I advanced with him, feeling rather lonely. The cat backed up a yard. We walked again. She retreated another yard.

Harry said quietly in Swahili to Kidogo, who was standing by with the spare rifle, "Get into the car. Then cover the bwana with your gun." He said to me in English, "Cover me. Then get into the car. Keep covering me from the car."

Kidogo got into the car, which Chabani—who had thoughtfully stalled it into a dead end of bush—had revived and driven up to us. I got into the car. The lioness stopped. Harry stopped. He made a step backward. The cat seemed inclined to follow him, but stopped, her face flat on the ground, her chest on the ground, her tail waving gently, her rump in the air. Harry walked backward slowly. He came alongside the jeep. He slid in. Chabani slid over to the center of the seat. Harry eased out the clutch. He hit the side of the jeep a tremendous whack with his hand and roared. I jumped. So did the cat.

"Begone, you surly slut!" Harry said, tramping the gas and whacking the door again. "Go back to your babies! Go back to your other boy friend! Away with you!" The lioness sneered and backed up. She walked reluctantly to the edge of the bush, across the broad savanna of grass, and stood at the edge, still looking unpleasant. We drove up to where the dead lion lay, his head pillowed on the haunch of the considerably disheveled topi. I looked then for the first time at Virginia.

"I hope you got pictures of all the commotion," I said. "It is so seldom that you have five lions to play with at once, one of them charging, in easy range of a camera."

Virginia stared at the camera in her hand as if she were seeing one for the first time. "Pictures," she said bitterly. "This idiot"—she pointed at Chabani—"drove this car into a dead end and stalled it. I looked over the side, and there was another lioness, with *more* cubs, right by the front fender. I have to watch my insane husband standing off another lion while three more bound around and one is flopping all over the landscape roaring and there is one more practically in my lap and then you two fools drive another one off like she was an alley cat and I am not accustomed to this many lions on an empty stomach and you ask me if I got *pictures*. No, I did *not* get pictures. I forgot I had a camera. I want a drink, and I will try to forget that my fate is in the hands of fools."

I looked at Harry. He shrugged and spread his hands.

"Too many lions at once apt to be unsettling," he said. "That was a very nasty lion. Thought for a second I'd have to shoot her."

"Why in the name of Christ didn't you?" I said. "By the time I'd finished with the big fellow she was practically sitting in your lap. I could see her come out of the corner of my eye and I kept waiting for the sound of a gun going off. Why didn't you belt her when she made that last jump?"

Harry looked at me in something approaching horror.

"My dear man," he said, "she had *cubs*. One doesn't go about shooting females with children—not unless it's absolutely necessary."

"When is necessary?" I said, bitter myself now, and still shaking.

"Oh," Harry answered, "I thought I'd give her another foot or so before I shoved one down her gullet."

"The *memsaab* is absolutely right," I said, sticking a cigarette into a dry mouth. "She is surrounded by idiots and fools."

We went up to see the dead lion. As we approached Gorgeous George in the car, Harry spoke over his shoulder to the gunbearers. "*Toa* .220 Swift," he said, and to me, "When we get out, give him one more behind the ear."

I got out and popped the old boy again with the little gun. It wasn't necessary, but it didn't do any harm, either. We walked to this fine redheaded gentleman, and sure enough, there was a fresh, ragged tear across his forehead.

"Thought so," Selby said. "Fight with the young bleeder after we left. I'd hate to see the other fellow. . . ."

He prodded the lion with his toe while the boys shook my hand.

"Very fine *simba*," he said. "Dead, now. Comes of being greedy. Never let your belly rule your reason."

We jabbered, released from tension, all the way back to Campi Abahati. As we got out Harry sniffed.

"I can smell that pig we hung up for the leopard all the way from the tree," he said. "Maybe tomorrow we'll go and

collect the leopard. Old Chui must be getting very fond of
that pig by now, to judge from the smell. He likes his cheese
ripe, does old Chui."

I remember how the fire looked that night, and the flicker
of the smaller fires on the shining black faces of the boys as
they squatted round, roasting their bits of meat. I remember
how marvelous the warm martinis tasted, and that we had
eland chops for dinner, and we drank far too much brandy
afterward as we sat in front of the fire in robes and pajamas,
saying the same triumphant things to each other over and
over again. I remember how the boys grabbed me by the
thumb in that queer handshake of theirs when we came in
with the second lion, and the almost reverent light in old
Katunga's mad eyes as he ran his thumb across the blade of
his skinning knife, looking first at the redheaded lion, then
at me.

"*M'uzuri sana, bwana,*" old Katunga said. "*M'kubwa sana.
M'uzuri, m'uzuri. Piga m'zuri. Bwana Simbambile.*"

It sounded very fine to be called Bwana Two Lions that
night, which is maybe why I am today dissatisfied with cocktail conversation and stale talk of politics and football scan-
dals and congressional investigations. Also, my taste in sports
has been somewhat spoiled.

This was a very fine *simba,* this last lion that I shall ever
shoot. He had this real red mane, as red as Ann Sheridan's,
and bright green eyes. He was absolutely prime, not an ounce
of fat on him, no sores, few flies, with a fine shining healthy
coat. He was the handsomest lion I had ever seen, in or out
of a zoo, and I was not sorry about the collection of him. Already I was beginning to fall into the African way of thinking:
that if you properly respect what you are after, and shoot it
cleanly and on the animal's terrain, if you imprison in your
mind all the wonder of the day from sky to smell to breeze to

flowers—then you have not merely killed an animal. You have lent immortality to a beast you have killed because you loved him and wanted him forever so that you could always recapture the day. You could always remember how blue the sky was and how you sat on the high hill with the binoculars under the great umbrella of the mimosa, waiting for the first buzzard to slide down out of the sky, waiting for the first lioness to sneak out of the bush, waiting for the old man to take his heavy head and brilliant mane and burly chest out of the bush and into the clear golden field where the dead topi lay. This is better than letting him grow a few years older, to be killed or crippled by a son and eaten, still alive, by hyenas. Death is not a dreadful thing in Africa—not if you respect the thing you kill, not if you kill to feed your people or your memory.

I was thinking along these lines when I went happily to bed, pleasantly drunk on brandy and triumph. The next morning we got up and drove back to see how the lady lion and the kids were making out. The old girl charged the jeep again. We spun Jessica about and took off. There didn't seem to be any future of friendship with this particular lion, and no point to pursuing further acquaintance. This girl purely despised jeeps named Jessica, and any humans associated with jeeps named Jessica. She had an ugly face for a lion, like Harry said.

Chapter 6

THE *memsaab* was adjusting very well to her new life. Her fears had given way mostly to fascination. She was happy in her khaki drill pants and her Russell Birdshooter boots. She was getting so she could tell the difference between a leopard's grunt and the bark of a baboon or the growl of a colobus monkey. She was fascinated by ants and anthills. She had made friends with all the baboons. She had found a dead cobra in the cook tent and had not screamed. She was taking better pictures all the time, and she had trapped Juma into the job of hairdresser to the queen. Juma, as head boy for safari for many years, was not surprised at assuming an extra added duty to replace the firm of Ceil et Paul in New York City.

It is no secret that Virginia is considerably blonder than she was born. She got sore at me once for some frivolity or other and dyed her hair a dazzling platinum. I can still remember when she turned up in Hawaii one morning with the new hair. A man named Don Beachcomber and I had been up most of the night before her arrival. We went early to the airport with some carnation and *pikake* leis to welcome the lady to Oahu. I hadn't seen her in three months.

Pretty well overhung, Don and I watched the passengers disembark, and suddenly here was this woman with a face I knew but hair I couldn't remember. A sudden thought struck me.

"Jesus Christ, Don," I said to Beachcomber. "She's brought her *mother* along with her." Virginia is a twin to her mother, except that Polly Webb's hair is natural silver instead of bottled silver. That surprise hair-dye job was a lot of years ago, but Virginia had liked it and she was still platinum, even in the Tanganyikan bush. And to stay blond when you are basically brunette takes work. It means a weekly anointing with some mysterious juju from a bottle.

Friday was hair day, and Juma would take great care to get his other chores done for the big event of the afternoon. There was usually a handful of locals from the nearest village around, waiting to watch the miracle of the ages. Friday was the day that Juma, using white man's magic, turned the *memsaab's* hair from black to white.

We had had a hard time explaining the nature of the trick. Harry consulted long with Virginia, and then mapped his lecture in Swahili.

"Look," he said to Juma. "*Memsaab's* hair is not really white. It is black. But *Memsaab* puts *medsin* on it to turn it from black to white every seventh day. You will take this stick with the cotton on it. You will put the *medsin* on *Memsaab's* hair, as she directs you, being careful not to get any of the *medsin* on the *ends*."

"*Ndio, bwana,*" Juma said, wondering at the madness of white people, who keep the head and horns of animals and throw the meat away, who continually court death and disaster for fun, and whose women wish to look old and therefore change their hair from black to white. Nothing a white man ever does is surprising to the African unless he does something that the African expects him to do, creating surprise by concurrence.

So the old lady was keeping her ersatz hair white with Juma's *medsin,* and she had supervised the washing and ironing processes of her clothes and found it satisfactory, even if Kaluku and Gathiru, the personal boys, were a little over-brusque when they beat her underclothes on a rock and the hand-hewn, glowing-coal-filled iron was somewhat less gentle than an electric appliance. She had been back to check on old Ali's kitchen, possibly expecting him to be serving us tarantula stew, and found the shriveled, gray old Swahili as clean as herself. In addition to which he knew a hell of a sight more about cooking, especially when you consider that he used a biscuit tin for a bake oven. The table service, supervised by Juma and implemented by Gathiru and Kaluku, was perfect.

Jinny got along very well with the blacks. When she sat alone in the hunting car with Chabani, the car boy, while Selby and I were off crawling after buffalo or some such nonsense, she and Chabani had long conversations in her sketchy Swahili and Chabani's mission-school pidgin English. I recall she came in one day, highly indignant. Chabani had asked her age and she had told him the truth, that she was in her middle thirties.

"Then the Bwana M'Kubwa must be a very old man," Chabani said with chill logic. "Else what would he want with such an old woman?"

The *memsaab* had shot a few things with the rifle—a topi bull for meat, which she shot capably, breaking his neck with the first bullet. She also came in from a photographic trip one day with a fine Thomson gazelle ram, which was only an eighth of an inch away from the world's record. But she had tried her luck on zebra and had managed to shoot the lower jaw off a big stallion, necessitating some extra killing, and she got a little sick. She never cottoned to the rifle any more but concentrated on the shotgun. And after a bit she never hunted but half a day with Harry and me, preferring to sit around the camp in the afternoons, reading some of the detective junk we had brought, watching the baboons, listening to the birds, and occasionally picking up the little Sauer .16 to provide the odd francolin or guinea for the pot. She said she was happy enough just being away from telephones and New York cocktail parties.

We drank quite a lot, for outdoor types. We'd roll back to camp about 1 P.M. after a hard morning's hunt, starved, thirsty, and dust-covered. The ginny bottle would be hanging, coolly beaded with sweat from the evaporation of the water bag. I was bartender, it always seemed.

"What'll it be? Dr. Ruark's nutritious, delicious, character-

molding martini, or one of those gin-and-nonsense things that
children drink?" Gin-and-nonsense was Gordon's elixir of life
mixed with Rose's lime juice or orange squash. Harry and
Virginia usually drank gin-and-nonsense. I am a martini man,
myself. Over six weeks we used up forty-six bottles of gin and
a little less than half a bottle of vermouth. I like martinis dry.

We drank, sitting in the comfortable camp chairs, with the
mess tent cool and breezy and the river trees green and
soothing for us to look at, and the fact that the martinis were
warm in their plastic cups and that the bees dive-bombed the
attractive nonsense drinks did not detract from the flavor or
the effect. We drank a lot. Three apiece before lunch killed
the whole bottle. But we never got tight. We never felt bad.

It is funny about booze. I have been drinking it constantly
since my first tentative sampling of North Carolina corn liquor
when I was fifteen. I love liquor. It has been a good and constant friend for over twenty years. I have never used the
bottle to hide in from fear or frustration, and I've never been
on a protracted bat. I just like its taste and the way it feels
and the wondrous atmosphere of celebration, of relaxation,
of pure festivity that it creates. Each drink in my book should
be an adventure, neither a dull habit nor a screaming necessity. There is no point to coming in out of the snow after a
long rough walking day after pheasant or deer, or coming in
wet from a duckblind, or coming in hot and tired off the
African plain, unless there is a drink at the end to com-
memorate the home-coming.

But there are places I do not like to drink in. New York
City is one. I do it, of course, but I am not happy with whisky.
I feel bad the next day. It depresses me while it's in me. New
York people drink to stay sober, to kill boredom, to drown
their nervous unrest and irritation at being forced to live in
that steaming, sweating, raucous, stinking, overcrowded as-

phalt purgatory between farm and farm. I can drink two bottles of wine at lunch in Rome or Paris or Madrid, top it off with three brandies, and feel marvelous all day. A glass of wine at lunch, two glasses at dinner, in New York, would keep me in bed with the miseries for half a week. I have never had a hangover nor have been really drunk in a place I like. I have never felt an unpleasant impact from liquor when I was happy —drinking with friends in front of a fire, drinking at the end of a good day's shooting or fishing, drinking to celebrate a new book or a raise in pay or the start or return of a trip.

Here by the little Grummetti River it was happy drinking. It was drinking with point. We were either applauding the beauty of the day or a good shot at a fine head or the prospect of lunch or the sheer wonder of being where we were, with more days to spend and a hope to return someday to spend more days just like the ones we were milking of their fullest potential at this time. Never in my life have I seen days of which I was so stingy with the hours. When I went to bed at night I felt beautifully tired and spent, but at the same time a tiny voice told me that this was another one marked off the calendar, that this one had subtracted another twenty-four hours from my sum.

We laughed and jabbered an awful lot in the pre-meal cocktail hour, retelling the morning's events, talking without caution, without the guarded carefulness of the city man who does not want to commit himself or become accused of naïveté or spontaneity. We didn't care what we said. There was no effort to be consciously amusing or brittle or ponderously wise. We jabbered as happily as our cousins in the swamps.

I never cared much for food before this; I had eaten to stoke my body with energy, not caring what it tasted like and hoping to get it done in a hurry. I have eaten alone a great deal, with a book or paper propped against a water tumbler, and people who eat alone hate food. I discovered food out here in the bush. I approached each meal with the reckless abandon of a small boy. What we ate was not tremendously varied. I can eat Tommy chops seven days a week with the same enthusiasm. I can eat cold guinea or cold grouse or cold spur fowl every day. I can eat sand-grouse stew or roast duck or broiled catfish with undiminishing appetite. I can also eat potatoes and tomatoes and spaghetti and beans and bread and butter and pickles and relish and mustard and House of Parliament condiment with no palling on my tongue. These things we ate, with tinned fruit and an occasional pie or pudding for dessert, and I found I was consuming five or six pounds of meat a day. A normal lunch was the breasts of two guinea fowl, accompanied by more starch than I ever dreamed existed, and the whole thing washed down with a quart of beer. I couldn't drink a quart of beer in a week in New York. Virginia ate comparably. Harry doubled me in consumption, and the blacks trumped Harry. We were burning up so much energy with 150 miles a day in Jessica, plus an average stroll of ten miles, that there just wasn't *enough* meat to restoke the furnace. I'd have eaten a cold boiled hyena when somebody yelled for *chacula* and Juma came out with a covered dish in his lean black hand.

The nights were the best, of course. The nights were when you were really tired. Harry Selby is the kind of hunter who squeezes the last drop of effort from the final moments of shooting light, and it was always seven or better when we started back to camp. You could pick up the pin-point gleam of the boys' cooking fires a half mile away from camp and see the big blaze of the *bwana's* fire in front of the mess tent. You could see the hot light of the pressure lamp that Juma would have hung from the ridgepole of the mess tent, and if Virginia hadn't hunted with us in the afternoon you would know she would be waiting and curious and satisfactorily questioning, with her first evening drink already in her hand. She would be *bathi*-ed and robed by now, with her pajama pants tucked down into her mosquito boots, and she would mix us one of Dr. Ruark's et ceteras automatically while we commiserated or bragged. We would have flung ourselves out of the jeep, filthy, weary, bone-sore from the jouncing and pounding that Jessica gave us, grasping for the drink and hurling ourselves into the camp chairs drawn up along the festive fire's rim.

People who are clean all the time and who take two showers a day are apt to forget the tremendous adventure of removing a couple pounds of topsoil from the body at the end of a man-killing day. By the time the first drink of the evening was done, one of the personal boys would be scurrying into the tent with a couple of five-gallon petrol tins full of hot water, to pour into the canvas tub that always seemed to be placed just over a thornbush. It was not the cleanest water in the world, and sometimes it was full of sticks, small fish, and other debris, but it washed off the alkali dust and it ironed the kinks out of knotted muscles and soothed the tsetse bites on the wrists and ankles. It took the powdered soil out of your whiskers and your hair and from between your teeth.

And it made the sight of clean flannel pajamas and fresh boots and a woolly camel's-hair bathrobe a beautiful thing. It made the beckon of the other drink, accepted leisurely now by the fire in a cold that was beginning to be bitter enough to stop the mosquitoes and discourage the flies, bitter enough to command at least two thick blankets on the cot, bitter enough to spur an appetite that was already going at full gallop inside you. Your breath was white against it, and the stars had a North Woods twinkle to them. Along about nine Gathiru and Kaluku would bring the mess table outside the mess tent, place it close against the fire, and start the evening meal with a smoking tureen of soup, liberated from a can or perhaps made mysteriously from sand grouse or the odds and ends of eland joints or the tougher sections of Tommy and impala. It scorched going down and tingled clean to your toes. Where the luncheon was nearly always cold, everything that came out of Ali's biscuit-tin oven at night was white-hot. And when it was over and the coffee served with a bite of brandy in it, we stretched out our feet to the fire, smoked lazily, and listened to the concert. All the sounds were fine, but the hyena symphony was the finest. Not even a hyena knows how many keys and registers and vibratos he owns. This was the last hour of the waking night and was generally devoted to question-and-answer having to do with the lives of the people and the animals that Selby knew and loved so well. He was taciturn by day. He was garrulous by night, and he loved to talk of what he knew.

We were sitting by the fire, with a low-swung sickle moon over the swamp, when a couple of dozen pairs of eyes came to within shoe-throwing distance of the fire. The symphony was now operating at close hand.

"Bloody cheek," Harry said. "I woke up early this morning and one of the blighters was sitting in the entrance of the tent, looking at me and licking his stupid chops. I also notice that one was in the mess tent last night, chewing on the camera bag. Buggers'll eat anything."

"One of them was whooping outside the tent and tripping over the guy ropes while Bob was snoring last night," Virginia said. "He butted into the tent half a dozen times."

At that moment a big dog hyena detached himself from the pack and sauntered over to the corner of the fire and sat there insolently, no more than fifteen feet away. He bared his big teeth and looked us straight in the eye.

"I'd say this was taking it a bit too far," Harry said. "Cheeky big bastard. Bite off a piece of your face, next thing you know. I think I'll just teach these gentlemen a little lesson in etiquette."

He got up and went into his tent and emerged with his battered old .416 and a flashlight, which he clamped on the stock of the rifle.

"Be back in a minute," he said, and strode off into the darkness. You could see the tongue of light licking here and there, and every time it steadied there was an explosion of the .416. I counted fourteen reports in as many minutes, and then Harry came back into camp, looking grim.

"I may've missed one," he said. "And some of them took off. But the growls you'll hear tonight will be the remaining cousins eating their own relatives instead of lounging about the camp. I don't like to shoot them, but once in a while you have to. They eventually get arrogant enough to be dangerous. I've known them to come into a native hut and make off with a child. And they're dreadful on the farm when the cattle are calving. Awful beast, and pathetic, too."

We sat a long time in the moonlight, listened to the snapping and snarling, and Harry expounded on hyenas. I found them fascinating. So did Virginia. Harry talks well, almost as in a lecture, when he is talking natural history. This is roughly what he had to say.

The African native, no matter what his tribe, is generally a grave citizen, seldom given to jokes and even less seldom stirred to laughter by the life around him. The one never-failing source of mirth is the hyena—Fisi—a ridiculous animal who could be called a dirty joke on the entire animal kingdom.

Anything a hyena does is funny to a native. Great humor is found in the fact that Fisi, fatally shot, will eat himself before he is dead. He will snap and snarl at his own festooned intestines or chew greedily on his own feet. His voice is always a subject for merriment, whether he is giggling hysterically in homosexual whoops, chuckling sardonically, grunting, groaning, howling, moaning, or snarling.

Fisi is stupid, and Fisi is smart. When he is smart he arouses almost frantic laughter. When he is dumb—say, for instance, when some wild dogs make off with a chunk of Fisi's dinner, and Fisi knocks himself cold running away by charging into a tree—the Africans hold their sides and scream with laughter, imitating Fisi at his worst and noisiest. Fisi is so low on the totem pole of life that even the scraggliest aboriginal, flea-bit, diseased, and scrawny, can lose his own misery when he sees a hyena.

I discovered pretty early where the humor lay. You will come upon natives with a portion of their faces chewed off, with horrid scars and welts healed over into grotesque masks. You ask them how come. The answer is always Simba—lion. It is seldom true. The truthful answer is Fisi—hyena. There is an ingrained fear of Fisi that is founded in all the dark hours of a savage existence. *Fisi* means death—meant it more, formerly, than now, but is still conceived as a symbol of the dark destroyer.

Many African tribes have such an overpowering fear of the spirits which attend death that they will not live in a hut in which death has occurred. A day's journey in Kenya or Tanganyika will always point out a handful of ramshackle, deserted huts, with the cactus *boma* gone to seed and the rafters sagging under disheveled thatch. A death has occurred here; the survivors have moved to avoid the attending ghosts of the dead.

So practical prudence, in the past, asserted itself, and when an aged and dying member of the family appeared to be on his last legs, he was lifted from his bed and taken out into the

bush. He was left there, to be attended by Fisi. The hyena
became a walking symbol of the graveyard in the native mind.
Many a mortally ill native was eaten by hyenas well before
normal death came to claim him. Not a small percentage had
the animal take a savage chop from his face and was cured,
except for the wound, of whatever illness beset him—cured by

fright alone. The native who laughs at Fisi is laughing un-
easily at the angel of death—he is giggling in the graveyard,
because the ingrown knowledge is ever present that one day
Fisi will have the last laugh on him.

The tremendous temerity of this stinking thief is such that
many a man has not needed to be critically ill to suffer a snap
of the most powerful jaws in the animal kingdom. Fisi grown
bold is the boldest of all African animals. He will not only
come into your camp, he will come and sit by your fire or

stride into your tent. And if the mood strikes him he will bite off half your face.

The African makes a tremendously potent beer, a thin, gruel-like liquor which is only half fermented at the time of intake. It continues to ferment inside the drinker, so that a native on a binge eventually accumulates a fantastic load. Instead of sobering, he gets drunker as the beer continues to work in his innards. The jag is only abated by prolonged and deathlike sleep, during some phases of which it is impossible to wake the sleeper. Here again is where the hyena is apt to relandscape your profile. A young native with hyena scars must have a record of drunkenness in his background—Fisi took a chunk out of him as he slept in stupor before a dying fire. The natives laugh at Fisi as the Europeans laughed at werewolves and vampires—from sheer uneasiness.

Of course the hyena is a ridiculous beast. God's mind was absent the day he built Fisi. He gave him a dog's face and a lion's ears and the burly body of a bear. He permanently crippled his hindquarters, so that his running motion is a slope-spined, humping shuffle. He gave Fisi the most powerful jaws, possibly, of any carnivore, and then made him so slow and so ungainly that the living meat which Fisi craves easily outruns him. With the potentiality of killing almost any creature with his enormous steel-trap jaws, the hyena has been forced to live off the stinking carrion of other animals' kills—forced to kill the sick and the crippled and the very young. He himself stinks like the corrupt meat he eats—and the final joke is that the hyena is hermaphroditic—a frequent blend of both sexes with the manifestations of both. Carr Hartley, a wild-animal collector, once penned up two female hyenas which could not possibly have been with young at the time he turned them loose together. Both females dropped a litter of pups. The hermaphroditism seems to be the last quirk of a grim joke on a pathetic beast.

The sardonic humor about the hyena is that he's so tragically, terribly *awful* that he inspires the kind of mirth that unfeeling youngsters derive from the presence of village idiocy or malformation. Fisi is such a terrible creature that he almost isn't true. If you own a farm you will hate him when one of your cows is found dying, hamstrung, or with an udder ripped off by one snap of those frightful jaws. You will despise him as you see him on the outskirts of a game herd, waiting for a sick or lame animal to lag behind. You will loathe him during calving season, when he attacks the female in the midst of birth pangs and makes off with the fresh-dropped baby. Fisi is an arrant coward nearly always, and anything whole and brave can chase him. Even a little jackal will drive him from a lion's kill. But he will kill the lion if the lion is sick.

His persistence is the persistence of Uriah Heep. Shuffling apologetically, he will return after repeated rebuffs. And of nights he sometimes acquires an arrogance that is frightening in its very dumbness. That is when you fear Fisi—he might be just dumb enough to walk into the tent and have a go at you.

But in a peculiar fashion this unwieldy, unhappy ghoul is such a vital part of African life that you would miss him greatly if he disappeared. Very few hunters shoot Fisi, although he is classed as vermin, except when he becomes so bold that he gets to be a dangerous nuisance around camp. For one thing, he is the head man in the sanitation corps. He will eat anything—you, his mother, himself. He will even eat a vulture, although sometimes the non-finicky buzzard won't eat a dead *fisi*, figuring that a deceased hyena is even beneath a buzzard's dignity. But between the hyena, the vulture, the marabou stork, and the ants, the great rolling plains of Africa seldom smell of carrion. Today's kill is clean bleached bone by tomorrow, a tremendous sanitation program that is part of the cycle of life-in-death of Africa.

It is uncanny how swiftly the legions of the cleanup corps appear. You will shoot a zebra for his hide and tallow, and almost before you have rolled the strips of yellow fat into the still dripping skin, a few round-eared, dog-faced, shambling *fisi* will be sitting, tongues lolling, a few rods away, while the vultures are beginning to slant down before you quit the carcass. The vultures and the hyenas snap and snarl at each other but seem to work together pretty well. More active competition occurs when a fleet of wild dogs come onto the scene, and the fight for the carrion becomes a personal issue between Fisi and his cousin, the big-eared dog.

In addition to his value as a walking incinerator, the hyena is fairly handy to the hunter. He follows the game concentrations and, more important to the hunter, he follows the carnivore. A large incidence of *fisi* generally means lions about. I have noticed that his abundance also bespeaks cheetah, the hunting leopard who is nearly extinct today. The cheetah kills freshly and feeds once from his kill.

Fisi has his uses as a decoy too. If you are trying to toll the most timid lion out of the bush with a kill, he will come like a shot when he gets a whiff of a hyena sidling up to that nice fresh topi or zebra you have thoughtfully supplied for Simba's lunch. If you are working overnight on lions with a kill, a concentrated, dedicated corps of hyenas screaming frightfully as they attempt to rip off a protective covering of thorns from the lion kill is almost guaranteed to attract the most reclusive *simba* in the area. The lion hates Fisi—because, like the native, the lion knows that the hyena will eventually get him. It is cynically humorous that, one way or another, the king of beasts always finds his tomb inside the knave. It is the crowning indignity to a regal life that the aged and weakened lion is pulled down and consumed, while still alive, by a stinking, snarling, cowardly outcast who is neither true male nor female, but an awful amalgam of both.

But without Fisi's admirable voice range and his ever-present attendance at camp, Africa would never pack the nocturnal wallop that makes night noises and a flickering campfire so wonderful. There is no way to describe accurately a dozen hyenas without the camp—the virtuosity of voices is too great. There is a bone-chilling insane giggle—the *heeheeheehee* of a madwoman—and there are enough roars and whoops and screams and growls to fill an album. Eventually you come to miss Fisi if he is seldom in the area. He has become a part of your life, like the moon and the bugs and the baboons and the scorpions.

I finally got fond of Fisi, and very sorry for him. He is such a dreadful fellow, hated by every living creature, loathed by all, shunned by all, laughed at by all, that I kind of adopted him. No living creature, I thought, should have so much bad luck and live so shamefully, so ignobly. All the other African animals have a dignity that lasts until Fisi, the undignified, has the last laugh over their cracked and crunching bones.

And then my friend Fisi betrayed my good will later on by eating up half my portable library, wrecking the booze supply out of sheer vandalism, and chewing up a perfectly good hat. He also made off with the skull and headskin of a greater kudu bull—as he once ate up a fine leopard Tommy Shevlin killed, leaving one wisp of tail to accent his gluttony. That is when you get all out of sorts with Fisi, remembering that next time, no matter how sorry you are for this dreadful monster, he may decide to dine on your face.

We sat quietly for one last cigarette, watching the fire bank down into gray ash over red coals. The snapping and the snarling had finished.

"I think I'll go to bed," Harry said. "Night, all. See you in the early bright."

"Good night," Virginia said, and then turned to me. "I have to go to the ladies'-room tent," she said. "This is one evening that a lady will require a gentleman to stand outside with a gun while she powders her nose. Honest to God, if I ever get home whole, I will never leave the 21 Club again. I might as well be living in a bloody zoo."

When we went to bed and crawled under the mosquito netting I couldn't help thinking, before sleep crept over me, that a few shillings' worth of net constituted no real obstacle to anything that was even reasonably hungry.

Chapter 7

THE NIGHT was cold and clear in the little camp at the Grummetti in Tanganyika. It was a sharp-flavored winy night, tangy like New England in the fall, with the stars distinct against the sky. The boys had reared a roaring blaze out of desert-dry thornbush logs. The dinner was responding graciously to a third cup of coffee and a cognac. Everybody was tired. Beat. It had been a day. It had been a hell of a day. There had been the big waterbuck in the morning and the redheaded lion in the afternoon, and the nasty business with all the lionesses and the cubs.

Suddenly the wind veered.

A smell raced down on the breeze, a dreadful smell.

"Oho," Harry Selby said. "Chanel No. 5, if you are a leopard. That delicious aroma would be your pig and your Grant gazelle. It may smell awful to you, but the bait has hit just about the right stage of rot to smell better than Camembert to our noisy friend of the fig tree. I was never able to figure why the cleanest, neatest animal in the bush waits until his dinner is maggoty before he really works up an appetite. Let's see. We've had the bait up five days now. The boys say your pussycat's been feeding since yesterday. He ought to be through the pig now and working on the Grant. He ought to be feeling pretty cheeky about his vested interest in that tree.

"I don't know what there is about that tree," the professional hunter said. "I think maybe it's either bewitched or else made out of pure catnip. You can't keep the leopards out of it. It's only about five hundred yards from camp. I come here year after year and we always get a leopard. I got one three months ago. I got one six months before that. There's an old tabby lives in it, and she changes boy friends every time. We'll go to the blind tomorrow and we'll pull her newest fiancé out for you—that is, if he's chewed deep enough into that Grant. That is, too, if you can hit him."

At this stage I was beginning to be something past arrogant. Insufferable might be the right word.

"What is all this nonsense about leopards?" I said. "Everybody gives you the old mysterious act. Don Ker tells me about the safari that's been out fourteen years and hasn't got a leopard yet. Everybody says you'll probably get a lion and most of the other stuff but don't count on leopards. Leopards are where you find them. We got two eating out of one tree and another feeding on that other tree up the river, and we saw one coming back from the buffalo business yesterday. They chase up and down the swamp all night, cursing at the baboons. You sit over there looking wise and mutter about *if* we see him and *if* I hit him when we see him. What do you mean, *if* I hit him? You throw a lion at me the first day out and I hit him in the back of the neck. I got that waterbuck with one through the pump, and I knocked the brainpan off that second *simba* okay enough, and I break the back on a running eland at plus two hundred yards. What have I got to do to shoot a sitting leopard at thirty-five feet with a scope on the gun? Use a silver bullet?"

"Leopards ain't like other things," Harry said. "Leopards do strange things to people's personality. Leopards and kudu affect people oddly. I saw a bloke fire into the air three times, once, and then throw his gun at a standing kudu. I had a chap here one time fired at the leopard first night and missed. We came back the second night. Same leopard in the same tree. Fired again. Missed. This was a chap with all manner of medals for sharpshooting. A firecracker. Splits lemons at four hundred yards, shooting offhand. Pure hell on running Tommies at six hundred yards, or some such. Knew hell's own amount about bullet weights and velocities and things. Claims a .220 Swift is plenty big enough for the average elephant. Already got the boys calling him One-Bullet Joe."

"So?" I said.

"Came back the third day. Leopard up the tree. Fired again. Broad daylight, too, not even six o'clock yet. Missed him clean. Missed him the next night. Missed him for the fifth time on the following night. Leopard very plucky. Seemed to be growing fond of the sportsman. Came back again on the sixth night, and this time my bloke creases him on the back of the neck. Leopard takes off into the bush. I grab the shotgun and take off after him. *Hapana.* Nothing. No blood and no tracks. Worked him most of the night with a flashlight, expecting him on the back of my neck any minute. *Hapana chui.* My sport quit leopards in disgust and went back to shooting lemons at 350 yards."

"How do you know the marksman touched him on the neck?" I asked. "Did the leopard write you a letter of complaint to Nairobi?"

"No," Harry said gently. "I came back with another party after the rains, and here was this same *chui* up the same tree. *This* client couldn't hit a running Tommy at six hundred yards and he couldn't see any future to lemon-splitting even at 350. But his gun went off, possibly by accident, and the old boy tumbled out of the tree, and when we turned him over there was the scar across the back of his neck, and still reasonably fresh. Nice tom, too. About eight foot, I surmise. Not as big as Harriet Maytag's, though. *He* was just on eight-four."

"If I hear any more about Harriet Maytag's lion, Harriet Maytag's rhino, or even Harriet Maytag's monkey, *Mister* Selby," I said with considerable dignity, "it will not be leopards we shoot tomorrow. It will be white hunters, and the wound will be in the back. Not the first time it's happened out here, either. I'm going to bed, possibly to pray that I will not embarrass you tomorrow. Even if I am not Harriet Maytag, I still shoot a pretty good lion."

There was an awful row down by the river. The baboons set up a fearful cursing, the monkeys screamed, and the birds awakened. There was a regular, panting, wheezing grunt in the background, like the sound made by a two-handed saw on green wood.

"That's your boy, chum," Selby said brightly. "Come to

test your courage. If you find him in the tent with you later on, wake me."

We went to bed. I dreamed all night of a faceless girl named Harriet Maytag, whom I had not met and who kept changing into a leopard. I also kept shooting at lemons at three and a half feet, and I missed them every time. Then the lemons would turn into leopards, and the gun would jam.

Everybody I had met in the past six months had a leopard story. How you were extremely fortunate even to get a glimpse of one, let alone a shot. How they moved so fast that you couldn't see them go from one place to another. How you only got one shot, and whoosh, the leopard was gone. How it was always night, or nearly night, when they came to the kill, and you were shooting in the bad light against a dark background on which the cat was barely perceptible. How if you wounded him you had to go after him in the black, thick thorn. How he never growled, like a lion, betraying his presence, but came like a streak from six feet, or dropped quietly on your neck from a tree. How if four guys went in, three always got scratched. How the leopard's fangs and claws were always septic because of his habit of feeding on carrion. How a great many professionals rate him over the elephant and buffalo as murderous game, largely because he kills for fun and without purpose. And how unfortunately most of what you heard was true.

I had talked recently with a doctor who had sewed up three hunters who had been clawed by the same cat. A big leopard runs only 150 pounds or so, but I had seen a zebra foal weighing at least two hundred pounds hanging thirty feet aboveground and wedged into a crotch by a leopard, giving you some idea about the fantastic strength stored under that lovely, spotted, golden hide. I reflected that there are any amount of documented stories about leopards coming into tents and even houses after dogs and sometimes people and breaking into fowl pens and leaping out of trees at people on horseback.

"A really peculiar beast," Harry had said when we jumped the big one coming back from the buffalo. "Here we find one in broad daylight right smack out in the open plain, when there are people who've lived here all their lives and have never seen one. Here is a purely nocturnal animal who rarely ever leaves the rocks or the river edge, standing out in the middle of a short-grass plain like a bloody topi. They are supposed to be one of the shiest, spookiest animals alive, yet they'll come into your camp and pinch a dog right out of the mess tent. They'll walk through your dining room on some occasions and spit in your eye. They're supposed to have a great deal of cunning, yet I knew one that came back to the same kill six nights in a row, being shot over and being missed every time. But they've a great fascination for me and for most people. The loveliest sight I have ever seen since I started hunting was a leopard sleeping in a fever tree, latish in the afternoon. The fever tree was black and yellow, the same color as the cat, and the late sun was coming in through the leaves, dappling the cat and the tree with a little extra gold. We weren't after leopard at the time, already had one, so we just woke him up and watched him scamper. He went up that tree like a big lizard."

I was getting to know quite a bit about my young friend by this time. He was a professional hunter and lived by killing, or by procuring things for other people to shoot, but he hated to use a gun worse than any man I had ever met. He has the fresh face and candid eyes of a man who has lived all his life in the woods, and when he talks of animals his face lights up like a kid's. He had nearly killed us all a day earlier, coming back from a big *ngoma*—lion-dance party—in the Wa-Ikoma village. There were some baby francolin, spur fowl, in the trail, and he almost capsized the Land Rover trying to miss them. What he liked was to watch animals and learn more about them. He refused to allow anyone to shoot baboons. He hated even to shoot a hyena. The only things he loved to shoot were wild dogs, because he disapproved of the way they killed, by running their prey in shifts, pulling it down finally, and eating it alive.

"You're a poet, man," I said. "The next thing you will be using the sonnet form to describe how old Katunga howls when his madness comes on him in the moonlight nights."

"It would make a nice poem, at that," Harry said. "But don't spoof me about leopards in trees. Wait until you have seen a leopard in a tree before you rag me. It's a sight unlike any other in the world."

We got up that next morning, and the stench of the rotting pig and the rotting Grant was stronger than ever. Harry sniffed and summoned up Jessica, the Land Rover. We climbed in and drove down the riverbank, with the dew fresh on the grass and a brisk morning breeze rustling the scrub acacias. As we passed the leopard tree there was a scrutching sound and a stir in the bush that was not made by the breeze. A brown battler eagle was sitting in the top of the tree.

We had made a daily ritual of this trip, after we had hung the bait the first day, in order to get the cat accustomed to the passage of the jeep. We had also made a swing back just around dusk to get him accustomed to the evening visit.

We always passed close aboard the blind, a semicircle of thorn and leaves with a peephole and a crotched stick for a gun rest. The blind was open to the plain. It faced the tree with its camouflaged front. By now it would seem that the leopard feeding on the two carcasses we had derricked up to an L-shaped fork about thirty feet aboveground, and tied fast with rope, was used to us. You could just define the shape of the pig, strung a little higher than the Grant, as both hung conveniently from another limb, in easy reach of the feeding fork. The pig was nearly consumed, his body and neck all but gone, and his legs gnawed clean to the hairy fetlocks. The guts and about twenty pounds of hindquarter were eaten from the Grant. They smelled just lovely, for the steady wind was blowing from the tree and toward the blind.

Harry didn't say anything until he had swung Jessica around and we were driving back to the camp and breakfast.

"You heard the old boy leave his tree, I suppose?" he said. "I got a glimpse of him as we drove by. And did you notice the eagle?"

"I noticed the eagle," I said. "How come eagles and leopards are so chummy?"

"Funny thing about a lot of animals," Harry said. "You know how the tickbirds work with the rhino. Rhino can't see very much, and the tickbirds serve as his eyes. In return for which they get to eat his ticks. I always watch the birds when I'm stalking a rhino. When the birds jump, you know the old boy is about to come barreling down on you. Similarly, you'll always find a flock of egrets perched on a buffalo. You can trace the progress of a buff through high grass just by watching the egrets.

"I don't know how they work out these agreements," Harry said. "Often you'll see a lion feeding on one end of a kill and a couple of jackals or bat-eared foxes chewing away on the other. Yet a lion won't tolerate a hyena or a vulture near his kill.

"Now our friend, this leopard which you may or may not collect tonight, or tomorrow night, or ever, has this transaction with the eagle. The eagle mounts guard all day over the leopard's larder. If vultures or even another leopard comes by and takes a fancy to old Chui's free lunch, the eagle sets up a hell of a clamor and old Chui comes bounding out of the swamp to protect his victuals. In return for this service the eagle is allowed to assess the carcass a pound or so per diem. It is a very neat arrangement for both."

We went back to camp and had the usual tea, canned fruit, and crumbly toast. It was still cold enough for the ashy remnants of last night's fire to feel good.

"We won't hunt today," Selby said. "We will just go sight in the .30-'06 again and you can get some writing done. I want you rested for our date with Chui at four o'clock. You will be shaking enough from excitement, and I don't want it complicated with fatigue."

"I will *not* be shaking from excitement or fatigue or anything else," I said. "I am well known around this camp as a man who is as icy-calm as Dick Tracy when danger threats. In nearby downtown Ikoma I am a household word amongst the rate payers. I am Old Bwana Lisase Moja, Slayer of Simba, Protector of the Poor, Scourge of the Buffalo, and the best damn birdshooter since Papa Hemingway was here last. I promise you, you will not have to go into any bush after any wounded leopard this night. I am even going to pick the rosette I want to shoot him through. I intend to choose one of the less regular patterns, because I do not want to mar the hide."

"Words," Selby said. "Childish chatter from an ignorant man. Let us go and sight in the .30. We sight her point-blank for fifty yards. They make a tough target, these leopards. Lots of times you don't have but a couple of inches of fur to shoot at. And that scope has got to be right."

"How come scope? I thought you were the original scope hater. At thirty-five yards I figure I can hit even one of those lemons you're always talking about, with open sights, shooting from a forked stick."

Harry was patient. He was talking to a child.

"This is the only time I reckon a scope to be actually necessary out here. The chances are, when that cat comes it will be nearly dark, well past shooting light. You won't even be able to see the kill with your naked eye, let alone the cat. The scope's magnification will pick him out against background, and you can see the post in the scope a hell of a lot easier than you could see a front sight a foot high through ordinary open sights. And if I were you I'd wear those Polaroid glasses you're so proud of, too. Any visual help you can get you will need, chum."

We sighted in the Remington, aiming at the scarred blaze on the old sighting-in tree, and trundled Jessica back to camp, pausing on the way long enough to shoot a Thomson gazelle for the pot. It was a fairly long shot, and I broke his neck.

"I think I can hit a leopard," I said.

"A lousy little Tommy is a different thing from a leopard," Harry said. "Tommies have no claws, no fangs, and do not roost in trees."

We slopped around the camp for the rest of the morning, reading detective stories and watching the vultures fight the marabou storks for what was left of the waterbuck carcass. Lunch time came and I made a motion toward the canvas water bag where the gin and vermouth lived.

"*Hapana*," Harry said. "No booze for you, my lad. For me, yes. For Mama, yes. For you, no. The steady hand, the clear eye. You may tend bar if you like, but no cocktails for the *bwana* until after the *bwana* has performed this evening."

"This could go on for days," I said. "Bloody leopard may never come to the tree."

"Quite likely," Harry remarked, admiring a water glass full of lukewarm gin with some green lime nonsense in it. "The more for me and Mama. A lesson in sobriety for you."

A bee from the hive in the tree behind the mess tent dive-bombed Harry's glass and swam happily around in the gin-and-lime. Harry fished him out with a spoon and set him on the mess table. The bee staggered happily and buzzed blowzily.

"Regard the bee," said Selby. "Drunk as a lord. Imagine what gin does to leopard shooters whose glands are already overactivated by fear and uncertainty."

"Go to hell, the both of you," I said. "Juma, *lette* the bloody *chacula*, and I will eat while these bar flies consume my gin."

The lunch was fine—yesterday's guinea fowl, boiled, cold, and flanked by some fresh tomatoes we had swindled out of the Indian storekeeper in Ikoma, with hot macaroni and cheese Ali produced from his biscuit-tin oven, and some pork and beans in case we lacked starch after the spaghetti, bread, and potatoes. Harry allowed me a bottle of beer.

"Beer is a food," he said. "It is not a tipple. Now go take a nap. I want you fresh. I *hate* crawling after wounded leopards who have been annoyed by amateurs. It is so lonesome in those bushes after dark, the leopard waiting ahead of you and the client apt to shoot you in the trousers the first time a monkey screams."

I dozed a bit and at 4 P.M. Harry came into the tent and roused me.

"Leopard time," he said. "Let's hope he comes early. It'll give the bugs less chance to devour us. Best smear some of that bug dope on your neck and wrists and face. And if I were you I'd borrow one of the *memsaab's* scarves and tie it around most of my face and neck. If you have to cough, please cough now. If you have to sneeze, please sneeze now. If you have to clear your throat or scratch or anything else, do it now, because for the next three hours you will sit motionless in that blind, moving no muscle, making no sound, and thinking as quietly as possible. Leopards are extremely allergic to noise."

I looked quite beautiful with one of Mama's fancy Paris scarves, green to match the blind, tied around my head like the old peasant women do it. We climbed into Jessica. Harry was sitting on her rail from the front-seat position. The sharp edge of her after-rail was cutting a chunk out of my rear. We went past the blind at about twenty miles an hour and we both fell out, commando-style, directly into the blind. The jeep took off, with prior instructions to return at the sound of a shot or at black dark, if no shot. I wriggled into the blind and immediately sat on a flock of safari ants, who managed to wound me severely before we scuffed them out. I poked the Remington through the peephole in the front of the blind and found that it centered nicely on the kill in the tree. Even at four-thirty the bait was indistinct to the naked eye. The scope brought it out clearly. I looked over my shoulder at Selby, his shock of black hair unfettered by shawl and unsmeared by insecticide. A tsetse was biting him on the forehead. He let it bite. My old Churchill .12, loaded with buckshot, was resting over his crossed knees. He looked at me, shrugged, winked, and pointed with his chin at the leopard tree.

We sat. Bugs came. Small animals came. No snakes came. No leopards came. I began to think of how much of my life I had spent waiting for something to happen—of how long you waited for an event to occur, and what a short time was consumed when the event you had been waiting for actually did come to pass. The worst thing about the war at sea was waiting. You waited all through the long black watches of the North Atlantic night, waiting for a submarine to show its periscope. You could not smoke. You did not even like to step inside the blacked-out wheelhouse for a smoke because the light spoiled your eyes for half an hour. You waited on islands in the Pacific. You waited for air raids to start in London, and then you waited some more for the all-clear. You waited in line at the training school for chow and for pay and for everything. You waited in train stations and you sat around airports waiting for your feeble priority to activate and you waited everywhere. From the day you got into it until the day you got out of it you were waiting for the war itself to end, so that it was all one big wait.

Sitting in the blind, staring at the eaten pig and the partially eaten Grant and waiting for the leopard to come and hearing the sounds—the oohoo-oohoo-hoo of the doves and the squalls and squawks and growls and mutters in the dark bush ahead by the Grummetti River—I thought profoundly that there was an awful good analogy in waiting for a leopard by a strange river in a strange dark country. I began to get Selby's point about the importance of a leopard in a tree— waited for, planned for, suffered for—and to be seen for one swift moment or maybe not to be seen at all. These are the kinds of thoughts you have in a leopard blind in Tanganyika when the ants bite you and you want to cough and your nose itches and nothing whatsoever can be done about it. Five o'clock came. No leopard. *Hapana chui,* my head said in Swahili. I looked at Selby. He was scowling ferociously at a flock of guinea fowl which seemed to be feeding right into the blind. He made a swift, attention-getting gesture with his hand. The guineas got the idea and marched off. Selby pointed his chin at the leopard tree and shrugged. Now it was six o'clock. I thought about the three weeks I sweated out in Guam, waiting for orders to leave that accursed paradise, orders I was almost sure of but not quite. When they came, they came in a hurry. They came in the morning and I left in the afternoon. *Six-thirty now. Hapana chui.*

It was getting very dark now, so dark you couldn't see the kill in the tree at all without training the rifle on it and looking through the scope. Even then it was indistinct, a blur of bodies against a green-black background of foliage. I looked at Selby. He rapidly undoubled both fists twice, which I took to mean twenty more minutes of shooting time.

My watch said twelve minutes to seven, and it was dead black in the background and the pig was non-visible and the Grant only a blob and even where it was lightest it was dark gray. I thought, *God damn it, this is the way it always is with everything. You wait and suffer and strive, and when it ends it's all wasted and the hell with all leopards,* when I felt Harry's hand on my gun arm. Down the river to the left the baboons had gone mad. The uproar lasted only a second, and then a cold and absolute calm settled on the Grummetti. No bird. No monkey. No nothing. About a thousand yards away there was a surly, irritable cough. Harry's hand closed on my arm and then came away. My eyes were on the first fork of the big tree.

There was only the tree to watch, a first fork full of nothing, and then there was a scrutching noise like the rasp of stiff khaki on brush, and where there had been nothing but tree there was now nothing but leopard. He stretched his lovely spotted neck and turned his big head arrogantly and slowly and he seemed to be staring straight into my soul with the coldest eyes I have ever seen. The devil would have leopard's eyes, yellow-green and hard and depthless as beryls. He stopped turning his head and looked at me. I had the post of the scope centered between those eyes. His head came out clearly against the black background of forest. It looked bigger than a lion's head.

You are not supposed to shoot a leopard when he comes to the first fork. The target is bad in that light, and small, and you either spoil his face if you hit him well or you wound him and there is the nasty business of going after him. You are supposed to wait for his second move, which will take him either to the kill or to a second branch, high up, as he makes a decision on eating or going up in the rigging. If he is not shot on that second branch or shot as he poises over the kill, he is not shot. Not shot at all. You can't see him up high in the thick foliage.

And Harry had said: *On a given night there has never been more than one shot at a leopard.*

I held the aiming post of my telescopic sight on that leopard's face for a million years. While I was holding it the Pharaohs built the pyramids. Rome fell. The Pilgrims landed on Plymouth Rock. The Japs attacked Pearl Harbor.

And then the leopard moved. Only you could not see him move. Where there had been leopard there was only fork. There was not even a flash or a blur when he moved. He disappeared.

He appeared. He appeared on a branch to the left of the kill, a branch that slanted upward into the foliage at a 45-degree angle. He stood at full pride on that branch, not crouching, but standing erect and profiling like a battle horse on an ancient tapestry. He was gold and black against the black, and there was a slightly ragged rosette on his left shoulder as he stood with his head high.

The black asparagus tip of the aiming post went to the

ragged rosette, and a little inside voice said, *Squeeze, don't jerk, you jerk, because Selby is looking and you only get one shot at a——*

I never heard the rifle fire. All I heard was the bullet whunk. It was the prettiest sound I ever heard. Not quite the prettiest. The prettiest was the second sound, which said BLONK. That was the sound the leopard made when he hit the ground. It sounded like a bag of soft cement dropping off a high roof. *Blonk.*

There were no other sounds. No moans. No growls. No whish of swift bounding feet on bush. A hand hit me on the shoulder, bringing me back into the world of living people.

"*Piga,*" Harry said. He was very excited. "*Kufa.* As bloody *kufa* as a bloody doornail. Right on the button. He's dead as bloody beef in there. We were as near to losing him as damn to swearing, though. I thought he'd never leave that bloody fork, and when he went I knew he was heading up to the crow's-nest. You shot him one sixtieth of a second before he leaped, because I could just make out his start to crouch. You got both shoulders and the heart, I'd say, from the way he came down. My God, aren't they something to see when they first hit that fork? With those bloody great eyes looking right down your throat, and that dirty big head turning from side to side. You shot him very well, Bwana Two Lions. Did you aim for any particular rosette, like you said?"

"Go to hell twice," I said. "Give me a cigarette."

"I think you've earned one," Harry said. "Then let's go retrieve your boy. I'll go in ahead with the shotty-gun. You cover me from the left. If he's playing possum in there, for Christ sake shoot him, not me. If he comes, he'll come quick, except I would stake my next month's pay that this *chui* isn't going anywhere. He's had it."

Harry picked up the old Churchill and I slipped the scope

off the .30-'06 and slid another bullet into the magazine. We walked slowly into the high bush, Harry six steps ahead and me just off to the left. I knew the leopard was dead, but I knew also that dead leopards have clawed chunks out of lots of faces. Selby was bobbling the shotgun up and down under his left shoulder, a mannerism he has when he wants to be very sure that there is nothing on his jacket to clutter a fast raise and shoot. We needn't have worried.

Chui—*my chui* now—was sleeping quietly underneath the branch from which he had fallen. He had never moved. He was never going to move. This great, wonderful, golden cat, eight feet-something of leopard, looking more beautiful in death than he had looked in the tree, this wonderful wide-eyed, green-yellow-eyed cat was mine. And I had shot him very right. Very pretty.

"You picked the correct rosette," Harry said. "Grab a leg and we'll lug him out. He's a real beauty. Isn't it funny how most of the antelopes and the lions lose all their dignity in death? This blighter is more beautiful when he's in the bag

than when he's in the tree. Lookit those eyes. No glaze at all. He's clean as a whistle all over, and yet he lives on filth. He eats carrion and smells like a bloody primrose. Yet a lion is nearly always scabby and fly-ridden and full of old sores and cuts. He rumples when he dies and seems to grow smaller. Not Chui, though. He's the most beautiful trophy in Africa."

"How does he compare with Harriet Maytag's leopard?" I said, rather caustically, I thought.

"Forget Harriet Maytag, chum," Harry said. "I was only kidding. As far as I am concerned, you are not only Bwana Simba, Protector of the Poor, but a right fine leopard man too. Here come the boys. Prepare to have your hand shaken."

The boys oohed and ahed and gave me the old double-thumb grip which means that the *bwana* is going to distribute largesse later when he has quit bragging and the liquor has taken hold. We piled the big fellow into Jessica's back seat and took off for camp. Mama nearly fainted when we took the leopard out of the back and draped him in front of the campfire. The wind had changed again and she had heard no shot. When the boys left in the dark with the Rover, she had assumed they were just going to pick us up.

The leopard looked lovelier than ever in front of the campfire. His eyes were still clear. His hide was gorgeous. Even the bullet hole was neat. He was eight feet and a bit, and he was a big tom. About one-fifty on an empty stomach.

"Tail's a bit too short for my taste, though," Harry said. "Harriet's had a longer tail."

"Harriet be damned," I said. "After you're through with the pictures, mix me a martini."

Harry took the pictures. He mixed me a martini. I drank it and passed out—from sheer excitement, I suppose. Because I hadn't had a drink all day.

The next evening when Harry and Mama went down with cameras to see about the female, she had already acquired another tom. This leads me to believe that women may be fickle.

The tom came in across the plain, which leopards never do, and passed within a few feet of the blind. He growled mightily as he bounded past. The *memsaab* gave up leopard photography. She said that Selby was obviously deaf or he would have heard the leopard coming through the grass.

Chapter 8

TIME was spinning out on our stay at Campi Abahati. We'd spent some ten days there and had had a
really phenomenal run of luck. Everything had been
much, much too easy. The long corridor of short grass was
overflowing with new hordes of game flocking in as the water

dried up on the Serengeti, as the grass towered high and dry in the long-grass country. The plains now were solidly swarmed with zebras and wildebeest. The little gazelles, the Tommy and the Grant and the impala, had increased by thousands. A big herd of buffalo had come in from somewhere, and the carnivores were all around. There were at least half a dozen leopards feeding up and down the Grummetti. You could hear the lions in a dozen directions. The grass fires were beginning to start—a patch here, a patch there. This was around the first of July. By August it would all be burnt and the tender green shoots would be coming up everywhere, waiting for the early autumn rains to send it plunging upward in almost visible growth, and taking the animals back off the plains and up into the hills, where they had enough to drink from the pockets and the little water holes, and where they would be safe for a while from the cats that sneaked the thick grasses.

There were only the twin young rhinos in the area. The buffalo had been numerous but meager in the horn. The best bull we saw measured only forty-three inches. But otherwise we had had this wonderful burst of luck. In a space of about five days we had taken two lions—one decent, one very fine— an entirely noble leopard, a fair buff, two exceptionally fine impala, a magnificent Tommy and Grant, the best waterbuck to be seen in those parts, and a damned good eland. I am no shooter for shooting's sake, and Harry was the kind of man who would rather not shoot at all than to shoot something unworthy of his reputation.

The *memsaab* had had a couple of days out on the plain with her cameras, while I stayed in camp and wrote, and there didn't seem to be much point to staying on. But we hated to go. I would have been content to stay there all summer, watching the baboons, watching the grazing game, shooting a piece of meat once in a while for the pot, and keeping track of the progress the ants were making in rebuilding one of their dilapidated hills. But it was a wrench to leave. I suppose it is always like that with your first camp in a new place, where the weather has been fine and the luck full and the new fresh wonders countable daily on the fingers.

I was even going to miss the black gentlemen in the nearby Ikoma village, especially the chief. The chief was a pompous type who wore a white solar topi as his badge of office over a reasonably clean white drill suit. He also carried a cane, and when he came out to meet us the day we attended the big *ngoma,* he was holding his fingers carefully away from his suit and blowing on the tips. The nails were bright red. In his other hand he had a bottle of Revlon nail polish.

"Hollywood," Virginia said, "is everywhere these days."

I was going to miss the pleasant Indian and his pretty little shy wife who ran the local *ducca*—the general store that is always to be found as the social center of any fairly populous village. He was a nice little bloke who lived a life of infinite boredom, leavened only by occasional conversation with his rival tradesman across the clayey street and *his* pretty shy little wife. They competed with each other for the local trade, out of the sparse, shoddy stores of their little tin shacks, taking a few goat and sheepskins in return for coarse Army hand-me-downs, tinned goods, and staple country-store provender. Business was never brisk. Both were clamorous with joy over the appearance of an occasional safari. *Our* Hindu was pathetically eager for us to accept his dead-grass cigarettes and cold beer in return for a few minutes' chat while we stocked a few canned goods and replenished the gasoline. It would probably be a long time before he saw another safari.

When we went by to pay a call on Kibiriti, the lion tracker, we received not much response. Kibiriti was drunk. He had been drunk since the lion dance. So had a considerable portion of the young bucks who had performed. It takes them two days and much beer to plaster on the paint, and a week at least for the paint and the *pombe* to wear off.

The last full day in camp I laid down some law and demanded the right to *my* kind of shooting. I am a compulsive bird shooter. Therefore I am accorded to be nuts by people who wish to slay large, angry animals every day. The natives especially regard a bird shooter as mad. They cannot understand a man spending time and energy blasting away at birds when there are two thousand pounds of eland over every hill and a sleepy topi standing under every bush. Harry was as nearly impatient. He is a trophy man and considers a six months' hunt with no armed activity as highly worth while if it yields one monumental head at the end of the struggle.

But I was raised on quail and matured on ducks and pheasant, and to me the shotgun is the noblest weapon yet devised. I had a hoary Churchill 12-gauge with me—a lovely piece as only the British make them lovely—the scarred Circassian walnut stock as slim as a girl's wrist, all balance and precision. It grew out of my face and pointed itself and I was beginning to itch to point it at something. There is more good and variegated bird shooting in Africa than anywhere else in the world, and by God I was going to have some. I was frustrated.

Every time I saw something worthy of the shooting, a flock of guinea fowl or a covey of big, pheasanty-looking spur fowl run across the trail and into a bush, I would look longingly at the shotty-gun and entreatingly at Harry. ("Best not spook the country with the shotty-gun, Bob," or "Best not bother with the birds now, Bob. We want a really good three-toed unicorn"—or some such disparaging talk.)

One day, coming back from Ikoma, I got mad and told the boys to *toa* the shotty-gun. A couple of francolin, those wonderful big partridge with all the white meat, even on the legs, trotted across the path and into a sedgy field. I got out and put up both birds simultaneously. I took the cock with the right and the hen with the left and glanced backward at the jeep, expecting some applause for a very clean double. Harry was looking at Kidogo and Adam, and all three were shaking their heads sorrowfully, as over the misbehavior of an unruly child. "*Ndege*," Kidogo said. "Bwana Ndege." I was the Bird Master from that time on. They used it as an epithet and only forcibly restrained themselves from tapping their foreheads to indicate my insanity.

Daft or not, I was paying for this *shauri*. So the last day I announced calmly that this morning was to be devoted to the *bwana's* especial pleasure, and anybody who didn't like it could damned well stay home. I kidnaped Selby, armed him with the little Sauer .16, took down the Churchill, and we bumped over the yellow plain to a water hole—to which, by personal and sneaky observation, I had noted that the sand grouse flocked in to drink at precisely eight-fifteen every morning.

The sand grouse is quite a wonderful little bloke. He is a desert bird and not a true grouse at all. The big imperial is heavier than a teal, and his little cousin, the pintail, is a few sizes smaller and a few knots faster. Both the imperial and pintail have long, back-swept wings, more like waterfowl than anything else, possibly, except hawk. The sand grouse is closer to the pigeon family than he is to a grouse, but he is stripped for speed and he is beautiful to watch when he flies and he is also beautiful to eat. He is a plump little fellow, deckled in brown, buff, and black, and while his meat is dark I never saw anybody curse him when he turned up in a pot roast.

For true sport, sand-grouse shooting touches a par with

high-pass shooting of teal in a high wind. A pintail sand grouse coming in with his eye fixed on a water hole is logging fifty knots or better, and when he swoops he make a Mexican white-wing dove look clumsy and slow. He comes just once a day to dip his sharp little bill in the water hole, and then he takes off to crouch in the hot sand or to hide among the rocks for the rest of the day.

When he comes, he comes by the millions, by the thousands, by the hundreds, and if you wanted to wait him out you could kill a hundred of him as he bunches up over the watering place. But if you shoot him for sport it is quite a different matter, unlike the habits of one particular Austrian nobleman who shot some 675 in one morning up on the Northern Frontier.

I doubt if I will ever forget this morning. It had rained briefly the day before, a slashing thunder shower that had cleaned the sky a well-washed blue. The sun was just beginning to warm itself, and the breeze was tremulously soft. A few animals—a Tommy or so and a couple of wildebeest—moved off lazily as Harry and I parked the jeep and walked over to the lone scraggly acacia that guarded the water hole. It was a morning so common to the African plain-country, the kind of morning where a man is highly content to be himself and nobody else at that particular time.

I broke open a couple of boxes of shells and placed one on one side of the tree, one on the other. I addressed Selby as sternly as he had been addressing me.

"You may be able to kill buffalo cleanly at six feet," I said. "You may be the devil's own choice boy on lions at six yards in thick bush. But in the shotgun department you will now pay careful heed to the master. We are going to pretend that we are standing under a eucalyptus tree on a muddy meadow in the outback of New South Wales, which is in Australia. We will pretend we are shooting ducks, the hard way. We will crouch as the flock of sand grouse approaches and we will let them get within range, and then we will stand up and expose ourselves fully. And we will shoot only at doubles. Nor will we shoot simultaneously. Each in his turn."

(I remembered suddenly that morning in Australia—hotter than this but as blue of sky and soft of breeze. I had gone out with a rancher named Keith Leahey on his vast Oxley Ranch, and he had posted me under a tree in a soggy meadow and said: "Shoot. I'll come and fetch you after a while."

(I thought he was plain insane. No blind, no cover, no decoys. But the ducks swept down in huge flocks, all the kinds of ducks I knew and a score of breeds I'd never seen. They zipped and swooped and passed high and skimmed low. After five minutes I was shooting only for sex, species, and in such position that they'd drop on a grassy hummock about thirty yards square. I've been telling that story to duck hunters for years. They never believe me.)

Presently here in Africa the air was full of a throaty chuckle-chuckle—and you could see the tiny spots in the distance. Five hundred there. Three hundred there. Two hundred over here. Scores and tens and fifties and pairs and an occasional single. Ahead of the flock came a lone big billy dove, swooping faster than he looked. I turned and casually shot him over my right shoulder. He dropped ten feet from the tree. It was a very simple shot, but impressive.

"That is how you do it, Hunter," I said. "Can Harriet Maytag do that?"

"You go to hell," said Selby. And then the birds came.

They came with whistles, like policemen summoning help. The sky darkened over the water hole. I shot blind into a couple of the big mobs, hitting nothing, but splitting them up into twosomes and foursomes. They made a great wheel and now began to return in shootable groups. There is nothing you can really do to discourage a sand grouse from his morning drink. Unless there is another water hole in the vicinity he will keep coming back all day.

We would crouch and let them almost in, and then stand straight up. They would veer and climb like frightened mallards, or they would bend into the wind and dart like bluewing teals. They would swerve and swoop and simply lay back their ears and pour on coal. Under those conditions they made the toughest and sportiest shooting I ever saw. You led a passing shot a dozen feet and got his tail feathers. He took off so fast you had difficulty stretching a gun by him and still keeping him in range.

In twenty minutes my gun was steaming hot. In between attacks I had scuffed my birds into a pile on my side of the tree. I was down to one cartridge from a box of twenty-five. I seemed to see two empty cartons on the Selby side.

"How many birds you got?" I said rudely.

"Eight," said Selby. "Fast little buggers, aren't they? How many for you?"

"Twenty," I said, with just the right degree of condescension. "I only got one out of that last double."

"How many boxes of shells?"

"One," I said.

"Let's go back to camp," Harry said. "I give up."

"It's only a matter of practice," I said. "Not like shooting leopard. Any bum can shoot a leopard. Just a matter of keeping your wits about you."

"Go to hell," said Selby. "And take your shotty-gun with you."

"When you write Harriet Maytag the next time," I said, "tell her that you finally found somebody who could top her in something."

On the way back to camp we saw a flock of guinea fowl scratching at the edge of the wet woods. Harry stopped the jeep. I tumbled out and dashed after the flock. They flushed with a great beating of wings, and I nailed one. Another whirled and came over my head, flying high, going downwind like a driven pheasant. I took a half twist and belted him. He came down with a thump and barely missed Harry's head as he tumbled dead alongside the jeep. I broke the gun and blew into the barrels, like the fancy pigeon shooters and skeet experts who wear chamois pads on their shooting shoulders and little badges on their hatbands do.

I handed the shotgun to Kidogo.

I lit a cigarette and looked at Harry.

He looked at me and started the car for home. He didn't say anything. Neither did I. I wasn't mad at Harriet Maytag any more.

It was a wonderful morning.

We broke the camp and policed the site, burning everything that could be burned, burying the tins and sweeping clean the campfire area. The boys climbed aboard the lashed tarpaulin top of Annie Lorry, and I noticed now that burlap bags, wound round with light line, with horns sticking out, were tied securely just behind Katunga, the skinner. He looked happy. He had had a lot of labor lately and had been forced to enlist the services of one of the locals, a dude whose sole article of attire was a kilt made of brown-striped blanket. Katunga was a real shrewd bargainer. He gave his assistant the bits of flesh he was able to scrape from the hides as the skinners sat on their hunkers all day long, crooning softly and flensing carefully each tiny particle of fat from each headskin and from the zebra hides. Katunga had taken over the lions and the leopard himself, and the delicate nostril-skinning of the antelopes. The cats are especially tricky. There is a plump drop of fat at the base of each whisker, and unless it is removed the whisker rots and falls out. It is also true of cats that, unless the skinning is done immediately after killing, the hide slips—that is, the hair falls out. A slipped leopard is not much of a trophy for the library floor.

If you could stand the hordes of flies, the skinning was fascinating. The flies buzzed round the heads of Katunga and his assistant, but neither seemed to mind. They skinned from early morn until late afternoon, working sometimes for as much as an hour around one nostril or eyelid, and removing every minute portion of flesh from the wrinkles and the crevices—slicing down the buffalo mask to reduce its bulk, and being very careful of the lions and leopards and the delicate antelopes. The headskins and hides were spread and salted and stretched under the shade of a low, umbrella-shaped thorn tree and a small *boma* of thorn built around the lowering branches of the tree. They were collected at nightfall, wrapped into small squares, and stowed aboard the lorry. The skulls were set to sweat in the sun after being flensed. The marabou storks ate the chunky, adhering meat. The safari ants picked the skulls clean, and the sun did the rest. In a few days the skulls were white, clean, and sweet-smelling. The skulls, too, were always stowed in the truck at night and the apron raised. We had been living in a hyena heaven, and the skulls are necessary for final mounting.

Little by little I was sorting out the aristocracy of my men. I noticed that Katunga's assistant did not eat with Katunga. He ate with the porters, who rank lower on the social scale than anyone save the kitchen *mtoto*, who is the Oliver Twist of the group. Katunga ate where he pleased; Juma, the head boy, ate largely alone. So did Chege, the lorry driver. Ali, the cook, ate with the two personal boys, Gathiru and Kaluku. Chabani, the car boy, drifted from group to group. Adam and Kidogo, the aristocrats, owing to their respected jobs as gun-bearers, ate together. They sneered at Juma, technically their boss. They made elaborate jokes about getting him out of camp and exposing him to buffalo and lions. Juma made no pretense of bravery. He was not a warrier; he was a factotum.

The gunbearers, I noticed, got first whack at the thick strips of yellow fat around the haunches and entrails of the plump zebras and the hog-fat eland. They also dived head-first into the viscera, carving the ribbons of fat from the stomach and around the heart, and finger stripping the dung from the large intestine to get at the fat-lined tube. They hacked off the best rib sections for themselves, and when we shot a kudu later, I observed *great* care in removing the tenderloin. I corrected this undue interest and commandeered the tenderloin for the *bwana's* table.

There was always an unholy squabble about the fat, but the gunbearers were on the scene of the killing and the others were not, and it was not long before their buttocks, where they store their fat, began to swell like those of zebras. But I noticed that old, mad Katunga got away with most of the lion fat and a good portion of the eland fat. Lion fat is highly treasured as a specific for arthritic joints and is almost price-less in a land where nearly everybody has a chronic gonor-rheal arthritis. The natives sell it to the Indians for a high fee, and the Indians sell it to the village natives, who have no hope of ever acquiring any lion fat except for a price. This is one of the few instances in which the black gets mildly even with his sharp-practicing neighbor. Eland fat and lion fat look re-markably the same and have the same texture. An inch of lion fat over a bottleful of eland fat is about the right proportion, and the Indian ducca keeper pays innocently through his money-mindful nose.

My boys got along wonderfully well, all things considered. They were an old, trained group, taken almost intact from the original safari crew of Philip Percival, the dean of the old-timers. When Percival retired he turned over his string to Selby, who had been apprenticed to him for a couple of years. Selby believed in keeping his tribal strains balanced, to prevent organized political action. Three of the boys were Kikuyu. Several were Wakamba. A couple were Swahilis; others were Nandis. Harry would have no Somali nor Masai in his entourage. He said he never saw a Somali whom he could trust, who would tell you the truth or not stick a knife in you in a fit of pique. He didn't fancy Masai because they were too proud, too nervous, too individualistic, and too prone to wander off when the mood struck them. The pure Masai is still almost untouched by civilization, and the sensitive, haughty *morani* generally fit poorly into safari.

Katunga was Harry's pet—and mine, too, I suspect. The old Wakamba was riddled by disease, and his age rode him heavily. He was utterly useless for general work around camp. He was even a demoralizing type to have around, because he was not only content not to work himself but seemed unhappy when anybody else put on a great burst of energy around him. As an artist with a knife, Katunga considered gathering firewood and policing camp undignified. Katunga's dignity was immense. He was called Bwana Katunga. Once, a long while back, he had gone to Philip Percival with a grievance.

"All white men are called *bwana*," he announced. "They are lords and masters. I am a lord and master too. I am lord of my knife and master of all hides that fall to my blade. Nowhere is there a skinner as good as me. I want to be called *bwana* too."

Bwana Katunga he became, and Bwana Katunga he remained, even to his safari mates. Sometime later, as the malady which afflicted his mind took a firmer hold on it, Katunga stopped crooning to himself and addressed the air.

"I am an old man," he said. "I have not long to live. But I

have left my mark. I am called Bwana Katunga because I am the best skinner in the world. When the safaris pass my *shambas* after I am dead and gone, they will see my wives and my children and my grandchildren and my huts and my sheep and goats and cattle and corn. They will look at the things I have left behind me and they will say: '*King-i* Katunga once lived here.'"

Katunga had not been content with a baronetcy. He had crowned himself king.

We loved Katunga, but the man we admired most was Kidogo. The bowlegged, high-nosed Nandi was a black gentleman of breeding, discernment, and bravery. Great bravery. He was fairly new to Harry's string, having come over from Frank Bowman's disbanding group when Bowman went back home to Australia, but he had dug himself in immediately as a top professional. Some superhuman store of strength lay in reserve in his stringy frame. He coughed dreadfully, but he could go on and on forever, seemingly, with no sleep, small rest, and no encouragement. He was a fine tracker, an excellent driver, a fine mechanic (very rare in an African), absolutely dependable, honest, decent, and possessed of another rare African attribute, a sense of humor. He used to drive poor Adam, the Mohammedan Wakamba gunbearer, near to spiritual prostration with theological arguments in Swahili. Adam was a good and simple soul, renowned mostly for the vehemence with which he blew his nose between his fingers, and a practical bravery that did not spread much outside his stated duties. He was never any good against Kidogo when Kidogo was feeling ornery about Moslemism. They got into an argument one day about whether or not women possessed souls, which kept the camp in a state of high debate for a week. Kidogo's logic was simple. He said that if a Nandi married a Wakamba woman, the issue was of course Nandi. Adam agreed. Well, then, Kidogo said, if you take a woman and a child is born, is the child a human if the child is a boy? Yes, said Adam. Well, then, Kidogo said, paring carefully at a zebra foreleg, the child comes out of the woman, and since he is half of the woman, does not that make the woman human, too, and if she is human, does she not have a soul? Adam said he wasn't sure.

"Have you got a soul?" Kidogo asked him.

"Sure," Adam said. "Of course I got a soul."

"Well," Kidogo said, "unless your mother was a human and had a soul, you are only half human, with only half a soul, and will surely go to Shaitani in Gehennum when you die."

Adam quit arguing. He was having a period of extreme devoutness, during which time he refused to sanctify meat unless it actually *was* still a little bit alive when he touched its eyeballs and then cut its throat. During his less devout periods, Kidogo accused him of *hallaling* meat that even the buzzards took a second look at.

Kidogo reached a point pretty soon where he would kid me about my bird shooting. One day I was blasting away at a particularly gaudy blue jay which Harry wanted as an ornament for his girl friend's hat, or dress, or some such. It was a beautiful jay, with a dark red crested head and feathers of a dozen shades of iridescent blues and purples. The damned jay bird would not die. I would take a belt at it with the little 16-gauge, and off it would fly to another tree. I chased after it and belted it again. And again. Feathers flew, but the bird flew too.

I felt a touch on my shoulder. It was Kidogo, who had taken the big elephant gun out of its case. He handed it to me.

"*Bwana nataka .470?*" he asked softly and innocently. Fortunately the little blue jay decided to die at that moment.

I was always impressed with the complete faith the men reposed in Harry Selby. Most of them were years his senior, but he treated them with the stern benevolence of an intelligent parent. He would take a sniff of snuff with Katunga, or lend him two bob to go to a nearby village to "get his back straightened," Katunga's euphemism for buying a piece of local affection. Harry would squat for hours around the boys' cook fire, gossiping with them, and incidentally keeping abreast and ahead of all developments, political, social, and otherwise, of his safari.

Some long experience with blacks had taught him when to joke, when to pitch in and help, and when to apply a swift kick in the pants. They accepted the jokes, the assistance, and the boot in the behind with equal relish. They were largely proud men and decent men, from Chege, who drove the lorry, to Mala, the porter. I liked my boys. I think in time my boys liked me.

It was funny, when we lurched out of Campi Abahati to head back across the Serengeti for Lake Manyara and the rhino country. Only two weeks had passed, and I knew something about all the people who made up my string—something about their wives, their diseases, their peculiarities, their bravery or lack of it, their industry. The faces were no longer just black faces, indistinguishable from each other. Their personalities had emerged from the shabby khaki and the shoddy castoffs which they wore over their black, dusty hides on safari. I knew already that Chege was the lady killer and Chabani the sea lawyer, that Juma was the Machiavelli and Ali the venerable gentleman, Katunga the character, Kibiriti the thespian, and Mala the strong silent man. They had decided that the *memsaab* was not the complaining type of female and that the *bwana*, while he had bad legs and great fear, had so far managed to control both at important moments. In two weeks they were beginning to joke me a little. I was very proud of that.

I felt like a hell of a fellow as the battered Land Rover clattered and bumped along ahead of Annie Lorry, who wheezed and lurched behind us. I was sunburned and my nose had quit peeling. I wasn't afraid of the guns any more,

nor of myself when I shot one of them. I had always wondered what I would do when I was faced with dangerous and
tricky game, and to some extent I knew. My safari clothes
were becoming weathered. So was my conversation. So was
my knowledge of what I saw. I was speaking some small
Swahili, and I knew a euphorbia cactus from a whistling
thorn, a Tommy from a Grant, a dik-dik from an oribi.

We swerved from course to say good-by to the lion pride.
The four females were still in the same place. The nasty
lioness stood her ground while the other three gathered up
the cubs and took them into the bush. We drove close aboard
the nasty lioness, and her tail started to wave and her head
went down again. At fifty yards she charged, and as Harry
turned the jeep under full steam, her jaws snapped about
three feet from my exposed rear end. Harry ran the camera
with one hand and swerved Jessica with the other. A great
many weeks later, when we saw the developed film, I wished
that he had been driving with both hands and to hell with
the photography. We have now a magnificent picture of a
lioness with her mouth wide open, narrowly missing the well-
padded rear of a visiting sportsman.

"We might as well face it," Virginia said as we headed for
the game ranger's house a few miles away. "There is one lady
lion who is never going to approve of the machine age or
anything in it."

The game ranger was home this time. He was a sandy
little man in shorts, who asked us in out of the heat for a
quick snap of brandy and a glass of cool water. It was
blessedly cool inside his thick-walled, heavily thatched house.
The sun was hitting hard on the dusty high grasses when we
stirred ourselves and inched Annie Lorry down the treacherous hill, over the rocky stream bed, and took a bearing on
the devilishly distant crater of Ngoro-Ngoro. It was going to

be a long and unpleasant, hot and tiresome two days. It was going to be distinguished by a series of balks and pushes and busted axles and off-loads and reloads of our tragic truck, Annie Lorry.

Annie's penchant for pig holes, soft cotton soil, red clay bogs, treacherous dongas, and top-heavy loading kept her in a state of permanent contusion. She snapped the leaves of her springs as easily as other vehicles snapped sticks in their paths. She boiled the water in her radiator for no good reason. She cast wheels as horses cast shoes. She gobbled oil. She staggered and fell on her side. She was more animal than machine and invited mercy shooting.

She dropped nearly dead in her tracks well after dark two thirds of the way across the Serengeti, far from wood, far from water. We went back to her and made a makeshift camp. It was bitter, searing cold, with an evil wind that whipped the lava dust from the bottom of what was once a volcanic lake into the pores of your skin. Your teeth grated on it. It kinked your hair and tainted your cigarettes.

We pitched the one tent only, its closed rear to the teeth of the wind, and dug a hole in the ground. Harry dripped a mixture of gasoline and crankcase oil into a dug pit, set it afire, and had Ali warm some soup over the blaze. We ate some gritty, cold Tommy cutlets, had a can of cold spaghetti, took a tremendous drink of brandy, and went to bed dirty.

The next morning we noticed that the wind had pushed a shifting hill a few more feet away from us. A lonely pregnant rhino cow was all that we could see in the way of game, and what the hell she was doing out there in her delicate condition not even Selby could say. We fixed whatever was wrong with Annie Lorry's cervix and started the hard, high climb up the shaly side of the serrated hills that led to Ngoro-Ngoro.

Chapter 9

THE sides of the mountains were talcumed with gray, choking lava dust, cobbled loosely with stones and small boulders, thinly wooded with starved thorn. The trail wound round and round on a slow rocky pull, with even the jeep in low or second, her gearbox groaning. Annie Lorry was suffering terribly behind us. We were averaging a good four miles an hour as we crept up the slopes. It got a little greener as we climbed higher, greener and colder. The few semi-Masai we saw, mostly small children, were a mangy and miserable-looking lot. We finally hit the top. Just before we stopped the jeep to wait for the lorry to come up, Harry pointed at an eagle. He was suspended against the cold, gray sky. His wings were churning furiously. He was headed into the wind and going exactly nowhere. I had on wool pajamas under my safari clothes. I was wearing a cashmere sweater over the pajamas. Over all was a heavy trench coat, and I was never colder in my life. It must have been somewhere

The grin on the author is three parts martinis. The grin on the memsaab *is a pleased one, owing to having gotten the author to the plane at all. Leaving for a safari is far more difficult than making the actual trip, because of last-minute complications and friends.*

TWA

TONY DYER

The boy is scraping **a** *skin. That's a typical jungle camp in the background. The car is not stuck now. It will be stuck later, and many times. Even this is simpler than getting out of town from New York.*

Now this is when it becomes worth while. That's Kilimanjaro, snow-capped and lovely, in the background. There's an acacia at the left, and the veldt is peopled by zebra. This is as pretty a picture of Africa as you'll see, because there's so very little nonsense in it. Or people.

This is Pop, looking stern and noble and full of vitamins. A fairly decent buffalo can always bring out the ham in a city boy, or any other boy who has just shot one. This is a long way from "21" and just a page or so away.

VIRGINIA RUARK

HARRY SELBY

Mama is looking pleased with herself again because she has transported the old man all those miles and now is mixed up in a lion dance, where her own mane mingles with the headdresses of the other savages. They're local kids from the Wa-Ikoma settlement, so far down into Tanganyika that you might as well not bother. It takes them longer to put on their paint than it takes a debutante, and they just let the paint wear off. Like debutantes.

PHIL SCHULTZ

This is known as the authenticating shot. The shabby character on the left has been in Africa so long he's lost his health again and seems to be just leaving the local Chez Dave. Couple in the middle are Mr. and Mrs. Armand Denis, the famous explorer-moviemaker, and his bride, whom he calls Poochy. Babe with the glasses is Mrs. Ruark, who seems to have retained her health.

VIRGINIA RUARK

Up top is how a white hunter looks when he is working in the bush. He is very tall, very broad, and full of confidence and strength. This is the man who keeps the lions from eating you.

Here is the same white hunter, but coming into New York now, where you have to keep the lions from eating him. Meet young Harry Selby, the best professional hunter in British East Africa, although he will not be thirty for a long time. When he left New York after this visit he swore he was through with sidewalks forever and would take his chances with rogue elephants in the musth *season.*

PAN AMERICAN

These are two cheetahs, hunting leopards, taking off for fun. When they whip past sixty miles an hour there is not much left to chase. They are an odd breed of cat, since zoologically they are a good half dog and make loving pets when they aren't biting you.

These are impala. An impala is a happy little bloke who is the color of a new-minted penny on his top side, brilliant white beneath, and black-barred on the sides. Sometimes, just for laughs, he will jump fifteen or twenty feet into the air. What makes this shot unusual is that you so seldom see so many so high in the air all at once. They aren't going anywhere. In a moment they will turn and leap back at you—just because they feel so good.

HARRY SELBY

This is a nice old boy, this papa lion, sore at nobody and wishing you'd feed him.

Can't say the same for Junior. Mama is suspicious, but Buster is just plain sore. He will grow up to have ulcers, but the snarl is sincere, and the tiny teeth are needle-sharp.

TONY DYER

You might just call this one lions at play, or in love, because the lioness is plainly kissing Papa at the top shot. It is a remarkable shot only in that so few people get so close to lions in love. Harry Selby was the eavesdropper.

HARRY SELBY

HARRY SELBY

Lions again, and an unusual Selby shot of four lads making a stalk against a herd of waterbuck. What you don't see is the lioness who will kill one. These boys in the foreground are just window dressing, and the buck doesn't care about them. Mama lion, downwind from them and off in those trees, will do the shopping with her claws.

The foot on the neck is ham again. Always there is ham in a man who goes against a lion and wins. This was a gorgeous simba *with a bright red mane and green eyes. The reason Kidogo and Chabani seem so pleased is that just a few seconds before there were five lions mixed up in this thing, and the issue seemed slightly in doubt. Kidogo, at right, was on the ground with the* bwana *and remembers that there was one lioness we should have shot and didn't, out of respect for females. But he's as nervous now as I am.*

You can barely tell the man from the beast here, except the beast is prettier. Difference is the leopard's dead. The man only looks that way.

TONY HENLEY

Above and over at the left there is some unusual leopard stuff. You seldom see them at all. You very rarely see them with a camera. And then you never see them in the daytime unless you are lucky like Tony Henley and have a camera with you and remember to take the cap off it. There's been one safari out fourteen or fifteen years now that still hasn't got a leopard to call its own, and most of the times you never bet on seeing one, let alone shooting one with a gun first or a camera second. Bloke on the right is chewing on either an impala or a Tommy. He seems happy at his task.

These are some more Wa-Ikoma warriors who have caught a slight infection from Hollywood about sunglasses. The sunglasses are phony. The lion manes that the lads wear on their heads aren't phony. The boys collect their own headdresses. With spears.

There is something powerful pleasing about baboons. Maybe because they think we look like them. And they smell terrible. Like we do.

The lovely African plain with its myriad beasts is marvelous to see. Everybody is in love and happy and gamboling about on the flower-scattered meadows.

Except when sex comes into the picture. And here we have two young Thomson gazelles slugging it out, just like in the Stork Club, and for the same reason. The dame'll go off with somebody else.

Grant gazelle at the bottom, and this is the way you'll most always see them, going away from you. Giraffe and some zebra up top, curious and alert. The giraffe is a real clown, and nobody bothers him much any more. But he has been known to kill a lion with his feet. We used to eat the Grant, but he has measles now, and his liver has its problems. I sympathize with the Grant.

TONY DYER

PHOTOS BY TONY DYER

You have to love the rhino, his horn is so long, and he makes such pretty pictures. The only trouble with him is that he's half blind, mad all the time, and isn't nearly so clumsy as he seems. He turns swiftly and smells well, and if he is as close as he seems at lower right, then he's dead a few minutes later. Else he'd have the photograph of you. It's a thing people don't understand about photography. Somebody had to tell the animal it was time to quit charging, and it wasn't the photographer.

Elephants are like this. Peaceful and happy and busy.

PHOTOS BY TONY DYER

PHOTOS BY TONY DYER

Elephants are like this, too. Coming quietly first, and then with a bustle of dust and a squeal of anger, and then like the boy at lower left. The fellow with the gun is Tony Dyer, a youngster who was protecting the cameraman in a recent film. Tony shot this fellow at six yards. From necessity. The elephant disliked actors.

HARRY SELBY

The big type on the extreme left above was snapped by Harry Selby on a reserve. The reason this Cape buffalo was on the reserve was that he knew what he was wearing on his head by way of souvenir. That horn spread is enough to make a collector weep.

Below you get some idea about how big a buffalo is. This one weighed a ton and scared us all silly. There is roughly as much room to sit on him as you will find in the average Pullman bar car.

VIRGINIA RUARK

TONY DYER

And above you see a fair example of the sanitation corps at toil. Nothing is wasted in Africa, and this is as fine a shot of vultures as Tony Dyer is apt to make. Or anybody. What he left out were the marabou storks, which will take the choicest bits away from the vultures. And the ants. They'll clean up the rest of the mess.

This is Memsaab Ruark proving that vanity can exist anywhere. Mama was steady set on staying blond. Juma, the head man, got the local equivalent of an Antoine assignment.

PHIL SCHULTZ

Every Friday was hair day, and Juma got awfully arrogant about it. You know what will happen to this boy. He has got to wind up in a salon.

TONY DYER

Nothing here but wildebeest, the bad-gag buffalo types who are really named gnu. Nothing stupider, uglier, or more prevalent. Their tails make fine fly whisks. Only hyenas prefer them as food. And I never shot one. Too much like shooting a relative.

PHOTOS BY VIRGINIA RUARK

Here we are finally in business. This baby is on my wall. It is a Tanganyikan waterbuck, and nobody you know has his peer on any wall. This is as noble a stag as if he were actually a stag. Harry Selby kissed him when we found him. So did Zim, the taxidermist in Nairobi, and Coleman Jonas, the taxidermist in America. So did old Katunga, the head skinner in camp. This is a hell of a waterbuck. That is why the author is weeping, at left, and so negligent of the skinning, at right.

We ate pretty good out there, if you like breast of guinea fowl, top—in the raw, but available—and those are grouse and spur fowl Mama is flaunting at the bottom.

VIRGINIA RUARK

HARRY SELBY

Mama got overbearingly arrogant as a shotgunner. But she kept us fed while Father was slaving at the serious work. God only knows how many she missed, because I have seen her shooting pheasant since.

That's a pretty pretty impala, and I expect his horns might buy him a place in Rowland Ward's Hall of Fame. I couldn't care less. It was a nice day, that day, and the boys needed meat, and I hit what I was aiming at. I would rather for me to have this impala than for a hyena to have this impala, because my memory is longer.

Here is a beautiful example of what the Marshall Plan has done to the natives everywhere and a great reaction to all peoples abroad. These kids are saying good-by. To their first jeep. And to them it looks awful.

around thirty degrees, with a sixty-knot gale going at nine thousand feet.

Harry pointed down into the vast crater of Ngoro-Ngoro, the extinct volcano, the fifteen-mile-wide walled meadow in which thousands of head of game roamed, a reservoir achievable mainly by a meandering wildebeest trail in which you could see some fairly fresh droppings—a trail that twisted and tortured itself thousands of feet below to the lush green of the volcano's floor.

"This was a hell of a place to shoot once," he said. "Used to pull lions out of this crater by the hundreds. It's still a sort of Shangri-La. Not many people been down into the bottom. Some bloke was going to lower a hunting car down into the crater, piece by piece, but I don't know whether he made it. Sometime, when I have time, I'd love to go down there and spend six months or so looking around."

"Next trip," Virginia said. "Let's creep down the side of this other hill and find a little warmth. This is more like Alaska than Africa. I'm froze."

"That's what makes it so fascinating," Harry said. "I'll be showing you baobab trees and bananas in another few hours. We'll camp tonight in a place so bloody Tarzany that you have to carry a Masai shield to shoo off the tsetses. Tropical butterflies and snakes in the bed."

"Snakes or not," Virginia said, "if it's warm, it's for me. Here comes Annie, sneaking up the hill behind us. To horse, my good man, and let us dig up that resthouse you were mentioning a bit back and have one of Dr. Ruark's nutritious deliciouses."

The lorry lumbered up, stopped, and Harry sent it on ahead of us. We gave her a mile's start and started down. About halfway down, or around, the crater, he turned off the trail into what seemed a picnic ground, a series of rustic huts overlooking Ngoro-Ngoro, with the grass green around them, the flowers bright, and such odd and miraculous things as taps with running water and stone fireplaces. There was even a three-hole latrine and what seemed to have been a shower bath before it rusted out of shape. A few citizens, white and black, had pre-empted most of the camping space. We pushed the jeep along to the lower end of the encampment and outspanned. It was still cool, as it is cool in the high hills of Australia in the wintertime, but not the freezing, blowing cold of the summit where the eagle hung suspended against the force of the gale. Chabani went off with the basins and found some water. We removed several pounds of lava dust, cut a bottle of gin three ways, and lazed back on the green grass. It was nice, there on the side of the volcano, seeing the tiny moving specks of game herds at the bottom, drinking the gritty warm martinis, and contemplating a hot bath no more than four hours away.

Harry puttered around in the chop box and came up with some cold francolin and cold beans, coarse cold bread and rock-hard butter. It had melted and frozen and looked like yellow lava. The taste was not unsimilar, either.

"You'll like Manyara," he said. "It's the real movie jungle, tropical, big trees, thick bush, and steamy-hot kind of Africa. The lake is a big soda deposit. When it's dry you can rip up and down on its bed at ninety miles an hour, if you've a vehicle that'll do ninety miles an hour. The shores are stiff with rhino and a kind of smallish, reddish buffalo. We ought to pick up a good rhino first day out—second day, anyhow. Then we'll have a look up in the hills around Kiteti for an oryx, kiss Manyara good-by, and shoot up past Kandoa to have a look-see at the kudu. We're over the hard part now, except maybe for the kudu. Might get a nice one the first day. Mightn't get one at all. But the rhino I can almost guarantee.

Lion and leopard are the tough ones, and we breezed through lion and leopard. Luck holds, we'll have a chance to get in at least a couple of weeks at the N.F.D. Then you can shoot your bloody birds to your heart's delight, and pull in an elephant as well, if you're so minded."

The Manyara side of Ngoro-Ngoro was considerably more cheerful to look at than the Serengeti side. The earth was a dark maroon clay, still slippery and treacherous from the recent rains. The vegetation was thick alongside the narrow roads. The grass we saw was dark green against the clay. These slopes were farming country. The road was fairly populous with both vehicles and strolling natives. It seemed strange to see Europeans again after a couple of weeks of complete solitude, and stranger still to see automobiles and busses with yelling natives hanging out of the rear end. The wet road, deeply torn with skid marks, crowded the lip of the sheer drop, and we could see where Annie Lorry had slewed seriously on several bends. We could also see a straight plunge down the side, dripping green and thick with baobab and creepers, verdant thorn and fleshy-looking underbrush. This was wet country—and there didn't seem to be any bottom to where you could fall if the jeep skidded too enthusiastically. I was beat from the night before and a little stupefied from the heavy lunch and the generous gin. I slept going down the hill and woke up just as we came into the little settlement off Mto-Wa-Mbu, the River of Mosquitoes. I had seen the town before, in Cuba, in Spain, in North Africa, in Mexico.

The bunches of bananas hanging outside the general store with its dobe walls and corrugated-iron roof, the potbellied kids and the starved dogs playing in the middle of the dusty streets, the stacks of sugar cane leaning against the sides of the shops, the busy sewing machines on the clay verandas,

the smoke and smells coming from the shabby mud huts—
this was the kind of country I knew. I knew the people too.
Tanganyika comes from the word *tanganya,* which means
mixed up. These were mixed-up folks. Negroes with a heavy
strain of Arab. Pure Arabs in fezzes and turbans. Indians,
Sikh and Parsi and lower grades of *babu,* in robes and swad-
dling-cloth pants and jodhpurs under caftans. The women
with the saris and the caste marks, alongside plum-black
local ladies with floppy bare breasts over cheap curtain-mate-
rial wrap-arounds. All the local ladies very brightly dressed,
and very conscious of their high style, but no more style-
conscious than the two or three effeminately surly Masai
morani, leaning arrogantly on their spears, smeared red with
ocher over coppery hides, their long hair greased and plaited
into thick pigtails. Maybe someday when I know them better
I will learn to love the Masai as today I love the Wakamba
and the Nandi. But every time I see one of those elaborately
got-up, sneering dandies with all the cheap-john jewelry, the
heavy-lidded eyes, and the supercilious sneer, I think of fagot
parties I have stumbled upon, and the toe of my boot itches.
A young Masai *moran* knows he's hot stuff, and he has a way
of flirting his goatskin cloak at you, of shrugging insolently,
which leads you to believe that he's been practicing hours
before a cheap hand mirror before he comes to town to give
the locals a break.

We went in to say howdy to the Indian *ducca* keeper, an
old buddy of Harry's, a portly citizen with a handsome wife
and pretty daughter. His stock was considerable. He had
more good gin than you could buy in Nairobi, and better beer
—imported Pilsen in gold-foil bottles—and any amount of
wines, vermouths, candies, canned goods, and cigarettes. He
had tennis shoes and dress goods and pickles and condiments
and Coca-Cola and Pepsi-Cola and Kotex and English soap

and hardware and Vienna sausages and hot mustard and bolts of dress goods made in England, of Indian patterns, to sell to the natives, and he had baskets and biltong and fresh vegetables and bananas and brandy and John Jamieson Irish whisky and a full stock of simple pharmacopoeia and shotgun shells and sweet tinned biscuits and hats and leather shoes and beads and copper wire and flashlight batteries and much, much conversation. It was only a wide place in the road, but the English, German, and refugee tea, tobacco, and coffee planters were always there in fair force along about dark for a quick beer and a packet of Virginia cigarettes. It seemed odd that the Indian Toots Shor was only half a dozen miles from Manyara, where the buffalo roamed and the rhino butted down the tent posts.

The Indian Toots Shor said that so far as he knew there was nobody at Harry's old camp site at Mto-Wa-Mbu; that there was another safari just pulling out which had shot a couple of buffalo yesterday, and that there were *mingi sana mbogo,* likewise lots of elephant, also myriad rhino. We bought a few staples, including a clump of sugar-cane stalks and a bunch of bananas, and headed past what seemed to be the local whorehouse, from the noise coming out of it, down a winding trail to the River of Mosquitoes. Two hundred yards away from the Indian and the local whorehouse and we were right back in the bush again—this time jungle bush. A million butterflies fluttered back and forth across the trail. Branches whipped at our faces in the open jeep. A couple of withes armed with thorns tore at my arm, and a branch bit me viciously on the ear. We drove two miles to a semi-clearing, topped over by big wild figs, baobabs, towering acacias, all thickly woven with lianas. The clearing had filled with high green grass and short, shiny, broad-leaved shrubs. There was a strong stink of baboons in the air, and the high trees were

full of baboons. Also monkeys. And birds. Annie Lorry was
waiting for us when we got there. The boys had started to
off-load her, and a couple of them were chopping at the
underbush with *pangas*. While they were setting up the tents,
we strolled a few hundred yards away down a well-defined
track to look at what I called Mosquito Crick. Mto-Wa-Mbu
was not the most impressive river I ever saw, being not much
more than thirty feet wide, but it was swift and swollen by
the rains.

"Take a look at that bridge," Harry said, pointing downward to what seemed more like a floating raft made of skinny
logs and leaves than a serious structure. "Everybody who
camps here builds a new layer on it. Once in a while it col-
lapses and everything goes into the drink, so we haul out the
vehicle and chop a few more logs and strap 'em onto the top.
Surprising how much actual weight this thing'll sustain."

A couple of black gentlemen with bundles of fresh-peeled
sticks on their backs and another carrying about twenty-five
pounds of just-caught catfish strolled by. They said *"Jambo"*
tentatively. They said the place was overrun with rhino.
*Mingi sana faro. Doumi. M'kubwa sana. Manamouki, mingi,
mingi sana.*

"Place is loaded with rhino," Harry said. "Always was.
They come down out of the hills for a little sunshine and to
graze. Last time I was here I saw fourteen the first afternoon
out. Shot a twenty-three-incher no more than three or four
miles from the camp site here. Can't tell, though, whether
we find them in the mornings or in the afternoons. Never
could figure it out, myself. Last time, nothing whatsoever in
the mornings, but the afternoons would find them fair swarming. Around four o'clock you'd have to beat a path through
them. We shouldn't be here very long before we collect the
faro and go up into the hills, about eighteen miles up yonder,

and grab off the oryx. Ought to be herds of them come down
to the plains, the high plains off the Rift, by now."

We strolled back to camp, which was beginning to look
pleasantly like home, with the underbrush chopped off and
collected for burning. Katunga had been forcibly inspired by
Juma to drag in an immense stockpile of dried logs for the
fire. Ali had the cook fire going. Somebody had driven a
wooden peg into the soft rough bark of one of the big yellow-
mottled trees, and the banana bunch was swinging happily
from the peg. The tents were up. Juma was setting the table,
and the canvas water bag was hanging off a wildebeest-horn
hook. The bag had bottles of gin and vermouth and beer in it.
A baby baboon was peering through a lofty crotch, scolding.
Gathiru and Kaluku, the personal boys, were sweating petrol
tins of water up from the riverbank, placing them onto a
separate blaze to heat up for the *bathi*. Kidogo and Adam
were squatting on a blanket alongside the jeep, field-stripping
the artillery.

And the mosquitoes and the tsetses. They were there too.
In companies and regiments and battalions and divisions and
armies. It was mutual-aid hour, the hour before the tsetses
knock off and the mosquitoes take over.

"Lots and lots of *dudu*," Selby said. "That's where the river
gets its name, of course. I have seen bugs all over this bloody
continent, but the *dudu* here are incomparable. The tsetses
have a special awl arrangement on their bills. They can take
a firm grip with their feet and bore through three thicknesses
of canvas. All the mosquitoes are four-motored. There are
varieties of little squishy, fuzzy caterpillars that roam into
your shirt and leave their tread marks wherever they pass.
They burn and itch like dammit for a while. Then they turn
black and yellow and blue, and then they ache like you've

been beat up by the flat of a buffalo's horns. If you are interested in bugs, I highly recommend this place."

I learned about bugs at Mto-Wa-Mbu, hard by the lake
called Manyara. Bugs do dreadful things to me. When they
bite me I swell. My face puffs, and my hands swell, and they
always seem to bite me near to bone. They bite on the
knuckles and the frontal bones and on the nose and under the
eyes. They get me on the shins. And bugs never seek fresh
territory once they've staked a claim on my pelt. They bite
on bites. And then they rebite the bites they've bitten on the
bites.

We were lavish with the assorted mosquito and/or tsetse
ointment I had bought, the stuff that Abercrombie and Fitch
guarantees repellent to any creature smaller than a crocodile.
Our *dudu* thrived on it. They got drunk on it. They whetted
their spears on it. They went through layers of clothing like
hot needles through vanilla ice cream. After the first evening
at Mto-Wa-Mbu, I was a man no more. I was a walking welt.

After dinner the first evening, we were sitting in front of
the mess tent, washed, full, well-bitten, and just tired enough
to dread the fifty-foot walk to the sleeping tents. Harry and I
were talking idly of bullet weights versus something or other
when he let out a shriek and started to fling off his clothes. He
continued to shriek, shed clothes, and leap high into the air
until he finally trapped something in his fingers and cast it to
the ground, where he jumped on it.

"One of those dreadful woolly caterpillars," he said, and
went shuddering, still near naked, off to bed.

"Some hunter," Virginia said. "Scared of an old caterpillar.
Taking off his clothes in front of a lady, and him so shy."

"Each man to his weakness," I said. "Let's go to bed. We
got a date to shoot a rhino in the morning, and I, personally,
am afraid of rhino."

Surrounded by a cloud of mosquitoes—the tsetses had definitely finished—we staggered down the path to bed. Inside the nets, you could hear the mosquitoes banging against the sides like raindrops on a yielding roof. The whine was more drill press than insect, but I turned over and died.

We were up early and excited; at least, I was excited. It was still gray when we got into the jeep and headed across the bridge on the River of Mosquitoes, a bridge which shook and shivered frighteningly under Jessica's tentative wheels. The forest, dripping, thick, and poison-green, with knobby roots like cypress knees threading across the track, lasted for about three miles, until we hit marsh, which was sopping still and impossible to cross in anything but a light four-wheel drive job such as our Jessica. You could see the deeply bitten tracks where the last safari's hunting car had gone just so far and then no farther. We put up a reedbuck and some sort of hog before we finished with the marsh and headed back into another patch of jungle—real jungle, this time, like Congo jungle in the bad television movies. This was not cheerful bush at all. It was sticky, butterfly-clogged, creeper-twisted, humid bush, with immense trees rearing out of the practically impassable underbush. You could see the raw stump occasionally where the elephants had broken the top off a tree. The trail was very narrow, crossed and recrossed with streams, and at every stream we had to unload and push.

"These'll take some digging," Harry said. "They've been washed out too steep even for Jessica, and she'll go anywhere. We'll shallow the banks some and cut some sticks for a tread at the bottom. Nasty bush, hey?"

We were crawling along through a sort of open-topped tunnel in the solid mass of vegetation when Harry was struck by a happy thought.

"I believe it was right here that Andy Holmberg and Chris Aschan were driving along when they ran head onto a bull elephant standing right in the track. Andy couldn't drive around him, and the bull was walking steadily at them, and I do believe Andy slapped his Rover into reverse and set a new record for backward driving. I hear he was hitting sixty when he came assward out of the bush."

I could believe it. In that compressed wilderness of malignant growth there would be no place to go except backward, and that highly unlikely, since the trail twisted and contorted in constant S-turns. If Holmberg made any time backward, his jeep had a flexible spine.

We burst out of the jungle suddenly, curved toward the lake, and passed through a sea of saw-edged grass that towered over the Land Rover by half a dozen feet. The showers of seeds added to general irritation of last night's bites. The sun was coming up now, and while it was still cool, the tsetses had relieved the mosquitoes of their watch and were working lustily. It did no good to swat them. You had to pull them off and pinch their heads, as you did with the lion flies.

We came out of the grass as suddenly as we had come out of the jungle. We rounded a point where some fishermen had erected a small palm-thatched lean-to, waved at the two scrawny locals who got up to stare at us, and passed through a point that looked exactly like the cedar and live-oak groves that grow, gnarled by the wind, along the Carolina coast line where I was raised. It had the same shaly beach, the same scrubby trees, the same damp projection of a wetter wood. A herd of impala was gamboling under the grove. They stopped to stare. They were quite tame and moved off slowly.

Harry killed the jeep on the point, crawled out, took his glasses, and scanned the shore line. "Nothing that I can see for a couple of miles," he said. "Anyhow, the wind's this direction, and the sound of shot won't carry. It'll be late when we come this way again, too late to shoot. I think you'd best get out and wallop one of those impala. In case we're entirely out of meat."

I took the .30-'06 and jumped out. The impala had worked into the thicker scrub, and the herd kept ambling tantalizingly just ahead of me. I could see the herd ram's big lyre-shaped horns pressing steadily through the bush as he drove his family ahead of him, but his horns were all I could see, and by the size, he would eat tougher than boot. I had all the impala I wanted for trophies, anyhow.

There was a wind-blown tree trunk lying at right angles to its stump, and I crawled up on it. The herd, about thirty or forty does and young ones, was no more than a hundred yards away in the bush. There was a bare place they seemed to be heading for. As they crossed it, one of the several two-year-old rams, with horns past the spike stage but not yet grown into the back-swept wonder of maturity, stopped and looked stupidly back at the herd ram. I suppose he was questioning Papa's right to hurry.

He was fat and pretty and bright gold as he stepped into the open. Balancing like a toe dancer on the log, I held and squeezed at his foreshoulder, shooting down through his back, and I managed to break his neck as he took a step away. He went over with a blat. Adam came running up with Mohammed's knife to make the kill religious, and I have no way of knowing whether the antelope was dead. Adam cut his head clean off and pronounced him fit. We opened him up and tied him to the bumper and proceeded along the twisty trail that goes by Manyara's shore line.

The lake was full. To the left, as far as you could see, it stretched with a peculiar, flat, silver-dull sheen. On the right was a sheer wall of hills, dropping steeply to a few hundred yards of indented, sloping grounds, so that at times you were riding along directly under the frown of the thickly forested cliffs, at other times half a mile or so away from them. Where it was flat or semi-flat it was either thornbush on soft soil or grassy marsh. Only the shingle was sandy and shell-speckled. We stuck to the shingle.

Up ahead was another headland, a sort of thumblike peninsula, which curved backward from its point to make a palm of ooze and heavy bush. Sticking out, farther on, as the inlet came around to another headland, was Majimoto, the hot-water mountain. Steaming springs in the hills cut downward in small waterfalls, to gurgle their warm waters into Manyara. Something like six small rivers, all difficultly possible to cross, were between us and Majimoto. It was only eighteen miles from Majimoto to camp. It took us, we learned as days passed, six hours a day to make the round trip of thirty-six miles.

As we drove along, a dozen ostriches, including two albinos, broke out of the bush and ran foolishly ahead of us, splashing through the water, not pausing even to defecate, slapping along knee-deep in the lake on their big splay feet. They were joined by a small herd of wildebeest, who bucked up and down, meeting other herds, reversing their courses to run back at us, snorting and plunging and acting exactly like wildebeest. A few zebras, fifty or more, hooked up with the wildebeest, and our escort was joined.

"Bloody reception committee," Selby grumbled. "They'll spook everything from here to Majimoto. If they don't, the bloody birds will."

"This," I said, "is known in my country as public relations. You announce the arrival of the honored guests. You send out invitations. Then you run around, waving your arms and squawking, and bollix up the whole works. I've been trying to remember what we have in New York that these stupid wildebeest remind me of, them and the ostriches. It's press agents. New York is loaded with their blood brothers, all running around in circles, yelling and waving their arms and screwing up the entire bleeding issue."

Clouds of waterfowl were rising along the oozy edges of Manyara. The black-and-white Gyppie geese were squawking. The curlews and snipe and plovers were screaming. The secretary birds were sailing up and down, trying to make up their minds to leave permanently. The ducks were setting up a hell of a clamor, and occasionally a flock of guinea fowl would run out, look indignantly around, cackle, and scuttle back. A hippo grunted offshore. A flock of flamingos rose and went dipping over the lake in an indescribable, improbable pink cloud. Up on the sides of the hills there was a crashing in the bush and a small herd of elephants squealed in displeasure.

"Christ," Selby said. "What with one thing and another, any rhino worth shooting will be clean over the mountain by now, heading for Yaida Swamp. Look at those goddamned ostriches. They'll run the whole fifteen miles ahead of us, picking up new chums as they go. I don't remember it like this from before."

We spun along, back wheels slipping and sliding through little rivers, wheels spinning in the sandy dongas, and rounded the first headland. Cutting back, following the heavy, scored wheel tracks of another, earlier vehicle, we ran around the rim of the hills in a crescent course and came out to the point of the second headland before Majimoto. Harry stopped Jessica and pointed.

There was a shapeless lump a thousand yards away. It looked like a big gray anthill.

"*Faro*," Harry said. "*Toa* .470. *Toa* .450." This to the boys. To me: "Well, first morning out and you've probably got your rhino. There he is, feeding down on the shore. Wind's right, too. Blighter's blind, and we can walk up close enough to take his pulse. This one's easy enough, so I'm asking Virginia along. Virginia? Care to go and collect a *faro?*"

"Better than that last time after the buffalo," Virginia said. "You left me sitting all by myself in this jeep and when I asked you what to do if the herd came my way, you said, 'Just stand up in the car and it's likely they'll run around you.' Yes, Harry. I will go along to shoot the rhino. Do I take the camera?"

"Sure," Harry said. "Let's go."

We walked along over the muck, not crouching yet. Harry and I were still letting the bearers carry the big double rifles.

"This is very simple," Harry said. "We'll stalk up as close as we can. If you take him head on, go for that little sore spot at the bottom of his neck. You'll see it. All *faros* have 'em where the armor plating rubs. It he's lying down—and this one seems to be—you can go for the brain. If he charges, you'll know, because the tickbirds'll jump just before he comes. Other shots, take'm in the shoulder, about a quarter the way up. Heart's a little lower on these blokes than on some others. Nothing to it, really. Up on the Northern Frontier, Harriet Maytag——"

"Let's not start that again," I said. "Let's go shoot this rhino without any assists from the fair huntress."

You may be a very brave man, and perhaps your breath

does not begin to hurry in your chest when you walk up for the first time on three tons of antediluvian armor plating, but I am not a particularly brave man and I was beginning to breathe jerkily although the going was fairly easy on the rough, fissured mud. The rhino had its head down. You couldn't see whether the horn was worth it or not. Selby had taken his .450 No. 2 from Adam, and Kidogo handed me the .470. Virginia was just behind the gunbearers, carrying the Cine-Kodak. She looked a little pinched in the face. I noticed I was breathing with my mouth open.

The rhino raised its head. The horn was nothing. Then a small gray blob of putty detached itself from the rhino's side. It was a calf, no more than six months old, if that.

"*Manamouki*," Kidogo breathed behind me. "*Mtoto.*"

Ordinarily you don't mind shooting a rhino cow if the horn is good, and quite often the horn is better on the *manamouki* than on the bull, apt to be longer and more symmetrical and less splintered from brawling. But this lady was too new-come to motherhood for us to leave a baby loose in the bush, even if her horn had been a marvel. Selby handed his gun back to Adam and took the camera from Virginia.

"Too bad," he whispered. "But the baby's young enough so she won't charge and leave it. Let's go and take some snaps. You can cover me, if you will. Don't shoot her unless it's absolutely necessary."

The cow raised her head wonderingly. The tickbirds were quiet on her back. The calf nuzzled irritably at her udders. The big stupid face swung back and forth, testing the wind, which was blowing directly at us. Her little pig's eyes blinked weakly. She walked slowly toward us, still questing with her nostrils.

There was a shallow pool of water in a half-formed donga between us and the cow. Harry had walked up to the edge of the water, and the camera was whirring. The rhino didn't like the noise. But she couldn't see us and she couldn't smell us. Harry kept taking pictures. I glanced back at Virginia, and she was following closely, frightened to approach but scareder still to stay behind. We had come to within thirty feet of the old girl now, and she was visibly upset.

All of a sudden the tickbirds hopped straight up in the air. The old girl stuck out her nose and started a gallop, heading directly at us. Her tail was still up. She couldn't smell, but she was fifteen feet from Harry, and she could make us out dimly with her poor weak eyes. Harry whirred through the film in the magazine and pushed the palm of his hand gently backward. I had the big bead of the .470 resting on the sore spot and was wondering less than idly if the famous rhino ill temper would conquer the mother concern long enough to take this one across that twelve-foot strip of shallow water, in which case I should certainly have to make an orphan of the child.

She made another half pass at a charge and stopped with her feet in the water. Harry was walking backward now, and out to his left so was I. The old girl muttered, tossed her head, checked her child, slewed off in a half turn, and stood rigidly, looking at us. The baby had come up and was butting between her legs. We walked backward another twenty feet or so and then turned, walking away but half facing her. After we'd covered a hundred yards Harry handed his rifle to Adam. I gave mine to Kidogo. Harry gave the camera back to Virginia. Virginia was white. A lady rhino looms very large at thirty feet when you are on the ground.

"I knew she wouldn't cross that water," Selby said. "Not and leave Junior unattended. A half-grown calf, yes indeed. But not the baby. Never the baby. Shame it wasn't a good bull."

Virginia was muttering, not unlike the rhino cow.

"Yes, Virginia?" Harry said politely.

". . . idiots," she said, with something bitter ahead of *idiots*. "Tormenting mother rhinos and taking me along to share in the fun. If there wasn't any danger, why did I see my husband slip the safety catch on that damned cannon and square off at the lady's neckline when she started to come at us?"

"Pure precaution," I said. "It's an expensive camera. I didn't want Selby to lose it when the foot race started. You know his reputation with rhino. He who looks and runs away——"

"Something about the Duchess of Grafton, wasn't it?" Jinny said. "Except here we'd no brawnches for the young man to send me to climb. Nothing but this lovely ooze."

"Seems to me there was another story about a half-grown rhino chasing this young man too," I said. "All over the bars in Nairobi. Tell me, did you actually ever shoot a rhino?"

"Not if I could run from one," Selby said. "I leave the shooting to the clients. Let's get back in the jeep and see if we can't scare this lady into the bush. We've got to pass where she's standing, you know. No other way to get around the point, and she seems a stubborn sort. Off we go."

We slipped and slid the jeep through the fecal ooze, sticking her once, twisting on our own tracks, and finally coming out just abaft the rhino cow and her calf. She was still standing close to the water's edge, turning her head and testing the air. We came up obliquely in the car, and she picked up the scent and charged a small way, with very little heart in it. Harry swung the car. The wheels squeaked and slipped and slithered on the hardened gray crust of the reeking mud.

"We'll outmaneuver the old lady," Harry muttered. There was quite a bit of muttering going on. In addition to Harry and the rhino, Virginia was muttering. So were Kidogo and

Chabani and Adam. Playing with rhinos in open jeeps is fun if the ground is hard, but the way we were maneuvering there wasn't any place to go except into the lake if she decided she didn't actually want to take her child back into the scrub.

Harry blew the horn. She swung her head at us again, facing us now, with her back toward the bush. The calf was beginning to totter into the thick low trees. Harry yelled and hit the door with his hand. The cow snorted. She made one more pass and then quit. She turned, rooting the calf ahead of her, and slowly and reluctantly walked into the bush. She gave one last snort and disappeared. We allowed her some time. We allowed her some time because we had to go through the bush she had disappeared into.

"Tricky terrain," Selby said. "Can't have any fun with rhinos unless you work on a terrain you can trust. This stuff we're driving on is suicidal. Never know when you'll stick or stall."

"That's nice to know," Virginia said. "Lead on, warriors, and don't mind me. I don't mind dying of acute rhino horn through the floor board of a stuck jeep. Let's go seek some more thrills, tomboys."

We picked up the wildebeest-ostrich-zebra convoy again and meandered down the shore line. My mouth was watering at the wildfowl. The ducks, black mallards mostly, were as tame as barnyard puddlers. They didn't bother to get up and fly. They just lifted themselves briefly from the water and flopped down again, gabbling contentedly. I didn't say anything about the shotgun. Lèse-majesté would be the best thing they'd accuse me of.

We came down under the lee of Majimoto. There was a broad green valley tucked under the mountain's steep side, angling backward out of sight into heavy bush, a mile or more in length from what we could see, and a half mile wide. It was rolling, lovely green, cool and inviting, like a park. On the near side, our side, was half a mile or so of very high yellow grass. Harry stopped the car and stood up with the glasses again. He swept the valley from lake to undetermined end.

"Rather a busy plot," he said casually. "I spy a small herd of buffalo just past that copse of trees down by the water's edge. There is a cow rhino just there in the center, with a three-quarter-grown calf. There are two bull rhinos having a hell of a set-to over there to the left in the high grass. There's at least one other rhino over to the right, under the trees at the bottom of the big hill. Seems a likely enough choice for a spot of amusement."

He started the car and drove, seemingly aimlessly, toward the general melee. We had come close to the two bull rhinos, who were making all sorts of ugly noises in the grasses. You could hear them grunt when they met under full steam. They made sounds I had never heard before. It was somewhere between a roar and a growl and a snarl and a gurgle and a grunt and a squeal. You could follow them through the grasses. They would square off, turn, run in opposite directions, and then come together with a smack, like a couple of heavy trucks colliding. The tickbirds, temporarily deprived of roosts, hovered around the battling pair, screaming helplessly.

One of the bulls backed out into the open, bleeding a little, but not seriously wounded, and the other followed him. Harry grunted disgustedly.

"Neither worth a damn," he said. "Young fellows. Neither one'll go better than fourteen inches. Waste of time to fuss with them. Especially in this high grass. Better horn, I'd either drive them out of the grass or risk going in after them. But

you don't want either of those fellows. Oho! Here come the
buffalo. Keep a sharp lookout, and if there's a decent bloke
among 'em we'll collect him later."

The rhinos had gone back into the grass and were having
at each other again. The buffalo, spooked by our noise and
the scent, were running the only way they could run—straight
past us. The herd was bearing down directly on us. Harry
had stopped the jeep. She was idling. We all stood up. It was
quite a sight if you do not have to see it every day.

The young rhino bulls were clashing and banging heartily.
The buffalo streamed past us like maverick freight cars, low
and bulky and long, their legs too short for the lengthy barrel
of their bodies. They were a touch smaller than the Grummetti buff, and a peculiar reddish-black in color. They came
past us, flirting froth, walling their eyes, pounding through
the grass with their sentinel egrets flying fighter cover over
them and screaming profanely. One bull passed within a few
feet. I could almost have poked him with the gun.

"Bloody awful," Selby said scornfully. "Not a decent head
amongst 'em. Can't imagine what turns 'em red, unless there's
a lot of iron in the earth about here. The zebras are reddish,
too, you've noticed. The ostriches are lighter. Even the wildebeest—if you'll look at that fresh herd—are buff-colored."

We looked at the fresh herd. Approximately fifteen hundred
wildly head-tossing wildebeest bore down on us in the trail
that the buffalo had left in the high grass. Snorting and pawing when they saw the jeep, they split around us and high-
tailed after the buffalo into the narrow end of the valley.

The two male rhinos continued to batter each other a
hundred yards away.

"Jesus," said Virginia.

"Let's go and pay a call on the lady rhino in the valley,"
Harry said brightly, and spun the jeep toward the cow with

the calf as big as she was. The other rhino—the one at the edge of the hill—had climbed upward and had disappeared.

The lady with the large child was in obviously a surly mood. She took one look at the jeep and charged. Baby, about two and one half tons of Baby, took us on a quartering shot. Harry hit the accelerator and we passed between them. Cow stopped. Baby stopped.

"*Hapana*," Harry said. "No good, either. Got a horn like a bloody banana. Let's have a bit of fun, though, so Mama can take a picture."

Harry used the jeep much as a bullfighter uses his *muleta*, to take the beast past him on quick swerves. The only difference was that we were all *in* the *muleta*. The old cow wouldn't quit. She came down on us in a fury, with Junior logging knots alongside her, and every time her stubby horn dropped for the uphook at the rear end of Jessica, Selby would spin right or left or put on a spurt of speed and leave the old lady with her forelegs spraddled and her dignity in a frightful state of frazzle. She made one last desperate, vengeful pass, missed us by six feet, and went grumbling off into the bush at full gallop, with Junior right on her tail. The young bulls ceased fighting and took off after her.

I had been bracing Virginia against the windscreen, pressing on the seat of her pants while she sighted the Cine-Kodak. When the rhinos chuffed off, I relaxed and let her slip back onto the cushion. Her face was pale, and you might have scraped her eyes off with spoons.

"Get a lot of good pictures?" Harry asked.

"If you mean close ones, I did," she said. "That old slut had her snout right in the spare tire a couple of times. Oh, my God."

She turned and pointed the snout of the camera at me. It was still full of the tissue paper with which she so carefully packed the lens to keep it from getting dust-smeared or scratchy.

"By God you're a great photographer," I said. "You forget to point it at the lions, and when we raise you some playful rhinos and buffalo and lay them right in your lap, you forget to take the blinders off that gadget. I wonder you bother to bring it along."

"It is just that I am not used to being charged by rhinos and lions every day," Virginia said with that watch-out-I-am-about-to-be-a-woman-and-cry expression. "God damn it," she said, "you two idiots may be a couple of Tarzans, but it is going to take some time to make a Jane out of me. Stop the car. I got to go to the ladies' room."

"There's a nice bush," Harry said. "Carry on."

Virginia came back from her bush and we shoved the jeep on toward the point under Majimoto. The ground was soggy. It got soggier. We pushed Jessica as far as she could go. It was about eleven o'clock in the morning. The sun had finally come clearly from the clouds. It was very hot and bright. A small hesitant breeze was blowing, and tsetses had knocked off for lunch. Ahead of us was a mile of marsh. Beyond the marsh was a patch of nasty-looking scrub thorn. On the sheer side of Majimoto you could see the little waterfalls glimmer as they ran down through the trees and rocks to cut small channels across the beach and into the lake. Around the patch of scrub, about two miles away, a third headland jutted. Selby used the glasses again.

"Seems to be a couple of rhinos in the middle of that last meadow," he said. "Just off that big point of rock. And what looks to be a sizable herd of buffalo down by the water's edge off the point of trees. Tell you what. It's two or three miles down there, at least, and the going's pretty mean. I know those legs of yours are pretty dicky. Suppose you sit here with the *memsaab* and I'll just slip down and check the horns. If they look like anything at all, I'll shoot Kidogo back for you and you can come and collect it. No use wearing out your legs for nothing. We're going to need them when we go after the kudu."

This was fine. The breeze was getting brisker, and I had a paper-backed, two-bit detective story and a bar of candy in my jacket pocket.

"Proceed, son," I said. "And don't forget your calipers. We don't want to make any quarter-inch mistakes on horn size. Be sure you get good and close now. None of this slipshod stalking."

Harry grinned. Kidogo fished the .450 out of the case again, and they swung off, long-strided and easy, through the marsh grass and the muck. As they entered the scrub of thorn I saw Harry take the big gun from the bowlegged Nandi bearer. He was carrying it at half-ready, diagonally across his chest. They disappeared. The wind was my way. There weren't any shots.

A little later I had a message which informed me that a certain amount of intestinal frustration was no longer frustrated. I snapped the .470 together and went off to find my own bush. I leaned the gun against a stone and became a vastly happier man. When I got back to the car my wife was—livid.

"You leave me alone in the car with this Kikuyu zoot-suiter," she yelled. "You leave me alone with no big guns, and you say nothing will happen. I can't shoot worth a damn and Chabani can't shoot nothin'. You send me off behind strange bushes when I got to go, in a place that's lousy with big ugly animals. I see the brave Selby take his gun when he passes through the same kind of bush I go unarmed to the toilet in. And when you—you—you—when *you* have to go to the john, you unlimber an elephant gun and take it with you! This one I am not likely to forget soon. 'Nothing to hurt you, Virginia,'" she mimicked. "'Just go over behind that bush. Don't worry about snakes. It's all right about the rhino. Just sit still and they'll go away.' But my hero takes his gun to his alfresco men's room. Wait'll I tell this around Toots Shor's when we get back. They'll read you out of the Campfire Club."

I calmed her down some and went to sleep in the sun, with a handkerchief over my face. When I woke up Harry and Kidogo had popped into sight. They looked cheerful. Harry waved an arm and beckoned, the way he had beckoned when he went to look at buffalo at Ikoma and had found an outcaste bull that pleased him. I picked up the blunderbuss and cut an eye at the old lady.

"Pray don't worry about me," she said. "I'll sit here in this zoo with nothing bigger than a .30-'06, and Chabani and I will swap recipes until you get back. If you don't find anything more than a few scraps of flesh when you return you'll know I died trying to save Chabani for the Communists to corrupt. I'll just be fine."

"For Christ sake stay in the car," I said. "This place is crawling with rhinos. If you need us, shoot a gun. We'll hear you. Try not to hit anything with it, though. Only serves to make 'em angry."

I walked off to meet Harry and Kidogo, with Adam following behind. The ground was oozy and watery and I sank up to the calves. The marsh grass was taut across the path and tripped you at every step. You could avoid falling down only by lifting your feet exaggeratedly high in a sort of goose step. This was fine for a left leg that had been painstakingly rebuilt by an excellent Washington doctor but which lacked a certain number of blood vessels and nerves from its original quota.

Halfway to the patch of scrub, Harry and Kidogo were waiting.

"There's a couple of bulls up there in the meadow," Harry said. "I stalked up on one who looked rather a decent sort. Couldn't see his horn very well, but I'd hazard that it's better than twenty. The other one fed off into the edge of the bush. But there's twelve or fourteen bull buffalo there, too, and you could use a better buff if we miss on the *faro*. Let's go."

The walking wasn't much better after we left the marsh. Both of us took guns as we threaded, half crouching, through the narrow elephant path in the bush. Harry grimaced to his right and pointed with his chin. "Spooked a small herd of elephant as we went through," he whispered. "Shouldn't care to meet one close up under these conditions. Too thick."

We made it out of the close bush and graduated to rocks and rills. We handed the guns back to the boys. The rocks were reddish, iron-heavy stones, small boulders, and wonderful round ankle-twisters. They formed small islands in the hot sand where hot water seeped through. The pools were red from the iron and green around the edges from the copper deposits. There was a fine healthy stench of sulphur, and the water, as it trickled down from the mountain, was just under steaming. This was Majimoto proper—Hot-Water Hill.

We crawled up some really respectable boulders the size of houses, lovely red, blue, black, and white rocks, with creepers growing over them. What breath I had saved was gone when we hit the summit of one special young mountain. The rhino had fed back while Harry had come to fetch me. We could just see the two bulls moving into the shade. The gray finally merged with the black of the thorn. I swore.

"This is the first and last time I ever send you off on any errand that I don't go along myself if I have to crawl," I said. "The only decent bull all day, and I'm sitting on my fat can reading Agatha Christie while you crawl up and carve your initials on him. How close did you get, by the way?"

"Not very," Harry said. "He was feeding down there in the wet—in that patch of bright green grass. I'd say I crawled up to within twenty feet of him. Rather an easy shot. However. Nothing to do now but wait three or four hours to see if they feed out again. Pity."

"Damn me for a lazy bastard," I said.

"I think I'll take a little nap," Harry said. "Lovely day, isn't it? I'll crawl down here and stretch out on that sort of sloping boulder. Wake me if you see anything." He scrabbled down a drop of thirty-five or forty feet, sliding like a mountain goat, and curled up contentedly on the ridge of the rock. If he'd slipped a foot each way he might have fallen sixty feet to some jagged and unpleasant-looking granite spikes. The possibility didn't seem to bother him any. Presently he snored.

It was a magnificent day to be sitting on a rock. Manyara was a sheet of tin in the sun. Some crabbed but kindly trees were spreading a little shade on my rock. The breeze had stiffened now into a wind.

I pulled out an ancient copy of one of the gorier Raymond Chandler mysteries, which make wonderful reading for people with a slim library at hand and who drug themselves with words. The best thing about the modern detective story is that no matter how often you read it you never remember how it comes out, and you never know why it comes out that way. All you know is that the private peeper gets slapped silly and kicked in the face, and he is always shooting people in the belly and talking tough. He gets injected with dope and set afire, and the cops handle him rougher than the crooks. And there is always sex rampant and blood all over everything. For a long time there has been a Krafft-Ebing hookup between sex and criminal violence, but the Chandler-Hammett-Mickey Spillane school just recently became aware of it. In today's detectives each man kills the thing he loves, and as painfully as possible. The over-all scheme is confused, but it saves thinking.

This salvage of thinking is an important new trend in the construction of the modern mystery. There was a time when the plot, though involved, was finally simplified by a rousing denouement, where the deteckatiff rounded up everybody in a room, eliminated all the likely suspects, and then turned with a snarl on the butler. The butler immediately leaped out the window, thereby saving the state a considerable sum in prosecution fees and electric current. The detective perforce was free to select a cigarette from his case, blow smoke whimsically from his nostrils, and send down for a dish of tea. The whole operation called for some fancy footwork with the story line and some small logic. You don't need that any more.

I defy anybody to step out of a modern hard-school novel and tell me simply what happened and why. The interlocking killings are always so tangled with the hero's libido, and there is so much necking, wrestling, and whisky drinking between kills, and there is so much cultism, archaeology, politics, abnormality, and frustration wound into the story structure that I am just forced to sit there and enjoy each excursion into sex or slaying as a separate peep show. All I am sure of at the end is that the hero will be battered. He will be standing fannydeep in corpses, and he will be languorously fondling the heroine, who, it seems, is also the villain, and shortly the police will come, take her away, and beat up on the hero some more. In looking backward, you can never tell why anybody had to die, except for kicks, and you can never figure why the detective didn't settle for one of the earlier mattresses and save himself a whole lot of trouble. There have been no clues and no deduction—just gunplay and erotica.

I heartily approve of this sort of entertainment, because it is so much more like modern criminal-coursing than the old classics of Mr. S. S. Van Dine and the other neat clippers of loose ends. Everything ends in a muddle now, with the wrong people dead, the wrong people in love with the wrong people, the cops beating hell out of everybody, the obvious suspects slipping free to kill and kill again, and innocent maiden ladies being coerced into conversation with rubber hose and matches under the fingernails. It is lifelike in that, after it's all over, nobody knows why or how, and when it ends on a sour note—well, hell, doesn't everything?

I was immersed in some wonderful dialogue that went briefly like this: "Sure, I loved her. But a private eye don't play it the way other people play it. I kissed her once, hard. I could taste her blood on my mouth. It tasted like saltines. Then I threw her off the cliff. She bounced once and quit. Then I poisoned myself with another slap of scotch. It tasted like iodine. I could feel it telling me that things were waiting for me to do 'em. They were weeping to be done. So I reached for the chopper. It felt sweet in my hands. I cut Joe in two pieces. I didn't like the way Pete's good eye was looking at me, so I shot it out of his head. I made Mike a present. Nine new navels. Then I went home. I belted myself over the head with another club of scotch. It tasted like quinine. I set a fag afire. It tasted like old rags. I went to bed. It felt like a rock pile. But I was tired. It had been a busy day."

I was thinking that this kind of a day would make anybody tired, when my brave companion aroused himself from slumber on the boulder below with a scream that made his shriek of the caterpillar incident seem a muffled squeak. He came off the rock, standing straight up, and seemed to soar upward some thirty feet. He was white and trembling.

"Now what?" I asked him. "Bad dreams?"

"Christ," he said. "I was catching a little nap and I put my hand over on a little stone in my sleep, to brace myself, I suppose. There was a sort of little coral snake—a red, yellow, and black thing—curled up on top of the rock. When I jerked my hand off it a scorpion crawled out from under the same stone."

"You're a brave man," I said. "I have seen you go. But you have the leaping fantods when you run against a bug or a tired little snake. I don't get it."

"I don't like oysters, either," Harry said. "I'd rather take on a wounded buffalo in thick bush than one of those woolly caterpillars. As for snakes, I might remind you that while there is an anti-venom kit in the jeep, the jeep is a touch better than two miles from here."

"I see your point," I said. "I beg your pardon."

We sat for a long time, watching the lizard playing ring-around-the-rosy on the rocks, listening to the birds, watching the duck flights and the billowing pink waves of flamingos as they passed over Manyara's sheen. It was very peaceful there on the high rock, with the breeze drying up the sweat inside your shirt and the thousand blended noises coming down from the hills. Finally Harry swept the big meadow and the outer rim of marsh with the glasses and looked at his watch.

"It's nearly four o'clock," he said. "I don't think that biggest rhino's coming back this way. The buff are still feeding down by the point, and there's one bull looks shootable. Let's stalk up on the *mbogo* and take one if he's bigger than your other one. If not, we can beat around that peninsula and maybe put up one of the rhinos on the other side. It's an old elephant wallow, and the *faro* might just be taking it easy in the mud."

Harry may be afraid of snakes, but buffalo give me the feeling of wishing they hadn't come up at all. There was nothing to say but yes. We slipped and slithered down off the rocks and started a stalk across the fairly open meadow, keeping to the six-foot, poison-green grass the rhinos had foraged earlier. It wasn't a very long stalk, maybe a thousand yards, but I was blowing and soaking wet again when Harry sank to his knees ahead of me and motioned for his gun. Pushing the rifles ahead of us, we crawled about twenty yards and achieved the protection of a small green bush. The wind was fine, coming straight down at us. You could smell the buff.

It was an old familiar farm smell, the cattle smell of dung and dirty, muddy hide. It wasn't strange we could smell them. When I peered around the corner of the bush, after my heart had come back down to its usual position, there were eight buffalo about twenty-five yards away—three bulls and five cows. There was one good bull, an old boy with a magnificent heavy boss and one horn that might have completed a formal measurement of at least forty-eight inches between the tips. If there had been more than one tip. The right horn was broken and worn down to a nubbin, its former point scuffed and many-ended, like a handful of sticks.

We hadn't been very careful in the stalk and had made as much noise as necessary, because the wind was dead in our face and the grass high enough to hide us. The buffalo couldn't smell and they couldn't see, but the old boy and one tick-ridden old cow were uneasy. The bull kept snorting and kicking up the water he was standing in. The cow kept swinging her head and sniffing painfully.

"No good," Harry said. "*Hapana.*" He stood up and motioned me up. We stood quietly and looked at the buffalo. The old bull took a couple of steps forward. He raised his head and stared through his bugged-out eyes. But he made no effort to run. All the buffalo had spotted us now, but the man smell wasn't there and they seemed puzzled. We stood quietly for at least a minute, maybe longer. Then the old bull seemed satisfied. He swung his muzzle as a man swings a foot against a ball, hit the nearest cow in the tail with his nose, and indicated departure. With dignity, looking back, they shambled out of the water and cantered off into the bush.

"Wonderful thing about buff," Harry said. "That half minute of curiosity. You can run smack into the middle of a herd, and they'll stand quite still for that thirty seconds or more. Just wait. All we've done so far is stalk. When the situation's right I'll show you how to hunt buffalo when a quiet stalk is impossible."

"I don't really want to know," I said. "I'm scared enough when we just stalk 'em like this."

"Well," Harry said, "long's we've come this far, we might take a little stroll around the end of this bit o' land and see if we can raise one of those rhinos. Better hang onto your weapon. This grass ahead is pretty thick, and we might jump something out of it."

I have mentioned a leg. Since they rechanneled the blood stream in it and removed certain essential portions of it, I have competed for no marathons. Selby runs up and over mountains for fun. He walks through marshes for fun.

This was a cute marsh. It was mostly of sword grass, which will take off a finger cleanly if you grasp it correctly. It was eight to ten feet tall. There were portions of this marsh in which the water came armpit-high if you missed a stout tussock and your foot slipped. For two more miles we walked, swam, and crawled this marsh. The sun, hotter around four than at noon, was a brass ball. Sweat rolled down my face in solid sheets, blinding me. I staggered, fell, caught myself, crawled, pulled myself semi-erect on stalks of grass, cushioned my headlong plunges by falling with the rifle across my body. The Westley-Richards .470 double weighed about eleven pounds when I entered the marsh. It weighed two tons when we came out of the muck and water into just plain elephant grass, fourteen or fifteen feet high, and as nice a covert for rhino or elephant as you're likely to see. A cow buffalo snorted at close hand and scared me witless. We conquered half a mile of this terrain and came to the shore with its hard ground and rocky shale. Harry climbed a tree and looked long around him. He saw nothing. We walked inshore a few hundred yards and found an old elephant trail which, by our stooping under the low-hanging branches, made quick and comfortable walking back to our big boulder at the point of Majimoto.

We caught a blower at the bottom of the boulder and smoked a cigarette. I looked rather reproachfully at Harry. He looked a little apologetic.

"I really didn't think it would be that bad," he said. "But certainly I'd never have taken you into that elephant grass if I'd not been reasonably sure that at this time of day, at this season, the elephants wouldn't all be up on the side of the hills in the shade."

There was a crashing in the bush some five hundred feet up the hill and a few hundred yards to our left, between us and the long two miles to the car. There was more crashing, some squeals, and the thin trumpet of a displeased bull elephant.

"You see?" Harry said. "In the hills."

We walked slowly back to the jeep. We skipped from rock to rock. We waded the hot-water pools. We took the guns again when we came to the section of thick bush and gave them back to the boys when we came out of it. I was stumbling and tripping again in the last half mile of marsh when Harry stopped and waited for me to quit playing tail-end-Charlie.

"Back there a bit," he said. "I saw you start and look at something. And then hurry a bit and come along. What did you see?"

"Nothing much," I said. "Only a cobra. 'Twasn't a very big cobra."

Harry squawked. "Why didn't you——"

"I didn't want to bother you," I said. "I know it would only upset you. Anyhow, at this season and at this time all the cobras are up in the hills with the elephants. This one was a little overdue. He was heading for the hills."

Actually it wasn't a cobra at all. I was just feeling a little mean. It was only a very few seconds later that one of the gunbearers let out a yip and jumped about five feet in the air, backward. This time it *was* a cobra. I presume he was heading for the hills, like I said.

We were pleased to get back to the car, where the *memsaab* had obviously not been eaten by the fauna. She had sandwiches and Cokes and water. I don't suppose I drank more than a quart of the water.

It is a long ride back from Majimoto to Mto-Wa-Mbu. It is a long ride and a ghostly ride. There were five rivers—rivulets or wet dongas—to ford, and one of them was deep enough to let the water rise a foot beyond Jessica's floor boards. Jessica likes water, as a rule, and can go most places a duck can go. This night she didn't like it and fouled up her transmission. This takes time to fix in the dark.

The rocky road, when it was not muddy, was serrated and full of small boulders. Each lunge that Jessica took dislocated something new. Each lurch and bump fetched into focus a fresh ache in pulled leg muscles, in cramped knees, in toothsore back. The mosquito bites and the tsetse wounds started to smart and ache and throb again. The plovers screamed like banshees and flashed ghostly white as they squawkingly rose ahead of the car. The snipe shrieked at us, and the nightjars swooped ahead of us. It was like a funeral procession to a madhouse in a weapons carrier on a rough road. The trail was visible for only a few feet ahead of us under Jessica's feeble candle power. Once Harry stopped the jeep, got out, and tenderly removed some object on the shale from the path of the hunting car.

"Nightjar's egg," he said. "Finding it and not crushing it means good hunting. Like finding a porcupine quill. That's my special fetish. If I find a porcupine's quill I know we'll have luck, just as I know that losing this elephant-tail-hair bracelet of mine is lousy luck."

Once we took a wrong turning in the dark and went down a strange pathway. Kidogo and Adam both yelled at the top of their lungs. The pathway we had innocently adopted led straight into Lake Manyara. We stopped three feet from the water's edge.

The last three miles, through the immensely tall grasses, through the velvet-black jungle, amounted to some sort of masterpiece of homing instinct on Selby's part. Trees and stumps became rhino and elephant. Animal trails and old native trails crisscrossed the only feasible track. We ran into blind alleys and had to back out of them. Three times the boys off-loaded and pushed as Jessica mired in streams. The itching seed pods from a specially accursed bush flew jaggedly into our eyes and down the front of our jackets, where they set up local irritations to rival the insect bites. We finally made the semi-floating bridge over Mto-Wa-Mbu, and Jessica lurched and snorted up the steep incline leading to camp. We had left before 6 A.M. It was 10 P.M. when we dismounted.

The fire was beautiful. The pressure lamp in the mess tent was beautiful. Juma in his white *kanzu* was beautiful. Even old Katunga as he came up to take the dead impala for skinning was beautiful, snaggleteeth and all. The gin bottle was especially beautiful, nearly as beautiful as Gathiru and Kaluku trudging by with the *bathi*. I don't remember what we had to eat or how I got to bed.

The next morning when Gathiru roused the *memsaab* she threw the *chai* cup at him and in clearly enunciated, beautifully concise words announced that her aching bones would remain in the sack, and that the Brothers Rover could go and hunt rhinos all by themselves.

This we did. We hunted them just as hard for the next two

weeks. The days began at five and we crawled into camp at ten. We saw in that time some twenty-eight rhinos. We stalked them all. We ran from most of them. We fired no shot, in anger or otherwise. We spoke very little. We were hunting now with a hard, stubborn, bubbling inner anger. It communicated to the boys, who stopped joking—who cleaned the guns and repaired the ravages to Jessica's springs and axles and motor and who staggered to bed at midnight to be up and on deck at five. Their eyes became red from dust and lack of sleep. *Hapana faro.*

Then one day even the cows and the calves and the immature bulls disappeared completely from Manyara. The last three days we hunted without seeing a pile of dung, without seeing fresh footprints, on a shore that is generally scarred and cut up like a cattle wallow from rhino spoor. The last night we dragged in at an early hour, something like 9 P.M. Virginia didn't ask us any questions. She just handed us the gin. Harry, hollow-eyed and turned-down at the mouth corners, his beard full of dirt, spread his hands.

"*Shauri mungu,*" he said, going back to the Swahili excuse for everything. "God's work. I never saw it like this before. I guess we'll break camp tomorrow and go up top by Kiteti and see what's in the hills up there. I'm damned if I can understand it." He glared in the firelight. "I wish," he said vehemently, "I wish I'd *run over* that goddamned nightjar's egg."

The next day we went bird hunting.

Chapter 10

ACROSS the wide pewter-dull Manyara, on the other
side of the lake, it was gray and barren as a plate
full of wood ash. The wood ash was a drifting lava
dust. There was little or no game about—a few spooky Tommies that had been shot over by every safari out of Arusha

that needed a piece of meat in camp and didn't want to rouse the rhino on the Majimoto side. We could see Majimoto distant and blue as we drove along, trying desperately to draw up within some sort of reasonable range of the panicked Tommies, who knew vehicles from the spurt a bullet makes when it kicks up dust under their feet, who knew what the report of a rifle sounded like and what it meant. We were meat-hungry. In the recent rage to find the right rhino, in the Ahab-like pursuit of a land-bound Moby Dick, we had been careful not to shoot. We had been living mainly off the birds the *memsaab* had been able to bring in from the low meadows where the Rift escarpment petered out. She had been taking Chege and the lorry and one of the personal boys and going out to hunt on her own.

We rolled over the soft gray lava soil, and the Tommies skipped ahead of us, usually a thousand yards or so in front. There was just one laggard, a youngish ram who seemed less spooky than the rest. He kept tagging behind the flock and looking back. He let us come up to four or five hundred yards and then did a very stupid thing. He turned his back, stopped, bowed his spine, and began to evacuate his bowels. Harry stopped the jeep in a hurry and I got out. I landed flat on my rear on the bare ground, wedged both elbows on my knees, and lifted the Remington. He was so far away that even with the scope, when the sight was on him, you couldn't see him over the aiming post. I sucked in a long breath and squeezed. Tommy was still bent over. When the rifle blast dissipated I looked up and I couldn't see him at all. The jeep drove up and the boys were whooping a hunger-whoop. They beat me on the back and said extravagant things in Swahili. Through some sort of outlandish fool's luck—certainly through no skill at over four hundred yards—I had settled this fellow's troubles for him. He was neatly bored through the shoulder. I expect he died happy.

Apart from the Tommies, there was nothing on this side of the lake except a few birds. We ambled back and forth in the Rover, close to the marshy edges of the water, jumping a few small ducks and the odd Egyptian goose, and having some mild fun with the shotguns. On the way back we ran into a considerable bait of yellow-throated spur fowl, and between us Virginia and I shot down a dozen or so, plus a sextet of minor bustards. Leaving the lake and crossing over the dwindled end of the escarpment, we came upon a small herd of kongoni, newcomers and tame. I walloped a young bull, and now everybody would eat hearty. The Tommy was for the white folks. The black folks got the kongoni, who was big enough to last at least three days, and the spur fowl we would save for the chop box, for lunch. We wouldn't have any more noise for a little while, anyhow.

We kept the camp at Mto-Wa-Mbu, on second thought, and decided to drive daily up to the high hills under the escarpment. It meant getting up an hour earlier, but there was a pretty well-defined track through the high, waving yellow grass, and we could do the twenty-five miles up to the top in little better than an hour. It was cold in the morning and cold coming home, and dusty all day, but at least we didn't have to ford any rivers. There was only one, anyhow, and it was easier to get out of the jeep and walk if anything popped up in the hills on the other side.

"I expect if we get on oryx we'll call ourselves lucky and push on up to Iringa for the kudu," Harry said as we drove up in the freezing morning, the lava dust in the track still settled by the dew. "Frankly, I'm not expecting much. There's still bags of water on the reserve plains and in the high hills, and from what we've seen, the game just hasn't come down yet. These hills are generally black with animals at this time of the year. This damned grass has ruined everything, everywhere, except around Ikoma in that pocket we hunted. Whoa!"

He stopped the Rover and screwed up his eyes to peer at the knobbly green-and-granite hill on our right.

"Looks to be a rather decent steinbok up there," he said. "He may be all we'll have of this area. Better get out and do for him. Use the .220 Swift. It's plenty big enough. *Toa* .220, Kidogo."

The Nandi gunbearer handed me the vicious little gun, which I hadn't touched since I abused the hyena with it. I crawled across the track, sat down in the usual nest of thorns, and picked out the little fellow out where he stood, poised like a corny table lamp, his four tiny feet jammed together on a rocky *kopje*. He melted into the side of the hill like part of the foliage, and you could barely see him without the scope. I held on what seemed to be his shoulder. The bullet made a soft whap and he jumped straight up off the rocky knob. That's the last I saw of him. We toiled up the hill and found a clump of neck hair. There was no blood.

"I hate this bloody gun," I said to Selby. "It's bewitched. I was cold on that little bugger. And don't tell me that I shot under him because I was shooting uphill. That's neck hair, off the top of his neck."

Selby shrugged. We got back into Jessica and drove on. We had gone possibly ten miles, past the strangely milky-musky-smelling settlement of anthills, and were working along to where the escarpment begins to look high and haughty, when Kidogo clamped his broad black hand on the back of my neck and whispered, *"Faro."* Harry stopped the car and got out the glasses. He was excited now.

"By God, I think we're going to have luck after all," he whispered, although the rhino was at least three thousand yards away. That Kidogo had seen him at all was miraculous. The green valley was studded with gray rocky outcrops and pimpled with thousands of anthills, each one of which looked exactly like a feeding rhino at a distance. This *faro* was browsing under the lee of a little red, black, brown, white, and green hill. They have very picturesque hills in Tanga.

"There's a good one," Harry said. "I can't make out his horn at this distance, but I think I know him. We killed a hell of a big cow here a couple of years ago, and there was a bull about then. We only got one swift look at him, and he was enormous. The cow went twenty-eight inches, herself, and he looked to be bigger. If it's the same old boy, you've got yourself a real one. This is the smartest rhino I know. He's evidently lived here for the last twenty years or so. Creature of habit."

We decided to drive down about three miles, leave the car at the river, walk over to the little hill, climb it, and come down on the rhino from over the top.

"He rolls there right under that hill," Harry said. "He holes up in that long donga off to the right, behind the hill. I'd judge he was feeding back. He'll take his dust bath and then bugger off to his hidey-hole in that grown-over donga. If we miss at the hill we can beat him out of the donga. Send the boys in with stones along both sides, and we'll stand downwind of him and wallop him as he boils out. That's how we did it with the cow."

We parked the jeep and picked our way across the tree-lined, swift-running clean little river, jumping from stone to

stone. It was a mile to the hill, and we nearly ran it. It was
a little hill to look at distantly, but it was a sizable mountain
when we reached the bottom, about a hundred yards straight
up. We took an old game trail and wound around a bit on
its circumference, but it was nasty climbing—slipping and
falling on loose stones, and pulling muscles in the thigh from
the stress of the climb. I was blowing and hurting in the
chest when we hit the top and peered over.

Hapana faro. We could see his rolling bed, all right, the
dust still loose and swirling in the mounting breeze. We clambered down the near side and walked up to his beauty bath.
There were fresh hoofprints the size of ash-can covers. There
was plenty of new dung, and the clear marks of his wallowing. The outlandish hoofprints led off toward the grown-over
donga.

"Wind must have changed a little on us and he heard the
car," Harry said. "Smack into the bush for this gentleman.
It's the same one, all right. Couldn't be two bulls in this neighborhood with feet that big. If he fits his feet, he's as big as
an elephant, and he's got to be at least forty years old. Lone
bull, now, too set and surly in his ways to find a new wife.
I'll bet he's a cantankerous old brute. Let's go and flush him."

We started to track. I can include myself in the we, because
following this lad was as simple as tracing a tractor in the
snow. He had great round pads, sunken deeply at the heel,
as if his head were so heavy he rocked backward to counter-
balance its weight. He had been in no hurry. He had used
his own deep-worn trail. You could see the shattered clay
uptossed in crumbles and the low thorn broken where he'd
passed. We followed him over two little mountains and into
the donga, at least three quarters of a mile long by a block
in width. He was in there somewhere. Doggo. And smart.

That's how you live that long if you are a rhino with a heavy horn.

We figured the wind, and we figured his point of entrance, and Harry figured where he'd bust out if he came. We went to where Harry figured he'd bust out. Kidogo and Adam went up to the end of the donga. Each took a side. They yelled. Kidogo cursed him in Nandi. Adam belabored him in Wakamba. For our benefit they translated into Swahili. What they said roughly was that somewhere in those thickly interlaced bushes was the father of all rhinos, a great beast to see but one who unfortunately had been born without testicles. *Doumi-manamouki*, they called him, bull-cow. They mentioned in passing that he lacked the courage to find another female, and that, unlike all the other rhinos they knew, only this one would scurry off to hide instead of charging out like a full warrior. They accused him of mésalliances with topi cows. Adam called him a Nandi heathen. Kidogo called him a Mohammedan Wakamba. Then they both threw rocks. He didn't bust out.

Harry and I stood at the edge of the donga, with the safeties slipped and the big doubles rocking gently up and down. He had to come out here, like the music that went down and round. There wasn't any other place for the big sonofabitch to go but out into the clear past us. And if he fit his feet, like Selby said, you could have shot him on the hurry with a bow and arrow, he would be that big.

We heard him snort and we heard him crash and we heard him turn and that is all we heard. We clasped insanity by the hand eventually and beat the donga upwind, our scent blowing straight to him, figuring maybe we would anger him into a pass. He didn't anger. He didn't pass. He went. He went quietly.

I know that Harry Selby is as fine a tracker as any native

loose in Tanganyika. He can track with Kidogo. He can track with Kibiriti. He can track anything from elephant to dik-dik on the strength of a blade of grass arranged the wrong way, a rumpled leaf, a suspicion of blood, a dissipation of dew, alignment of dust or loam. He can also smell. Especially he can smell fresh rhino. I had seen him stretch a neck and distend a nostril and say in his schoolboy English: "Bob, there's a rhino just over the rise there, in that patch of bush. A female on heat, I'd say." And sure enough, there would be a cow in season.

We tracked this *faro*. We tracked the big blundering behemoth most of the day. We lost him on the seventh hill, where the sun-dried rock showed no passage. This *faro* got lost.

We turned up late for camp again. Later than we'd planned. We stopped off at the Indian *ducca* to buy some cigarettes and have a beer to wash the lava dust loose from our throats and got hooked up with a local farmer and his Canadian house guest. They were feeling festive.

"If it's rhino you're after," the local said, "you must stop and pay a call at my farm as you go up past Ngoro-Ngoro again. My fields are simply teeming with the creatures. Buffalo, too, any amount. And elephant. Come and shoot over the farm a few days."

Selby put on his mysterious, displeased, wary-of-strangers look. Later he said: "Best never to have anything to do with these farmers. They see one rhino a year and make it into an epidemic. They hear an elephant in the bush and make it into a herd. All you ever get out of visiting anybody is headaches. You'll sit around and yarn all night long over a bottle of your whisky. They'll smoke all your cigarettes and then call you a bloody bounder in the morning if no animals show up for you to shoot. It suddenly becomes your fault that the elephants tread down the mealies and the rhino breaks into the fencing. Let us bid these gentlemen good night and be vague. Else we'll have the whole bloody lot for dinner."

We drove down toward the camp, and as we went past the whorehouse a familiar-looking native was running down the track, his khaki streaming in the wind, with some giggling girls coursing after him. We gave the fugitive a lift and foiled the pursuers. The fugitive was Chege, the lorry driver, the dude, the ladies' man. He was escaping with his virtue. Or else he was escaping without his virtue and without having paid for the loss of it. We didn't ask him. We just scooped him up and took him home to dinner. The fires glimmered beautifully in a small and jewel-like way as we approached Mto-Wa-Mbu. The butterflies fluttered before the headlamps. You could smell Ali, the cook, at work half a mile down the road. The big anthill on the right smelled like bread in the oven.

"You know," Harry said seriously, "I read all I could about the old hunters, Karamojo Bell and Selous and the rest. I read about the old-time elephant shooting, where the professionals used small-bores and how they used to shoot one beast and then climb up on it to shoot a dozen as the herds milled. I know one old bloke who has killed more than one native who crossed him—and this, mind you, less'n twenty years aback. I've read all the hunting literature of this country, and you know the one thing sticks out in my memory? Karamojo Bell. Bloody old ivory-poacher, mass murderer of animals that he was, he still wrote a line makes me want to cry. He had a bit about the small-gleaming campfires at the end of a hard day's hunt, and that, by God, is the Africa I love. The small-gleaming campfires at the end of a long day's hunt."

"Son," I said, "you are a sentimentalist and I forgive you. I also forgive you for trying to kill us all coming home tonight when you were having that stake race with the bat-eared fox. Some clients would be annoyed when you nearly capsize a jeep at forty miles an hour to keep from hitting some bloody stupid little animal that charges the jeep out of sheer bravery. When that fox turned and snarled and charged—all three pounds of him—I knew you would turn Jessica over and kill you, me, Kidogo, Adam, and Chabani rather than run down the bat-eared little bastard. I forgive you because I am a tiny-gleaming-campfire man myself. When man made fire he lifted himself up, over, and above the animals. Fire is actually too good for people. Let us sit in front of one of these tiny-gleaming blazes and drink a little gin."

"It is nice to hunt with a philosopher-poet, especially on my birthday," Selby said. "I am now twenty-seven years old, battered and worn from clients."

"Happy birthday, little man," I said, and wondered if Virginia and Juma and Ali had done right by the celebation. They had, it turned out. I had sent them after cakes with candles. They were short on candles but long on cakes. They had bought out the Indian's candle store. They had two candles and about twelve cakes. Ali had made one. Juma'd bought eleven more, of all shapes and sizes. They all tasted like browned sawdust with lard frosting. Birthdays are an umplumbed art form in Tanganyika.

The dinner was fairly festive. The *mem* had had Juma hard at work on her coiffure that afternoon, and she showed up blonder and tighter-curled than usual. We had the ripened Tommy chops—Tommy had been dead a whole day—and we had stringy duck and some exotic bland canned goods from the Indian and a lot of Danish beer with the dinner and a lot of brandy after. Harry blew out the candles and manfully strove to eat the rubbery cakes, and then we had a ceremony. I summoned the faithful—Adam, Kidogo, and Chabani—the brothers in frustration. I was going to make a big gesture to celebrate Harry's birthday.

Juma was the custodian of coin, so I went and collected seventy-five shillings from him and fetched the faithful. We had been attempting an experiment of weaning the black brethren from their expected harvest of money every time the *bwana* shot something of woofed and warped celebratory stuff. That kind of free-handed dough-throwing can louse up a camp's morale, because the hunters are finally hunting for pound notes, and a lion is no longer a lion. He is baksheesh to the crew that collects him, and this sours the cook and off-browns the personals and curdles the rest of the camp. We had decided to pull a switch. I wrote the speech and Harry rehearsed it in Swahili.

Adam and Kidogo and Chabani came, like dutiful subjects awaiting the dub, and crouched by the fire. Harry dipped into my hat, which was resting on the mess table, and took out handfuls of silver. He blessed each boy with twenty-five shillings each. I am afraid that Harry was a little shikkered on his birthday. What he said was fulsome. This is roughly what he said:

"Oh, you bloody *nugus* and direct descendants of *nugus*. I am hunting with an insane Yankee *bwana* whose brains have been boiled to porridge by the sun and whose reasoning has been unhinged by a severe shortage of shootable rhinos. His kidneys now dwell under his armpits, due to punishment from Jessica, the jeep. He has hunted unavailingly for a fortnight, and now he makes a supreme gesture to prove that all Yankees are completely mad. He wishes to give you money for nothing.

"As trackers you could not follow a gut-shot hippo through the lobby of the Norfolk Hotel in Nairobi. As scanners of the mountains you could not see a greater kudu if it had radio

antennae on its horns. Under your care the guns rust and the
bullets fly falsely due to leaving too much oil in the rifle barrels. A wounded dik-dik would send you all into hysteria, and
I doubt very much if any of you could conquer a female
guinea fowl in single combat.

"But for some strange reason this *bwana* thinks you have
worked hard and hunted well for the last two weeks, although
meat in camp has been short and all we have shot for trophy
is *shauri mungu*. Although we have no rhino horn to sell to
the Indians to make them look longer at women, although we
have seen no *beisa* oryx, although nothing has happened at
all worth remembering, this *bwana* wants to say *asante sana*
for the effort you have put forth.

"This *bwana* has rewarded laziness with money. Lack of
ability he pays for in pounds sterling. Bad luck he celebrates.
He does not curse or kick you at the end of a day in which
nothing happens but boredom. He is a very simple *bwana,* but
he is not a *bwana* who wants me to shoot it or for you to lie
about it.

"So you will be kind to the *bwana* in his madness, and you
will be goddamned appreciative in your actions or I will take
the toe of me boot to you all. He rewards you for nothing in
the deliverance; he pays you for lack of performance. Twenty-
five bob each the *bwana* gives you for what he calls in his
strange language the good old college try. This is a new kind
of *bwana,* and I warn you. If you don't drag your asses into
the ground from now on to get the *bwana* what he wants, you
will all be left to starve with your whorish wives in Nairobi
next trip out. Come get your money and say thank you."

Harry turned and looked at me.

"This'll completely bewilder 'em," he said. "They're used
to the odd bob when you kill something big and difficult.
They're used to drunken clients throwing money all over the

camp. But never before have they ever been paid for *not* accomplishing anything. Being bonused for effort instead of delivery is a new one in the book, and they'll probably just accept it as white man's madness. But on the other side, they may start to think and wonder a little bit about what manner of man they've got here, and if they even have a germ of thought you have bought yourself a faithful retinue for a few lousy bob."

Harry was right in his latter estimation. A man who paid for intent instead of meat on the block *was* completely new to simple thoughts. Thus incentive pay came to Tanganyika. The only trouble was, thereafter I had a hard time getting the kids to quit at all. They wanted to work all night as well as all day for the peculiar *bwana* who showered shekels for muscular activity, with or without horns to sanctify the sweat.

We were up and hungover from the birthday and into the hills early to look after our friend in his red dust wallow. We climbed the little garish hill again, and he had been back but he was gone. He was not gone to the donga but up into the high hills. We tracked him for three or four hours until his trail got onto the hardpan again, and cursed him and went back four or five miles to the car. We headed for the top again and came onto a very fine herd of Grants. They were spooky and did not indulge in the looking-back habit. I followed the ram into some high grass on foot. All I could see were horns cutting a wake through the grass. They were fine-looking horns.

The old boy finally reached a shorter stand of grass and stopped to look back. I could see his chin and a little piece of neck, so I popped one at him offhand and accomplished nothing except to run him out of the grass and up the foothill of a minor mountain. He stopped behind a bush, leaving me his insolent tail and saucy hindquarters for a target. I did a quick calculation as to where his neck might be and winged one at him on pure speculation. I was speculating well, because I broke his neck. There was about as much credit due me on this one as if I'd touched off a .45 at a flying quail and managed to hit it. He was measly when we cut him open, like all the Grants are measly these days, but his horns were heavy and more than long enough and shapely enough for Mr. Rowland Ward's Bible.

"We finally score something out of this blasted area," Harry said as we waited for the boys to take the headskin. "I've not seen a better Grant in years. You're not going about saying that you made that shot on purpose, are you?"

"Of course I am," I said. "I always break the necks of Grant gazelles when they stand behind bushes at a four-hundred-yard minimum. Have you ever noticed that nobody ever kills anything out here that wasn't a measured four hundred yards plus? Someday somebody must shoot something that staggers up to within rock-throwing range, and he ought to shoot him early in the day, not courting desperation in the dark. It must be against the law to ever get a good shot close—at least it's against the law for American *bwanas* to tell about anything that wasn't hard come by. Lessens the worth of the story. As for shooting this thing on purpose, you know and I know that anybody who hits anything in the neck is jerking his gun one way or the other. I just fired blind at where I thought his shoulder might be if he had a shoulder."

"Such honesty will have me weeping in a moment," Harry said. "Let's go scare us up an oryx. Ought to be a few up top here, anyhow, no matter what the weather."

It was pleasant driving along up top with the escarpment stern and beautiful and blue and the little hills green and pretty. The broad rolling meadows were yellow as wheat ex-

cept in the bottoms, where there was still some ooze and the grass was virulent green. There was a nice stretch of green grass all along the river, and the country was laid out as neatly as farmland in the Middle West, except it rolled and was occasionally accented by blunt hills. There were birds everywhere.

The bright blue jays swooped back and forth from the scrubby trees. We put up thousands of quail every time we crashed through a high-grass field. They didn't make much noise when they rose, and flew more like flying fish than birds. They would scud from under Jessica's wheels, level off, sail with stiff wings, and suddenly plop into the grass again as if paralyzed by effort.

Over the tops of the low hills, where the trail was well

defined, hundreds of the francolin, the spur fowl, scratched as busily between the tread marks as chickens. They ran down the trail ahead of us, looking curiously back at us, until they ducked into the brush and froze themselves. Close alongside the trees, scratching in the shade, there were countless guinea fowl, and the trees along the river were full of doves. The weaver birds, like swarming bees, dipped and rolled and wavered in flight, a million tiny birds all in one pattern big enough to move across the brilliant blue sky like dark clouds.

"Nice place for a man who likes the shotty-gun," I ventured as a couple of black-bellied floricans, the bustard's cousin, squawked and flew from beneath the Rover's nose.

"No shotty-gun right now," Selby said. "Look yonder."

Yonder was a herd of oryx, the first I'd seen. They look enormous at a distance, bigger than they actually are. They are fawn-grayish, with a black stripe down their back, with a black, brown, and white face shaped like a mule's, big flop ears, and a mule's tail. They look more like mules than antelopes. The straight, rapier horns make an oryx look as if somebody had pasted them on a jackass, daubed him with black and white, and turned him loose. These animals, an old bull, a couple of youngsters, and a herd of cows and calves, were swinging along at a steady loping trot a thousand yards up front and heading for the steep hills. Harry fed Jessica some fuel, and we barreled after them, occasionally losing teeth when the Rover springboarded off a hidden rock in the dense grass. We had the windscreen down, to lessen the concentration of dust, and grasshoppers as big as bars of soap hurtled backward and struck us in the face. I was wearing broad contour sunglasses, and you could hear the steady rapping of razory grass seeds on the panes. Harry doesn't wear glasses when he drives, and I am always amazed that he isn't blinded daily. But he squeezes his eyes half shut and makes a protective hedge of thick, dust-crusted lashes, and so far has gone along unblinded.

The oryx were very wild. They kicked their heels occasionally and ran at a steady swinging gallop—not panicky but very wary, as a herd of eland is wary and always moving.

"These are pretty tough beasts," Harry said. "They're a desert animal, you know, and they've a hide a good inch and a half thick around the back of the neck. They'll take an awful lot of lead and still go, and they're one of the few antelopes who're really dangerous when they're hurt. You never go up to an oryx from the front when he's down. They've accounted for several natives with those thin straight stickers they wear on their heads. Go through you like a double bayonet. Up on the farm at Nanyuki I've seen them carrying dogs around, stone dead, skewered on their horns. For my money, they're more dangerous than sable when they're hurt."

"It don't look like we are apt to hurt these babies very much, friend," I said. "Every time they stop, they start again. We haven't shortened the gap very much in the last half hour."

"I know it," Harry said. "I'm going to cut across that patch of meadow and come out ahead of that piece of bush about a mile up to the right. They'll be coming out about the same time, and all you can do is hop out and snap one offhand, like you did when you got lucky with that eland bull back at Ikoma. It'll be the only chance you'll have at this crew, because they're going right up the side of that escarpment, where we can't follow with the Rover."

Selby jammed his foot on the accelerator, and Jessica bucked and flattened out for the chase. We careened over the field, jouncing two feet off the seat when we hit a pig hole or a boulder, and when we came out of the woods the oryx were trotting amiably along about two hundred yards ahead of us. They picked up the tempo of the trot. Harry squeezed a last burst of speed out of Jessica, closed to a hundred yards or so, and clapped on the brakes. I went out the door in an arc, lit miraculously on my feet, and threw up the .30-'06. The herd bull was running last, quartering away from me. I forced the gun ahead of him, pulled it out in front of him on a level with his shoulder, and squeezed off. The bullet made the right slapping sound, and the oryx bucked and jumped with all four feet off the ground, and then he straightened out and was last seen going like hell in the general direction of Rhodesia.

The car came up and both Harry and the boys were yelling. The boys were yelling *"Piga!"* and *"Kufa!"* like they yelled the day I took a running whack at an eland at about three hundred and managed to take him up the rear end and break his spine. I didn't bother to tell the boys that day that I thought I'd led the eland enough to get him in the shoulder. If they wanted to think I was a hell of a rump-shot artist I wasn't aiming to disillusion them any.

"You hit him," Harry said. "That was quite a shot, offhand, on this bloke. He was a good 250 when you cut down on him."

"I don't think I hit him," I said. "I would love to believe it, but he was quartering more than I allowed for. I thought I was going to stick one up his tail, but I think I shot just behind him. There was a little puff of dust right behind him that I don't think his feet made. If he jumped I probably sprayed him with some ricocheting pebbles. But it didn't say whunk like it ought to. It sounded more like a slap than a whunk."

"The boys say you hit him," Harry said. "Hop in and we'll go look for some blood."

"You ain't going to find any," I said. "This isn't my day. Mind what I say. There won't be any *damu*, or bloody dung, or anything."

I was all too right. Somehow you know. Weeks later when I shot another eland for the boys to make biltong to take back home with them, the whole carful shook its head sadly and said "*Hapana.*"

"I hit the sonofabitch," I said. "He was standing head on and I had a rest on a thornbush and the damned bullet said whunk. I hit him where I was holding."

"I didn't hear any bullet slap," Selby said. "We can still collect him, but I don't think you hit him."

"I know goddamned good and well I hit him," I said, getting mad. "When we pick him up you'll see. Hell, you couldn't even see him standing under that thorn. If you can't see two thousand pounds of eland standing under a thornbush in broad daylight, how are you going to say I didn't hit him when I know I was cold on his chest?"

"There, there," Selby said. "No temper, please. There he is, loping around that hill. Dismount and try your luck again."

I held about six feet ahead of the eland and squeezed, and the bullet slapped again and down he went, tail over horns. He struggled up, and I could see that the second shot had broken his right foreleg just below the shoulder. The big ones can't travel much on three legs, and I took a lot of time squeezing off at his neck. You could hear it break even that far away, and his head went down. He was a beauty, better than my first one. We turned him over, and there was my first bullet where I said it was. It had taken him a little low and to the right on his chest, had gone through the bottom of his heart and wound up in the lung cavity.

"I told you I hit him," I said. "He'd have been deader than Kelsey's knuckles in another thousand yards. Don't tell me when I hit 'em and know it that I didn't hit 'em."

It was like that with this oryx now. I knew damned well I hadn't touched him. We went up to where the band had been when I fired at the bull and they had torn up the grass getting across the field and over the river and up into the high hills. If there had been any blood we could have seen it as clearly as ink on a sheet. There wasn't any blood.

"*Hapana damu*," Kidogo said. "*Hapana piga.*"

"You're so bloody right," I said in English. "When I *piga* I will know I *piga*-ed, and I will be the first to announce it. Let's go eat some lunch."

We swung over by Kiteti Swamp, with lunch about an hour away in the blinding, brassy sun, across the hot, dusty plain. There were a lot of giraffes—eighty-some in one bunch—and a few ostriches and the occasional sand grouse crouching in the hot rocky sand. But there wasn't a scrap of common game —no Grant, no eland, no kongoni, even. Not even a lousy zebra.

"It's got me beat," Harry said as we whizzed down an open track making a fairly well-worn road. "Last time I was here, with the Maytags, these damned hills were crawling with stuff. Bob and I got a marvelous lesser kudu bull over those hills there. We tracked him for about six hours. You could track then. It wasn't so dirty dry and high-grassy. The soil wasn't so rock-hard. But trying to track this country now is just a plain and simple waste of time. You can't track when you can't see sign. Apart from the lesser kudu, there were bags of oryx even as far down as the road to Babati. Bob Maytag saw one in a low field just as we were pulling out of Kandoa Irangi. I stopped the car in the road. Bob got out, stalked up along the road, and walloped him with little or no trouble at all. And the plains were filthy with Grants and kongoni and buffalo and stuff. But she's a dry hole right now."

We swung down the road past some big baobabs and turned off to go into Kiteti. It was a big cool swamp. We started to park under a clump of high mimosas, but Harry sniffed and said a rhino had just left the locale and we didn't particularly need it busting in on the luncheon party. It was a cow, anyhow, he said, and not a very big one. This he ascertained with his nose. A little later along we saw the hoofprints. It was a cow, and not a very big one.

We wound on into the swamp and came to an old and favored camp site of Harry's, a big amphitheater under huge liana-draped trees, with a staggering reek of baboon and a loud orchestral arrangement of hippo grunts coming from deeper into the swamp. The roots of the trees were gnarled and crawled along on top of the ground and made fine chair backs. It was cool and cathedral-dark under the sheltering umbrella of green, with just a few arrows of light slanting in from holes in the leafy canopy. There weren't many bugs, and the ground was clean, clear of brush, and cool. Elephants had been at the place fairly recently, for some of the shorter, smaller trees had been ripped apart at the top for fodder, leaving bright sharp spears of raw wood sticking up. There was a porcupine quill on the ground and another sticking into one of the trees.

"Luck," Selby said. "We can use some." He wedged the quill in his professional hunter's badge and unsnapped the chop box. Juma had stuck a couple of bottles of Tusker beer into the box, under the red plastic plates, and it was pleasantly cool. Anything that wasn't boiling would have tasted cool after that long morning under that sun and in that dust. My lips felt woolly, like somebody else's, and my nose was a brilliant cherry-red from the sun.

We ate the staple cold boiled francolin with the mustard pickles, and I polished off half a can of beans mixed with half a can of spaghetti, both cold. You could feel the peace spreading through you, hand in hand with the beer, and I lay down under one of the big trees, propped my head up on one of the kneelike roots, and went happily to sleep. I woke up when a baboon misconducted himself high up in the trees over me and a portion of his misconduct hit me on the head. It was time to go, anyhow, about four o'clock.

It was after five when we made the low hills, down toward the bottom where the escarpment begins its long low slope, and I had decided to shoot a few francolin. The stupid but delectable little semi-pheasants love this time of day. They sit on anthills, looking forlorn, and say "quarank-quarank" back and forth to each other in the waning light. It is as lonesome a sound as any. I was out of the car and walking over to a covey of anthills which held a dozen or more lonesome quarankers when I heard a whistle, and Harry was waving me back. He grabbed the shotgun and handed me the Remington.

"I was sick for fear you'd shoot that blunderbuss," he said. "There's a wonderful lesser kudu bull just jumped as you got out, and he's over there in that donga. Wonderful head on him, and I don't see how we can lose him. Let's go. The wind's just about right."

We half ran across the stubbly savanna to a long, low black strip of stubby thorn that made an island of the dry donga. Creeping round the lower edge, I saw a blur of gray that walked up to a bush and stopped. Harry pointed. I crouched down on my thighs for a steadier rest, and all I could see was bluish-gray rear end. Kidogo and Adam were both on the other side of the donga. I didn't know where. But my Grandfather Adkins took a sound switch to me when I was very young for shooting blindly into bushes when I couldn't account for the rest of the party, and it's a lesson I still remember. I lowered the gun and began to crawl around to the front of the bush. The lesser kudu bull barked once and leaped. He headed straight into the donga, and you could hear him crashing. Then he stopped.

I walked on up a quarter of a mile over the rocky earth, turning ankles and swearing monotonously. I stationed myself on a stand at the head end of the donga and waited for Harry and the boys to drive this sportsman at me. There wasn't any other place he could go, for the donga was a peninsula which led to another donga which linked up with still another, to make a series of islands for intelligent kudu to hide in as they slip back to the hills.

This was not an intelligent kudu. He reversed his engine and ran the wrong way in the donga, almost knocking Kidogo down. I could see the bull streaking across half a mile of completely open plain, going the wrong way, away from the hills, away from the interlocking dongas, away from the river and the thick bush along its edge.

We got the jeep going again and spoored him as well as we could in the now rapidly fading shooting light. His sharp tracks led into a lonesome donga with no connecting strips of bush to any other place of refuge. I took up a stand again at the other end of it and sent my black bird dogs in to beat this junior-grade *tendalla* out past me. He reversed his engine again, ran smack over the boys against the stiff breeze that carried their scent into his flared nostrils. He barked sarcastically again, crashed out of the heavy thorn, and romped across the plain, heading for home and mother. It was so dark by the time we got back to the jeep that we went the last five hundred yards holding each other's hands to keep from falling over the little boulders and loose rocks. It was bitter cold when we passed the thousand sentinel anthills. They smelled milkier and muskier than ever in the frost.

We belabored the high hills and the Kiteti area for a week. We kept a faithful tryst with the old bull rhino for five more mornings. For five more mornings and five more afternoons he outsmarted us. Selby finally lost his temper.

"I told you this old bastard was a creature of habit," he said. "I told you it was only a matter of getting onto his habits and we'd collect him. I still say it's only a matter of fitting ourselves into his pattern. But I haven't got the next thirty years to spend trying to adapt myself to his schedule. He's got more alternates than a war map. I say the hell with him. We'll stop off at Yaida Swamp or someplace on the way back from Iringa and do the rhino there. Or if we're lucky with the kudu in Frank Bowman's new country we'll have time to whiz up to the N.F.D., and I'll guarantee you a big rhino there in less than three days."

"Like you guaranteed him at Manyara," I murmured.

"Yah," Selby said.

We drove and we looked and we saw only one other band of oryx in a week, and the bull in this group had horns like railroad spikes. We saw another lesser kudu bull, a fine one, finer than the other, and he was a cinch. All we had to do was stalk over two little hills and make the summit of the third. A steady rest on a thorn and I would have him nearly point-blank as he stood on the top of Hill No. 4, surrounded by three wives and a small son.

It is a long way over three little hills when you are scrabbling over sharp rock and sharper thorn on your hands and knees. We made the summit of Hill No. 3. The bull had fed off, as per kudu habit, leaving three cows and Junior in his wake. They fed slowly down the slope, no more than seventy yards away. They didn't know anybody was around. They didn't care. I could have killed all three of them if there was any point to shooting females for fun. We let them walk into the bush. Then we went down the steep slant of our hill and up the steeper slant of the kudus' hill to see if we could spoor the bull and track him to his next stopping place. When we got to where the cows had been and crouched to examine the tracks, there was a crash and a bark in the bush fifteen yards away. Father had remained.

"I will just be goddamned if I ever saw anything like it," Harry said, throwing down his hat. "Everything I know about kudu tells me that the bull is going to lead off and drift, letting the cows follow him. Instead this blighter decides to back off and feed in that bush, letting the *manamouki* wander away ahead of him. If we'd known he was staying, all we'd have had to do was wait where we were, behind that big thorn, you with a steady rest, and this dumb bastard feeding out across the open within five or ten minutes. *And* at a range of no more than seventy-five or eighty yards. You could have whacked him with a two-two long rifle at that range. It's all wrong. Everything is running wrong. Let's see if we can follow this lad on this lousy rocky, dry terrain, where tracks don't show on lousy sunbaked soil and lousy rock."

We tracked him. We tracked him over four more hills. We tracked him for four hours. We lost him.

It was like that for a week. Everything went wrong. Harry threw away the porcupine quill he was wearing in his hat. The *memsaab* had troubles and was half fainting in the heat when she tried to hunt with us. Everything disappeared, even the bloody giraffes. Even the shootable birds got scarcer. The small band of oryx never showed again. The kongoni went elsewhere. The impala that played around the camp on Mto-Wa-Mbu left the neighborhood.

We had invested three weeks in nothing. We broke the camp and packed the lorry and headed up the road for Babati. We saw fourteen lions as we left. They looked hungry. We had gone a miserable twenty miles when we pulled off at the side of the road to wait for the lorry, to see if she was faring all right. She didn't show in half an hour and so we went back to find her. We found her on her side like a sick pig in a bog. She had thoughtfully broken an axle and splayed all her springs. We got her fixed at last and passed Babati, where we had a Coke with the Indian in the *ducca* and spoke kindly to the missionaries. We passed Kandoa Irangi and made a temporary camp by the side of the road in the lee of a little hill. It was a very nice camp and the object of much concern by the local ladies and gentlemen. They were intrigued with us. They were so intrigued that one of them slipped into camp after we went to bed and removed from the back seat of the weary Land Rover one camera bag containing an Ikoflex, a Rolleiflex, a Leica, and a Cine-Kodak. Each camera was full of exposed film.

They also stole a pair of brown tennis shoes I had bought Chabani from the Indian at Mto-Wa-Mbu that morning. This appeared to grieve Chabani considerably. And somewhere in the shuffle Harry Selby lost his last remaining lucky charm, the elephant-tail-hair bracelet. The hell with Kandoa Irangi.

Chapter 11

WE BROKE THE CAMP at Kandoa Irangi and headed up for Dodoma. There were altogether too many subservient blacks about the camp, begging for old tins and bottles, but we were leaving the locality and there wasn't going to be any necessity for warning them away. It was their country, anyhow.

We made Dodoma by the middle of the day, over good

clay roads that were rain-wrinkled and corrugated into wash-boards. Jessica jolted painfully in a constant toothaching jog trot. The bush alongside the road was sparse and dusty and unprovocative. There were bridges every few miles—fine, sturdy, concrete-and-iron bridges the Germans had built before World War I. They stretched across the sandy dongas as true-plumb and reliable as the ancient day the shaven-headed, red-necked overseers whipped the blacks to build them.

"Say what you want to about the Hun," Harry said, "he was a great engineer and he did more to open up this country than anybody else. When he put down a road he put it down to stay. When he put up a bridge he put it up on purpose. It's funny how the people you conquer sometimes do the most for a foreign place. We'd no decent roads to speak of in Kenya until the Eyetie prisoners of war started working on road projects. Then the war quit and so did the road building."

We rolled into Dodoma and did about some new supplies and things. I strolled round the big square market close by the railroad station and looked at the natives with their goods spread flat on blankets and skins. The tobacco they sold was twisted into hard, dunglike lumps. They had little mounds of beans and some sweets that even the flies tended to ignore, and some dust-gray strips of biltong that the hyenas might have thought over twice before tackling. The Masai men were lounging around, as usual, looking haughty and elegant and aloof as they leaned on their spears. Only a few of the women were bare-breasted. This was a metropolis.

The sun struck white and hot on the plaster buildings. The white dusty streets were full of greenish-swarthy Indian boys in shorts, pedaling furiously on bicycles. The shops were all Arab and Indian, with possibly more Arabs than Indians. They were fine-looking old men, the Arabs, white-bearded and hook-nosed, heavy-headed in turbans or *khafiyehs*, wearing the gabardine caftan over baggy white pajama-cloth breeches caught tightly at the ankles. They looked disdainfully at the Indians, and the Greeks, and the Negroes, and the Masai, and at us. They seemed mostly to be dreaming of an older, gentler civilization, but they had created Tanganyika and were stuck with her.

Dodoma is a pretty little town, its streets rimmed with the brilliant Nandi flame-flower trees, its walls looped with great purple and red and white bougainvillaea. There are schools and churches and a cinema, a good hotel and restaurant where you can even eat the greens without fretting too much about dysentery.

"Too many people," Harry said, coming out of a *ducca* where we'd drunk an iced Coca-Cola and bought some new gin and other vital necessities. "Let's shove off and have our lunch outside of town. *Juma! Kwenda!*"

Half the boys weren't around the lorry. They had straggled off for their own purposes—Katunga to get his back straightened, Chege in search of less commercial romance, the tea hounds away to the teahouses, and the secret drinkers to the *pombe* palace. They straggled back in front of the jeep, with Kidogo driving them ahead like balky Masai donkeys.

We jounced down the dusty road, admiring the flame trees, and I had another of those attacks of unreality. It no longer seemed strange that I was in a town called Dodoma in Tanganyika, surrounded by a motley of filed-tooth, stretched-lobed, cicatriced Negroes, henna-and-ochered Masai warriors, wrangling Greeks, bickering Indians and haughty Arabs, and weary-looking, sun-parched *pukka* British in floppy terais and rumpled khaki. It seemed strange now that it no longer seemed *strange*. I felt that I didn't stick out from the mob even a little bit. If anything, I felt cramped, as did Selby, in a city, even such a small and insignificant city as Dodoma.

We rolled along, glad to be quit of the tumult and the crush, and Harry drove up alongside a handsome baobab the size of a water tank. It had pegs stuck into its soft, fleshy bark, where the locals had hammered them so that they could swarm up easily to collect the water that gathers in the pits and craters of the baobab's vast trunk. I looked slantwise at Virginia and saw her heave a small sigh of relief as Chabani unbuttoned the green chop box and Harry handed me the gin and the lime and the vermouth and the gay red and green plastic cups, with the checkered red-and-white napkins to wipe the dust out. It was ritual now, Selby bending over the chop box and slapping slabs of the cold guinea on the plastic plates, unscrewing the mustard jar and the House of Parliament sauce bottle, slicing hunks off the coarse loaf, prizing the cover from the butter jug, setting out the bottles of Tusker beer. Virginia sat down on the hard cushion from the Land Rover, rested her khaki back against the baobab, and took a long belt at her warm martini with the fine dust settled on the bottom of the cup. She sighed again. She was uneasy around civilization, too, and glad to be back in the bush again.

We drank two martinis apiece and ate. Nobody spoke much. Then we cleaned the camp site and drove on toward Iringa, high on the high plateau of Tanganyika, up to Iringa where the giant kudu and the roan antelope lived, up toward Frank Bowman's secret country.

The lorry had her usual number of mishaps. We were frightened blue when a local safari rig came past us and announced that a lorry had overturned just outside Dodoma and the people said they thought some of the people in it had been killed. Then they drove off.

We wheeled Jessica around and headed back as fast as we could push her, leaping over the corduroy road in great bounds, like an impala in a panic. Harry was white around the edges of his mouth. It had not been so long ago that another lorry under his command had turtled on him, killing a couple of boys and mangling some more. We were tense as we came up to Annie Lorry, on her side again, like a dead cow with its feet stiffly in the air.

Nobody had been hurt. Chege, God bless his Kikuyu intuition, had felt a tremor of fear and slowed her to a mere amble just a few seconds before the right front wheel had bitten clean through its lugs and sheered off the hub. The wheel had spun down the road and Annie rolled over gently, hurling the boys a short piece without killing anybody. We jacked the old bitch up, propped her on even keel, and fitted her with new shoes. Harry, greasy to the armpits, was flat on his back under her, her axle held up off his chest by a mound of stones, and the air was gently blue around him. He had been trying to lose this particular truck for the last three safaris, and the office kept sticking him with her. We had expelled her in shame from Mto-Wa-Mbu, but they sent her back just the same, and Selby was livid.

Annie's indisposition slowed us up, so instead of making Iringa for the night we quit at dusk on the far side of the Great Ruaha River, a really respectable stream that flows at ten knots over boulders, is spanned by a noble German bridge, and is maggoty with crocodiles. This was fine, lovely country now, high and cold and Swissy in its green slopes, with little blue lakes alongside the road and severe blue hills on both sides.

We crossed the span and curved the caravan in a half circle

to return to a cool cluster of big trees on the edge of the sheer drop into the river. The ground was mostly clear and trampled under the trees, and the boys scythed it clearer with *pangas* while we broke off some dead thorn twigs for the fire. This was a night you needed a big fire, because even at dusk you could see your breath cold and distinct in clouds ahead of you, separate from the cigarette smoke. We ate fast and turned in, with Harry not bothering to pitch the mess tent or his own sleeping quarters, but bunking in with us, and all of us eating in the open.

"Can't get over that other bloke, that social fellow you know," Harry said. "Kidogo tells me he insisted on pitching the mess tent and dining in lonely splendor even in temporary camps. Also made the boys carry him across streams on their back. Six foot four and he makes the boys carry him. What we call a high-spine-shot man. Nothing else is good enough. Cries and curses if he doesn't hit it high on the spine, first crack, and won't take the trophy if he has any collaboration. One of these skeet shooters."

"Got a pretty good kudu, though," I said. "I've seen it."

"Not with Bowman up here he didn't," Harry said. "They didn't shoot a kudu on that trip. Didn't even hunt them. Frank only came in here once, the trip before he packed up and went off to Australia. Was with a fellow named Bill Something-or-other. Shot a fifty-nine-incher, the damnedest kudu I ever saw. At least I saw the pictures of it. Kidogo was still with Bowman then. Says the kudu came down onto the river like impala. Saw one herd of sixteen bulls, all good, and as tame as bloody topi. Saw one bull better than the one they shot. I find it hard to believe, but Kidogo swears it's so. And he doesn't lie, or even exaggerate, like most of them. Must be a different kind of kudu altogether from those blokes that hang out in the Kandoa hills."

"I hope we get one," I said, "but I'm not willing to believe we will. This luck we had couldn't stretch forever. We loused up the rhino, and that was supposed to be easy."

"Frankly, I'm not prepared to bet on anything any more. This grass has changed the whole complexion of everything else, and I don't see why it mightn't change the kudu business too. You read that note Tony Dyer left for me at the *ducca* in Babati. 'Lost in a wilderness of bloody grass with a French purist,' he said. 'Seen little, shot nothing.' I really don't know."

"Let's turn in and pray," I said. "I'm beat."

"We'll know tomorrow," Harry said. "Night, all."

We made Iringa about eleven and stopped at the machine shop for some nuts and bolts and information. Iringa was a prettier town than Dodoma, smaller, more Englishy, with a neat white hotel and a Ford agency and a modern movie and even a sprouting housing project. It had an airfield and a once-weekly plane. It was Sunday, and everything was closed as tight as a watchcase except the machine shop, where we managed to knock up the owner long enough to dig a direction out of him. We pulled out of Iringa, headed for a village by the Ruaha, and a few miles out of town we stopped for the lunch ceremony.

"I love these picnics," Virginia said, nibbling happily at her nutritious delicious. "I always loved picnics as a kid. We used to go down into Rock Creek Park and have them on Saturdays when I was a little girl in Washington. There were always a lot of sex fiends loose in Rock Creek Park, and Mother was always afraid I would get raped or something, but I used to slip off and have picnics anyhow. Never thought I'd have a picnic three times a day, every day, though. Let's take some pictures, this is such a lovely spot."

"Fine," I said. "We've got nearly enough game shots now after that big day you and Harry had with the cameras at Ikoma. We better start shooting some fill-in stuff from now on—camp stuff and old Annie stuck in the mud and the like. Kidogo can take some footage of all of us together while we're eating. *Kidogo! Lette picha qua memsaab!*"

Kidogo walked over to the jeep and rummaged around in the back, where we kept the camera bag and the film. He looked a long time, and when he came back he was just a touch pale. He talked furiously to Selby, waving his arms and walling his eyes. Selby was disturbed. He got up and went over to Jessica and looked for himself. He walked back, frowning.

"Looks very much like we've been had, chums," he said. "No sign of the cameras at all, at all. *Kuisha*. Either we've lost them somehow or those types in Kandoa Irangi pinched 'em. Let's see what else is missing."

They had got Chabani's new tennis shoes and all the cameras except the little short-order Polaroid with which Virginia had earned such a reputation as a witch doctor by producing the finished print one minute from the snapping. The guns were all there, and the rest of the gear.

"Makes it a definite theft by one of those gay lads around Kandoa," Harry said. "First time it ever happened to me. Never lost so much as a packet of cigarettes before. I'm dreadfully sorry. This must have been one of the gentlemen who'd been in the Army and knew the value of what he was pinching. He could never dispose of a rifle, but he could sell the cameras for five quid to a local Arab, and they'll turn up in a bazaar in Nairobi six months from now with the serial numbers filed off. What makes me furious is my Leica. It had thirty-five very fine exposures of game in it—that whole day's work Virginia and I put in while you were writing in Ikoma. And the Cine was full of film too."

"So were the Ikoflex and the Rollei," Virginia said. "I shot a lot of still color and black-and-white of the boys around the camp and left the exposed stuff in the cameras. Damn it to hell. All that work wasted, and now we're stuck out here for three more weeks with no cameras."

"I am most awfully sorry," Harry said mournfully. "So are the boys. Look at 'em. In a way it's a reflection on them. Not that we would ever suspect them, but they feel terribly careless, especially since you've been so nice to them."

Kidogo seemed to be debating hara-kiri. Chabani was moping away off from us. Juma's usual air of impudence had melted and he looked two sizes smaller.

"Ah, the hell with it," I said. "I'm glad they're gone, and there's no use spoiling lunch. This camera business is a damned nuisance, anyhow. Always wanting you to stop and pose and testing the bloody light and fiddling with light meters and slowing down the hunt. I'm relieved, myself. Now we can get on with the kudu and forget the *piga picha* business. Let's all have another drink in celebration of no more damned nonsense with f-7's and apertures and the rest of that rot."

Harry turned and said something to Kidogo, who brightened.

"I told him the *bwana* didn't blame him and that the *bwana* was really happy that the cameras were stolen so that now we would have more time to hunt kudu," Harry said. "He thinks the *bwana* is completely nuts, but he admires this kind of insanity. He fully expected to be fined or beaten or both.

He says most *bwanas* would have raised hell for the next three days and held him personally responsible."

"Tell him I think he is a black Daniel Boone who is too valuable as a hunter to bugger about with cameras," I said. "Tell him cameras are women's work, that only the *mana-mouki* should mess about with this *piga picha* routine. Tell him if he ever kids me about shooting birds again I will remember to remind him of the cameras."

Harry said something swiftly. Kidogo grinned and ducked his head at me. He said something fast and furious.

"Kidogo says that he will get out the whole Nandi vote any time you run for office," Harry said. "He says that next to

Kingi Georgi you are his favorite white man. He says he will personally attend to getting you a sixty-five-inch kudu." Harry snickered. "He says his life is yours to command."

"Tell him if he ever carries that elephant gun so I am looking down the barrels any more I will command his life, all right. I aim to shoot him in the tail with the shotty-gun *'Mkubwa*. Let's knock off the dialectics and eat. I'm starved."

We had some cold impala chops from the yearling buck I had shot yesterday by the roadside with Harry's little Mann- licher, and as I chewed I was thinking that I really was glad the cameras had been swiped. You can hunt or you can take pictures, but you cannot hunt *and* take pictures. The two techniques are completely conflicting, and one bitches up the other. The camera bugs are always fretting about the light and trying to maneuver closer so that the animal will be squared off just so for the lens framing. They like to stir up the animals and always they want to get a little bit closer and wind up by spooking the whole neighborhood. And they always say: "Just one more. No, no, stand over there. Not *there*. Over *there*."

Then they always brag about how they are so stinking humane, they wouldn't think of killing one of the lovely beasties that God made so beautiful, and they don't see how a hunter can be so horrid as to shoot something when all they want to do is imprison its beauty on film. This is of course a lot of crap.

Every time some brave camera hunter drags you into the living room after dinner for two tedious hours of blinking at his amateur African film, you can reflect that the rhino which charges directly at you from the screen did not stop charging after the shutter snapped. You cannot say to a rhino: "Knock off, bud, your picture's took and you don't have to charge any more." Some poor harassed professional, standing affrightedly flat-footed while the camera hound runs, has to shoot the poor old *faro* as he comes barreling on, whether he's any good or not as a trophy. This applies to any dangerous game that gets itself annoyed into charging for the selfish benefit of the camera. The self-admittedly humane Martin Johnsons killed more game than rinderpest in getting their pictures, and the animals were slaughtered after deliberate incitement to nervousness and a final charge. Some black boys got killed, too, in some of the numerous lion-spearing shots that have been made by sundry photographers, because when you take on lions with spears some laddy-buck has got to get chewed.

It is the same way with all those lovely, peaceful shots of the happy lions, bloated, contented, and kitten-purring-playful for the camera. They are happy because their guts are distended with nice fresh zebra or topi, slain callously to serve as bait to beckon the carnivore in close. The zebra is just as dead as if you had shot him for his hide.

Harry strode into my thoughts.

"I mind me a couple of camera hounds came out here one time, going to get the last word in lion charges. They went out without a professional and they deliberately gut-shot a lion, wounding him just enough to make him sick and nasty. Simba departed into bush, and they went in after him, one with the gun, t'other with the camera. Going to make an epic, and didn't mind deliberately wounding the animal to do it."

Selby spat and curled his lip, like a lioness when you get too close to the cubs.

"Some natives chanced by the next morning," Harry said. "Found the two camera blokes ripped into ribbons and dead as mutton. Lion was dead a bit farther on, but his mouth was bloody and his claws were full of—things. I felt most awfully, dreadfully sorry for the lion. Didn't feel so damned sorry for the two fools that were willing to hurt him on purpose just to make him sick and angry. Lion's too good for people like that.

"I'm never going along on another one of those Hollywood picture safaris, where they want you to rile up the elephants for day after day, and finally you have to shoot some old cow that gets nervous, splits off from the herd, and chases the cameraman. Tony Dyer had a devilish near thing up on the Tana River while they were making some bloody cinema or other. Old bull finally got tired of being annoyed and tore loose at the camera group, and Tony had to shoot it offhand at about nine yards. Same thing with Stan Lawrence-Brown while they were making *King Solomon's Mines*. That bull you see shot in the opening sequence is no Hollywood fake. Those spurts of dust off the elephant's head was old Stan, standing and shooting while the electric cameras ground."

Selby spat again, scornfully and angrily.

"I can understand killing something you want so badly that you are willing to go to weeks of trouble and great expense to collect it, so that you will have it and enjoy it and remember it all your life. But this wanton stuff gravels the devil out of me. I hate conscious cruelty. Some bow-and-arrow bloke out here, breaking lions' backs with a rifle first, so's he could shoot it safely with his bloody play toy. And popping elephants in the knees to pin them down while they get the right pictures of our hero and his bow and arrow. Yah! I'll never make another one of these things where the first object is camera, with nothing but dirty work to be done with the gun, mopping up after the humanitarians."

We finished the lunch and drove down the rutted, rock-strewn, eroded road toward Bowman's last big camp, with Kidogo standing in the back of the jeep, exclaiming and pointing as he saw landmarks he remembered. There were about thirty miles of it to do, and in midafternoon we came to a village where Kidogo seemed to know everybody. They gathered round the car and grabbed his thumb, jabbering nine to the dozen, and subsiding slightly when a character stepped out of the main hut, as full of dignity as a hustler who's just married the cop on the beat.

This type was a Somali, delicately slim, light, one-eyed, scarred in the face, and overfull of manners. His name was Abdullah. He was the head cattle wrangler for an Englishman named Ricardo. He was the kind of native who carries his own candy. He affected shorts with his snood and looked as if he expected you to ask him for the next dance. He had a couple of stooges with him, and very soon his pretty light brown wife, with her head in a kerchief and wearing a dress of many iridescent colors, stepped out to abet the welcome. Abdullah also wore a knife to match his shorts and was so extremely unctuous he turned your stomach.

Abdullah pointed down the trail to where the river lay, uttered many phrases about how many million kudu could be killed by a backward child armed only with a sjambok, and allowed us to proceed. Harry wrinkled his nose. He didn't like Somalis.

The other villagers were nice enough. They were very black and twice as ugly as home-cultured mud, but cheerful and gently stupid. They didn't have much company there by the river, unless you counted the cows as company, because this Abdullah was too damned grand for anything but the governor's bazaar, and they were glad to see the safari. It was the second one they'd ever seen. Katunga pointed out later that these were very backward natives indeed, because he'd borrowed two shillings to get his back straightened and the girls were so unsophisticated that he had one of the shillings left over to buy beer.

They trooped after us as we drove the half mile to the Ruaha and clustered around while we set up the camp. Selby was feeling a little surly. He told them to push off and stay bloody well pushed, a sentiment re-echoed by Kidogo. They were both thinking of the cameras.

Here on the interior ford of the Ruaha the ground was high, sloping sharply into the water. Here, twice a day, the women drove the black-and-white and red-spotted cattle down to drink, creating all sorts of noises. We pitched the camp off the trail to the right, a hundred yards from the river, under a tremendous green-leaved tree whose name we didn't know. It was a lovely camp. Even the elephants liked it. One came and left his calling card in front of the mess tent the first day. The monkeys liked it too. They capered overhead and impressed us with their presence by depositing their droppings on the flap of the tent which served as an awning in front of the mess. It sounded like gentle steady rain on a tin roof.

There was an old man, a real *'mzee,* come to call in the early cool of the evening, after we had resighted the guns and scared the green pigeons out of the trees in enormous clouds. The old man was grizzled. He limped against his knobby stick. His goatskin toga was dirty and mangy. His feet and legs were sore and scarred with the white remembrances of ancient sores. His beard was clotted and filthy.

"*Jambo, 'mzee,*" Harry said. "*Iko tendalla hapa?*"

"*Hapana,*" the old man said sadly. "I have lived here for 120 years [this would make him sixty, because the Africans have two full seasons each year] and I have never seen a kudu. I am an old man, and if there were kudu here I would have seen them."

"How about across the river?" Harry asked. "How about down by the Little Ruaha? Are there *tendalla* there?"

"I would not know this, *bwana,*" the old man said, sadder

still. "I have never been across the river. What would I be doing across the river? The *shenzis* live across the river. The 'Ndrobos, the wild men and the bee chasers, they live across the river. There are no kudu here."

We gave the old man a cigarette and he limped off. Harry turned to Kidogo.

"This is the country where Bwana Bowman got the *doumi* 'Mkubwa? You sure?"

"*Ndio, bwana,*" Kidogo said, pointing. "*Pandi hio.*"

"Where else?"

"Also back there," Kidogo said, pointing at the road behind the village, the road down which we had just come. "*Mingi sana tendalla. M'zuri.*"

"It looks all right," Harry said. "I don't know. Let's try and get the jeep across the river before dark. We can leave her there and wade over in the morning."

Jessica didn't like this river, this swiftly running, rapid-rippling Ruaha River, with its slippery boulders underfoot and its current fit to pull you down and drown you. She made a heavy effort to crawl across and stalled when she went in over her dashboard in the shallowest part. We sent Adam back to the village to press a gang of locals and broke out the tow line.

The locals arrived and peeled their breechclouts, and about thirty of them breasted across the stream to the far shore. They horsed on the tow line, and the jeep surged a bit and then the tow line snapped. It was a two-inch line. We spliced the line and heaved again, and it snapped again. All together it snapped four times before we sweated the jeep up on the far bank and mopped out her vitals so she would run again. There was still time for a small hunt, and we aimed off into the bush, following Kidogo's directions until we came to a clearing of hard-baked clay with a little *shamba* in it—a few goats, three seedy huts, and another old man sitting in front of the biggest hut.

We stopped and asked him about *tendalla* and the Little Ruaha. This was an adventurous old man. He said he knew the trail, only eighteen miles, as well as he knew the body of his wife. He said he would like to show us how to get there. He said he was sadly in need of meat—that he was too old to hunt any more and that the game would not feed close to his *shamba*. He said that a few miles farther on the *tendalla* would trample you unless you were careful, and that the bulls were even tamer than the cows, and that the cows were even tamer than the chickens.

The old man was right. We got only two thirds of the way to the little river, along the grown-over trail that Bowman had made, but we saw fourteen kudu in ten miles, not so spooky as eland, as nearly sloven in their movements as topi. There were two immature bulls we might have shot with a .22. There was one big bull with a retinue of cows, who moved slowly off into the bush just at dark. There was a fine big red, black, white, and blue hill in the middle of the scrubby mesa which gave an admirable view of the country. Harry scurried up the side like a baboon and reported another herd of kudu, and also that he had located the river and it all answered to Bowman's sketchy description. His eyes were shining when he scurried down and turned the Rover's nose toward home and *campi*.

We came back in the chilly black night and dropped the old man off at his shabby *manyatta*, with a packet of cigarettes for his trouble and the promise of meat tomorrow. We fought through the low thorn scrub to the river's edge and left Jessica high and dry to spend the night by herself. We didn't figure anybody was apt to steal her. There wouldn't by any place to take her if they did steal her.

Crossing the river was very cold and very scary. Juma had come down from camp on the opposite bank with a lantern to light us across, but the water was well past waist-high and the current was now a good twelve knots. The stones were sharp and mossy-slick and loose underfoot, and even with Adam on one side of me and Kidogo on the other, we all slipped and went in to the armpits three or four times. I kept thinking about crocodiles, but obviously the water was too swift for them, Harry said. I still kept thinking about crocodiles.

We limped barefooted to the camp, accumulating thorns in the process, and staggered in wet and cold and beat and starved. Gathiru and Kaluku had the *bathi* steaming and Mama had the whisky on the hob. There was a big fire blazing and the night sounds had tuned up and there were certain smells coming from Ali's cook fire. The sky was as frosty-looking as Connecticut in the fall and the stars twinkled coldly and I felt a great upsurge of confidence. This was going to be another Campi Abahati, despite Abdullah the Somali and his grand airs, despite the pessimistic old man, despite the freezing crossing of that river twice a day. I was going to come out of here with a kudu bull bigger than a stud mastodon. I knew it. Harry knew it too. We had some drinks and ate the impala and turned in. I went to sleep smiling. Tomorrow had to be a lovely day.

Chapter 12

THE Ruaha was bitter cold again as we stripped and bundled our clothing, held high overhead as we staggered through the rushing waters to cross to where the jeep was waiting. Harry carried Virginia on his back, which must have been an awful job of balance-maintaining. We dressed, shivering in the pre-dawn gray, and got into the jeep. It was just coming on light when we stopped to pick up the old man. He was sitting in front of his hut before a small blaze of thorn branches, waiting for us.

"*Jambo, 'mzee,*" Harry said. "*Kwenda nataka piga tendalla?*"

"*Ndio, bwana,*" the old man said, grinning. "*Doumi mkubwa.* Horns like this." He stroked the back of his head, made a graceful double curl with his hand, then carried the hand backward until it passed his buttocks.

"God save us," Harry said. "If there are bulls here so big their horns pass their rump when they run, we must have found a sanctuary."

The jeep swept along, following its own track as far as the gaudy little red, blue, black, and white hill, and as it rolled it passed through a sort of Eden. I thought I had seen wild life before. I had not seen it this way.

The first indication of something special was the guinea fowl. We passed through flocks of hundreds. By the time we had reached the river we had seen five thousand or better. They were not scared, not in the slightest spooky. They trotted along, heads held high like pacing horses, but moving as unconcernedly as chickens. They cackled until the whole bright, sunny world seemed full of that harsh "potrack-potrack" sound they make.

Then there were the impala. I thought I had seen impala. I had not seen impala. They ran a hundred to the herd. The herds joined one another every thousand yards. There were hundreds of herds. They stood still at the side of the track, sniffing curiously. One bright gold chap was feeling the frost in the morning. He paced us tentatively at twenty miles an hour, moving easily in great arcs, and then jumped completely over the jeep—just to see if he could, I suppose. Then he stood still, waiting for applause. We applauded. He bowed and skipped away, his tiny heels catching the sun as he turned cartwheels out of exuberance.

And then there were the eland. For all his big bull's bulk, the eland is shy. He grazes at a canter, and he almost never stops still. He moves, and always away, in a swinging lope that grows into a gigantic hop. Here we saw a herd of eland, with a magnificent bull, about two thousand pounds of bull, his hide gray-gold, horns heavy-twisted and worn round and smooth at the tips from age and use. There were a dozen younger bulls with the mob, and more than two hundred cows. We stopped the car to watch them, and the eland walked up toward us, to stand, finally, huge necks stretched, horns laid back along their spines, nostrils jumping at our scent, but standing still and unafraid, and then taking tentative steps toward us. I could hear Harry exhale.

"I never expected to see this," he said softly. "I never saw an eland that wasn't moving, and moving away, unless you were downwind from him and blinded in lots of bush. I don't believe these beasts ever saw a man before."

We left the eland staring at us like cattle and drove quietly along to Harry's hill. The game thickened as we went, and the occasional oases of clay were scarred and rutted like a barnyard with tracks.

Harry drove the jeep in a tight circle, slowly around the track-bitten mud, and then he stopped the car and got out to look more closely. He kept shaking his head, muttering. Kidogo was with him, dropping occasionally to one knee to put his fingers into a track and crooning very softly to himself. After a while they both got back into the car.

"I never saw anything like it," Harry said, still shaking his head as if to clear it. "There's one kudu bull passed here last night got a hoof on him as big as a flatiron. There's any amount of small bulls and *mingi sana* cows. There's a herd of buffalo lives around here, and if the bull's got horns to match his hoofs, he must be fifty inches.

"A pride of three male lions and about eleven females is using around these parts, and there were three separate sets of leopard tracks out in the open. There's no elephant out here, of course, but the old man says the bush on the other side of the river is stiff with *tembo*. There seems to be everything in the world here, and none of it seems to have been shot at. Kidogo says that they only shot a couple of times when they were here before, and got right out again. I'm beginning to believe everything Bowman told me about this place, especially since I saw how the eland acted. Let's go on down and check along the river."

We drove easily through the short yellow grass, making our own track, with the old man pointing and saying "*Kishoto*" or "*Kulia*" as he directed us left and right. After this trip we wouldn't need him. Our own track would be plenty signpost.

As we came closer to the river we passed a deserted native *shamba* to our left. The thatch was half stripped from the wattle huts, sagging and forlorn. The cactus *boma* had gone to seed. The gardens were tangled and overgrown. Someone had died there, and the survivors had moved away to avoid the evil spirits. As we passed there was a short, sharp bark, and two immature bull kudu, followed by a harem of six cows, broke from the deserted garden and went for the wood. We followed slowly in Jessica and came up to them standing no more than a couple of hundred yards away, their nostrils flared and their huge mule ears flanged forward. They were curious and perhaps a little startled but not afraid. They were in easy gunshot.

"Two youngsters," Harry said. "But they'll go forty-five or forty-six easy with only one curl to their horns. And they've already grown the ivory. Give 'em another two or three years and they'll both touch sixty inches. My God, my *God*. I never saw anything like this."

The kudu, still frozen, suddenly unfroze and began to graze. Harry swung the jeep gently away and we left them feeding. We went on again toward the river. As we came to within half a mile there was a vast plateau of white, soft sand, studded here and there with scrub thorn, old logs, and a few cacti. It was again a barnyard, its large acreage almost entirely marred by tracks and sign.

"It looks like Johnny North's circus has wintered here," Virginia said. "There's enough manure to fertilize a truck farm. There must be about eight million of everything using this place. I still don't believe that there are enough wild animals to make all this mess and all these tracks. We must be in some extension of Texas."

Just as Jinny said "Texas" a bull kudu, his horns laid straight back along his spine, broke from the bush behind us and ran along parallel to the jeep. I saw him first and pointed.

"Holy Mother of God!" Selby said, and slammed the brakes. "*Toa* anything!" he yelled at Kidogo. I had trouble opening the door of the jeep, and by the time I got out the bull had crossed ahead of us and was going away in unhurried jumps, pausing briefly as if he were trying to make up his mind. As I fell out Kidogo handed me the .375 and I sat flat on my tail, wedged elbows on knees, and tried to cover the running animal. Harry had driven the jeep away.

The big bull almost stopped, at maybe 150 yards. His horns were very fine—at least fifty inches, maybe more. He looked bluish as he cantered, and I finally got the sights on his shoulder and a little ahead of him. I was squeezing when he dived into a patch of thorn and I lost him. I swung the gun some more to where he was supposed to come out, and when he came I touched her off at what I thought was a respectable lead. The bull barked and lunged, diving upward into the air and seeming to soar. He smacked into the heavy thorn, and you could hear him crashing as he went through the cover.

"I think you got him," Harry said, excited. "The boys think so too."

"*Piga, bwana,*" Kidogo was saying over and over while he was hitting me on the back. "*Piga m'zuri. Piga. Piga.*"

"*Hapana piga,*" I said. "God damn it to hell. I missed him. He started that bloody jump just as I squeezed off, and jumped right over my lead. There wasn't any bullet whunk. I'd know it if I hit him. I didn't hit him."

"Let's go look, anyhow," Harry said. "I still think you walloped him. He jumped awful funny. He jumped like that big waterbuck jumped when you socked him that day at Ikoma."

"You won't find any blood," I said. "Remember the oryx. You aren't going to find any blood."

We walked over to where the bull had crashed into the thick thorn, and we saw the ground scored deeply where his hoofs cut it when he took off. We saw some broken thorn branches and a few patches of gray hair stuck to the wait-a-bits. The boys fanned out like pheasant dogs, spooring and circling and crisscrossing each other. They went a couple hundred yards into the bush and came back crestfallen.

"*Hapana piga, bwana,*" Kidogo said. "*Hapana damu.*"

"I told you," I said. "There isn't any blood and there isn't going to be any blood. I missed that bugger a long mile. In a way I'm glad. I don't want this thing to end before it starts. Make it too easy and you cheapen the whole business. I want to work some for my kudu, and when I get him I want a good one. This is one I want to really earn."

"I'm glad," Harry said. "There's no point to shooting these things if they're easy as topi. Beast's too noble to just bash the first day out. Wants a bit of work to make him immortal on your wall."

"I bet *I* could have hit him," the *memsaab* said.

"None of that, please," Selby said. "Leave the *bwana* be. Any man with two lions and a leopard and a waterbuck as good as his needs no backchat from the *manamouki.*"

"Yes, master," Virginia said. "In retrospect I don't think I might have hit him after all."

We got back in the jeep and turned her into a point of land where Kidogo said he and Frank Bowman had made their camp. It was under a huge grove of palms that grow those little round red nuts the elephants love—palms and towering thorns and figs and baobob. The thorns were the flat-topped acacia that make a flat canopy over a long, clean expanse of trunk. The trunks reached upward a hundred feet or more before they began to branch and form their roof. The ground was flat-trampled straw. Elephants had stood beneath these trees since there were elephants to stand beneath trees. The straw was as clean and dry and sweet-smelling as the packed needles in an Italian pine forest down around Fregene. A slight breeze rustled the treetops and passed sweetly through the clearing. There was no reek of baboon. The sun, coming through occasional gaps in the foliage overhead, made little hot pools of light, slashes and crosses and islands of golden light on the golden straw, piercing the green shade as it pierces the windows of a church, leaving slanting streams of light in which the motes were swimming.

There were two piles of dung in the middle of the five-acre area. One was conical, two feet high and still smoking in the morning cool. The other, also smoking, was scattered in pellets the size of small golf balls. Harry pointed.

"Elephants," he said solemnly. "Kudu. Just here. Took off when you shot back there. Man, you don't have any problem with kudu. It's just a matter of shooting the first very good one we see, and then hanging around a few more days to see if we can better him. I've been hunting this M.M.B.A. since I was a boy and I never, *ever* saw anything like this for game. Especially kudu. Place is simply stiff with 'em, and if they hang about the river like Bowman said, we've no problem. No problem at *all*."

We didn't really seem to have a problem about anything. Harry walked me down to the edge of the Little Ruaha, which was slow-moving when compared to its big brother, and a half dozen crocs just raised their snouts, blinked, and took their time sliding reluctantly into the water. The guineas were everywhere, squawking their "potrack" symphony and not bothering to fly. The big goosy doves were clamoring in the trees. We started a herd of waterbuck which didn't even trouble to jump before it ran. Across the river you could hear the elephants bugling at each other in an amiable sort of way.

We strolled back to the clearing under the palms and the thorn and fiddled with lunch, but nobody ate much. We were too excited. The excitement that Harry felt, that Kidogo felt, that even the phlegmatic Adam felt, was too electric to permit much indulgence in food. We wanted to go and see it all, everything in it. As we finished the beer a leopard sawed no more than a hundred yards away. This was high noon, when God-fearing leopards are supposed to be sleeping off last night's excesses in the swamp.

About two we clambered back into Jessica and started down the river's edge. By river's edge you mean maybe half a mile away from it, because a thickish swamp and a broad donga divided the first swell of the hills from the actual water. We wound in and out of this swamp, all of which was elephant swamp, kudu swamp (for all we knew), but certainly baboon swamp, impala swamp, waterbuck swamp, leopard swamp, guinea swamp. Even to call it swamp is insult. It was a series of interlocking groves, shady and cool and clear underfoot where the elephants kept it trampled down. The troupes of shrieking *nugus* were even very tame for baboons, because you could stop the car and they wouldn't panic and dash off, the kids clinging to the mamas' backs and the old dogs looking surly and apprehensive in the rear-guard action. It was a hard bit of bush to describe. We had the groves, and we had the river, and we had the glades and the hills, and occasionally we had the bush, all laid out like somebody landscaped it that way. There were some peculiar laurel-looking bushes growing down around the river, and we wondered if maybe the kudu didn't come down at certain times of the year to cram themselves with a certain leaf that for all we knew contained a kudu-type aphrodisiac.

Still coughing and spluttering and retching a bit from her bath, Jessica indicated by jeep sign language that she thought she ought to rest a bit and have her diaphragm looked into, so we stopped under one of the big elephant groves to tidy up her innards. Then we heard the elephant orchestra. We never saw the herd, even when we walked down to the banks of the river. What we saw were buffalo standing placidly on the bank, but what we heard was the awful crashing of the elephant bulls as they waded through the deep bush we couldn't get to, with the river as high as it was. What we heard was the trumpeting like a Philharmonic composed entirely of Harry Jameses. What we saw was the turmoil in the tree-tops as the herd threshed about.

And the buffalo. Yes, the buffalo. I looked at one bull for twenty-five measured minutes across twenty yards of water. I looked at him. He looked at me. When I left he was still looking. So were the two or three hundred friends he had behind him. They never seemed a dime's worth of alarmed.

We found a shallow sand bar where the sand grouse flighted to drink, and I marked it down against the morrow. We jumped five or six kudu cows and a couple more young bulls just across the donga that separated the swampy part from the brown hills. We walked up one bull we never saw. He barked throatily and crashed just ahead of us as we stumbled back from the riverbank to the jeep. He sounded old and he sounded big.

We rolled on some more and came onto a small *shamba* with some scared kids and timid wives in it, and they said that the boss man was off with his gun, trying to shoot the *tendalla* out of the corn patch. We achieved this fellow eventually and he was carrying a wire-trapped, sewer-pipe-barreled, muzzle-loading flintlock which was undoubtedly loaded with rocks, nails, and pieces of broken glass. He said yes, there were *tendalla*. Between the *tendalla* and the *tembo*—the kudu and the elephants—he was just about to be et out of house and home. He had seen three big bulls this morning, but the bachelor coteries of bulls had not yet come down from the high hills. They were still with the cows, each man to his dames, and it would be maybe next month, September, before the big stag parties started on the banks of the river, and the bulls would desert the cows to hang stupidly about the river to eat some shrub he had not yet been able to identify. He said he would appreciate it very much if we would shoot twenty or thirty kudu just to keep them out of his yams. We said thank you very much, we would try to save him some trouble.

We wheeled the jeep around and headed back, fighting our way through the baboons and the hyenas and the impala, and suddenly came onto another herd of buffalo. There was a herd bull out in front that made my mouth secrete furiously, but Harry said no, we wouldn't shoot anything around here until we'd collected the kudu. All of us—Harry, Virginia, Kidogo, Adam, Chabani, the old man, and me—got out of the car without guns. We walked toward the herd of buffalo. The herd walked toward us. At about twenty yards both herds, human and buffalo, stopped walking and looked keenly at each other. The old bull stretched his neck and sniffed. He didn't paw the nervous way they do, and he didn't snort. The cows with him that had the little calves at their sides didn't snort and nudge their kids back behind them. The calves walked ahead of their mothers.

We squatted down on our hams and smoked a couple of cigarettes each, and the smoke drifted straight away from us toward the buffalo. Eventually they stopped staring and began to crop the weeds around them. The calves played and butted each other and kicked up some fuss. The herd bull was still serious. He looked and looked and looked and finally said the hell with it, these people have no importance. He turned his back, and the herd began to feed away. Somewhere down the swamp two more leopards sawed, a crew of baboons scolded, a kudu barked, and a lion complained. This was still bright day.

"I've seen enough," Harry said. "I want to go back to camp and think about it. I have always laughed at this business about untouched country, because every hunter is always sounding off about secret territory, but I'll be damned if this isn't the secretest territory I ever saw. Not an animal we have seen today ever saw a man before, bar a few natives maybe, and these natives aren't hunters. They're bee robbers and agriculturists. Not even old Joe with the blunderbuss counts as a hunter. He couldn't get close enough to kill anything with that sewer pipe, and even if he hit it, he wouldn't hurt it. Might blow up and kill him, but that's all.

"What I think we'd best do is bring a few pieces of gear over tomorrow and camp there by the river, under that fine grove, and not have to bother for a few days with fording the big Ruaha and making the eighteen-mile run twice a day. We'll just hunt up and down the river from the camp until we've got our kudu. If we don't like the first one too much we can switch back across the big Ruaha and hunt the road in the high hills backward to Iringa."

We drove slowly back to the old Bowman campsite, watching the game and hearing the noises and feeling the sun still warm as the breeze stiffened and grew chillier, as content as seven white and black people can be. We stopped for another look at the camp, and as we walked into it another young kudu bull barked, leaped, and streaked across the ground on which we would be living tomorrow. The shady grove still looked like a cathedral. We walked to the river again, and the same crocodiles looked bored and slid into the stream. The same elephants, I suppose, bugled across in the deep green thicket across the way. There were two or three other piles of fresh dung, deposited since we had left that morning.

"You know," Selby said, "I am not a particularly religious man, but there's an awful lot of God loose around here."

I noticed then for the first time that nobody had raised his voice above a whisper all day long.

Bending back to camp in the bloody-streaked sunset and the creeping chilliness of the dusk, we passed Harry's ornate hill, and he climbed it. When he hit the summit, maybe two hundred feet of sheer drop aboveground, he turned and waved at me. I lost a lot of breath getting up to the rock where Harry was sitting contemplatively like an old baboon. While I panted the ache out of my chest he pointed. In the fading light you could see the shimmer of horns—big, back-twisted horns—a couple of hundred yards away and off to the right in the thorn. There was a steady wake behind the horns. We counted. There was the one big kudu bull. There were two youngsters, and then there were twelve cows.

"Too late to go after them," Harry said. "By the time we're down the hill you couldn't see to shoot in that thick there. We'll see 'em tomorrow. But my God, Bob, have you ever even imagined anything like this?"

When we climbed down over the square chunks of rocks and walked to the car it was nearly black. We drove home quietly and carefully, with the yellow from Jessica's headlamps tonguing out ahead of us hesitantly as we picked our way through the hardened ruts of the wallows and skimmed over the sedgy grass. We dropped the *'mzee* at his *shamba* and told him that tomorrow we would shoot him a piece of meat, for very sure, before we went into the kudu country where we didn't want to make any noise. The *'mzee* looked doubtful, but another pack of Chesterfields happied him up a little.

We beat through the heavy bush and made the riverbank of the Great Ruaha. It was still as cold as I remembered it. We had a drink and ate quietly. We didn't want to talk too much and mouth up what we had seen that day. I was going to be the very first load tomorrow, when we started to shift the camp by carrying the necessities through the rushing river, moving what we could by a series of trips to the solemn camp by the Little Ruaha. I didn't know what was apt to come after me, but I did know that I was going to be the first one to go and the one to stay there by myself, with a gun, a table, a typewriter, and a bottle of beer.

We packed the first necessities into Jessica in the early dawn and said *"Jambo"* to the old man as he sat in front of his meager little fire. We didn't need the old man any more, but there was a small herd of zebra fidgeting around a half mile from his *shamba,* and I remembered that the old boy said he was sore and sick for meat. There was a big fat stallion who seemed overly curious for his own good, and we were twelve miles from the main kudu country. I hopped out of Jessica's lap and found myself a tree with a crotch in it and bored a small hole through the *punda's* ears, so's not to spoil the meat for the old man. Then we hitched a rope around the zebra's neck and hauled him back a half mile for the 'mzee to skin and cut up, to eat the first day's meat and dry the rest, and carve the fat off the bulging intestines, and to be happy over it and with it and to remember us kindly. The whole sweetness-and-light operation took a half hour, and nobody was unhappy except perhaps the zebra's first three widows and a flock of concubines he was undoubtedly cheating with when the legal mares weren't looking.

The old man was surprised when we showed up dragging the zebra. His experience with white folks had led him to expect nothing in the way of the fulfillment of a promise. He looked a little disappointed at his miscalculation of worth. But he lost the disappointed look when he saw how fat the dead *punda* actually was. We told him "*Kwaheri*" and absconded. That was a nice old 'mzee.

We traveled through the zoo to the campsite and unloaded the jeep. There wasn't much to unload this trip. I had the mess table and the big double rifle and the .375 and the chop box and some beer and my typewriter and some odd bits and pieces of equipment. The main stuff would come on the next three trips, and the last trip would bring Virginia. Harry had the Mannlicher and he was going to shoot a piece of meat for us to eat on the last trip, far away from here, where the noise wouldn't bother our friends. He had the little shotty-gun and was going to assassinate a couple of guineas just outside the 'mzee's *shamba,* and that would feed us for half a week. Shooting around the camp on the Little Ruaha seemed very wrong unless it was awfully important or necessary.

I stacked the guns against a big tree's butt, set up the mess table, opened the typewriter, pried the top off a bottle of beer, untangled a camp chair, and sat down to look and listen.

I would write after a while, maybe after I had finished lunch and a nap. There was nobody around but me, nobody else in the world but me and a million animals and a thousand noises and the bright sun and the cool breeze and the shade from the big trees that made it cathedral-cool but a lot less musty and damp and full of century-old fear and trembling. I got to thinking that maybe this was what God had in mind when He invented religion, instead of all the don't and must-nots and sins and confessions of sins. I got to thinking about all the big churches I had been in, including those in Rome, and how none of them could possibly compare with this place, with its brilliant birds and its soothing sounds of intense life all around and the feeling of ineffable peace and good will, so that not even man would be capable of behaving very badly in such a place. I thought that this was maybe the kind of place the Lord would come to sit in and get His strength back after a hard day's work trying to straighten out mankind. Certainly He wouldn't go inside a church. If the Lord was tired He would be uneasy inside a church.

I was very happy to be here, and very grateful to be here, all by myself with a bottle of cool beer and some peaceful thoughts, and presently I would try to put some of them down on paper. I was awfully grateful to have been allowed to live long enough and to have made enough money to allow me to take this trip with a man I liked and admired and the only woman I had ever been married to and a baker's dozen of black men whom I respected and who respected me. I was especially glad that ship didn't blow up that day in the Mediterranean. I felt very sad for my best and oldest friend, Jim Queen, who loved this sort of stuff as much as I did but who was never going to be able to do it with me because a JU-88 came over a hill at Salerno one day and laid one into Jimmy's stack and that was all there was of Jim, then and forevermore.

I was grateful that it hadn't worked that way with me, because the opportunity was equal.

I was never going to forget that day, a little east of Oran, about four-fifteen in the afternoon of a gray day, when the subs came and the low-level boys and the torpedo bombers, long, sharky-looking Heinkels, came up from around the Balearics and started to blow up the convoy. They got square onto the midships of a lad in the column to my left and just abaft me, and he blew like a firecracker, because this was an all-ammunition convoy and there were about seven thousand tons of bombs under me, and tetryl detonators, and another two thousand tons of aviation gas in one hold of my ship, and if we got hit that was all she wrote.

There were about ninety big ships, not counting the escort, in this convoy and they all had twin three-inchers forward and five-inch thirty-eights after and bristly clumps of Oerlikons in tubs fore and aft and on the bridge. The air was suddenly full of iron and fire, and the shrapnel was rattling down like hailstones, except sharper. I saw one ship, panicky, fire directly onto the bridge of a sister ship. The corvettes and destroyer-escorts were close into the African shore, dropping big, geysering depth charges. Occasionally a ship would blow or a plane would glide smokily down and explode in the gray cold sea. Then the Spits came out from Africa and started working upstairs, and a DE chased a submarine in close and walloped him with the ash cans. The attack was nearly over and my kids were shooting at one last tenacious Heinkel who was unleashing a fish into the convoy when the entire starboard side of the gun crew yelled: "Torpedo on the starboard bow." You could see whatever it was bucking through the gray chop, and I yelled down to the Old Man to give her all the right wheel he had so we could head into the torpedo and let it slip past the fantail. But the old bucket was belly-heavy and sluggish, and although she began to swing she didn't swing fast enough, and this thing belted us just at the No. 2 hatch. The deck plates popped and flames came up and there was a great crash where the thing struck. This was going to be the end of the trip I hadn't wanted to make—the one more run before we were relieved. This was the trip I wasn't supposed to make, because I already had seven months of ammo runs to tough places and we were supposed to get off in Baltimore the last time home, but nobody relieved us and here we were, dead.

The things you think about when you have a second or so of life left are not noble. I remember feeling a vague and misty sadness that all I loved of life was over and I would not be twenty-seven years old until the next month. *What a pity,* I thought, *to leave it so soon and with so many things undone.* I did not pray and I did not ask God's forgiveness, nor did I rail or weep or raise my mental voice. The thought flickered that I would shoot no more quail, love no more women, drink no more whisky, eat no more steaks. I was a little sad for Virginia's sake. I hated to leave her a widow because she would feel so bad so long and she was a peculiar kind of dame who would probably never find anybody who got along with her as well as I did. These are the thoughts I thought when I was already dead, because I had seen so many ammo ships catch the big horn and I knew what happened to them. Pinwheels and skyrockets and one big boom.

But the ship did not blow. She listed, moaned, and some fires flickered and went out, but she did not blow. Nobody knows why. For the longest thirty seconds of any man's life she was potential explosion and she didn't explode. I was an older man when I went round to the ladder and yelled down at the Old Man. The Old Man was a quiet Dane who never flustered.

"What are you going to do about this pot?" I yelled into the wind. "Do we get off and walk, or what?"

"Vell," the Old Man said calmly, "she don't blow and she's still answering de veel. If she's answering de veel I guess ve vill just stay aboard and see what happens."

She answered de veel all the way to Malta, where we got bombed, and all the way up the Adriatic to Bari, where we dodged mines and got bombed, and all the way back to Bizerte, where we got submarined and missed and then hit by lightning. She answered de veel all the way to Oran, where they sank a ship as she came out to join us. She answered de veel all the way home, as far as Philadelphia, where it was Thanksgiving Day and nobody was working on Thanksgiving Day in the States, and we had to stay in the stream. Then I got off her and was a little mad for a period of days, having noisy trouble with waiters and hitting a Pullman conductor and drinking too much and not sleeping at all. It was going to be a long time before I could hear an airplane in the night without coming full awake and reaching blindly for tin hat and pistol. I remembered undressing one afternoon to take a nap at my mother-in-law's house, and she was having a hen bridge party. A commercial plane came over, flying low, and I hit the stairs, running. That I was entirely naked seemed to disconcert the female guests.

I thought of all the stuff about the Pacific, the Japs living in caves and in the woods on Guam, and coming up at night to drink from our freshly erected outdoor shower baths and to steal what they could and occasionally shoot a Marine or a Seabee. I remembered that ghastly hop all the way from Guam to Melbourne in a two-motored aircraft, and waking up with a hangover in the middle of the Owen Stanley range in New Guinea and not knowing where I was, and landing blind at a place called Owi or Ebi or some such, landing with no radio on a field that had no lights at night. I thought about the long, painful hospital time in the Solomons and later in San Francisco, with a shattered arm that could just as easily have been a shattered back. I thought of all the landings and take-offs and the near squeaks when the motors cut out that time over Brazil, cut out first and then caught fire, and we were just lucky to be right over a place called Barreiras when it happened, the only decent emergency field between Rio and Belém.

I believe that this was when I said a short and simple prayer of thanks to Whoever it was that had been keeping His eye on me all these years. It was sort of like a delayed bread-and-butter note, way overdue, but nonetheless well meant and sincere. I hoped God would understand that I had been awful busy and was sorry I hadn't gotten around to thanking Him earlier. I hoped He would keep on looking after me so I could live to be an old, cranky man and come back to Africa many more times.

I suppose I must have dropped off to sleep a little bit because when I woke up there was a nearly naked native leaning on a spear and looking at me with considerable interest. He had on an old moth-bit goatskin, as filthy as he was, if that was possible. His beard grew in scabby patches, and he had no front teeth. There was a bow and a quiver of arrows on his back. He was barefoot, and his legs were sore and scabby from insect bites.

"Jambo," I said. "Pray do join me."

"Jambo, bwana," he said. "Wapi Haraka?"

I said as best I could that Harry was off at the other camp

on a highly secret mission involving the fetching of tents and other gear. I didn't bother to ask him how he knew Harry's nickname was Haraka, meaning "hurry."

"*Wapi Memsaab?*" he asked. "Where is the lady with the white hair?"

I told him that the lady was back at the other camp, too, waiting for Harry, so that they could shoot me in the neck and run off to live on my millions. I didn't bother to ask him how he knew there was a *memsaab* and how he knew she had white hair. Except the goose-pimples started to form and my neck hairs bristled. Harry had never been here before, and we had never been here before, but here is this black Robin Hood calling Harry by his Swahili nickname and asking after Virginia's dyed hair. Then I remembered the drums going loud all the way along the line and reckoned pretty accurately that the locals were alerted as we traveled, sort of alerted that some live ones were en route and could be depended on for tips, tin cans, bottles, food, tobacco, and in some instances employment.

I asked this character what manner of man he was and what tribe proudly claimed him.

" 'Ndrobo," he said. "Wa-Arusha 'Ndrobo."

If he was a Wa-Arusha 'Ndrobo he was a hell of a far piece from home. The 'Ndrobo, maybe you don't know, are out-castes of all the tribes. They have been expelled for one sin or another, like Robin Hood's men, and they live in the high hills. They live by stealing and robbing bee bikes and trapping and shooting animals with their bows and arrows. They are generally magnificent woodsmen. They have to be, or starve.

This laddy-buck said that the birds had told him that we wanted a *tendalla,* and that he was the local expert on *tendalla.* He said he had seen two big bulls this morning, back over yonder—with a wave of the hand—and three big bulls yesterday, away down yonder—with the other hand sweeping down the river. He said he knew a salt lick, back over yonder —with the finger pointing back across the big Ruaha—that was so populous with *tendalla* that the horns made a thicket all by themselves. He said that for a remarkably small amount of money he would slave for us, guarantee us a fine *tendalla*, and otherwise richen our lives by his constant attendance. I said I would think it over and we would wait for Harry. He allowed me to give him a cigarette, which he stuck in the hole in his ear, and went happily off to sleep.

I built myself a spot of lunch from the chop box and opened another bottle of the Tusker. Then I got out the writing paper and unlimbered the typewriter, to try to tell the folks back home what all this was like. I don't imagine I was very successful at it.

Harry rolled up after a bit, with the cook and one personal boy and Juma packed into the Rover, together with the sleeping tent and the cooking gear. There was an impala buck tied on the bonnet, and he tossed a couple brace of guinea fowl out of the car. He woke up the 'Ndrobo, questioned him a long time, told him he was hired, told Juma to give him something to eat, and went back to get Virginia and the rest of the duffel.

It was nightfall when he got back, with a story about having seen another big mob of kudu and some more tame eland. He looked tired and happy. He knew and I knew—we all knew—that we would get a kudu tomorrow.

Chapter 13

I DO NOT KNOW if I can explain a kudu, or *tendalla*, except possibly by the drawing at the head of this chapter. The drawing is done fuzzily, an impression rather than a sharp delineation—a gray blur, partially seen, swift to vanish. A kudu is definite only when he is dead.

There is something about this lovely beast that makes him a hunter's grail. Perhaps it is the tremendous sweep of those double-curling horns, as brown and clean as rubbed mahogany, heavy-ridged from the base around the curls, and ending in polished ivory points. Perhaps it is the chevron on his nose, or his clean, gray, white-barred hide, the skin thin as parchment. Perhaps it is the delicacy of his long-legged deer's body, the slimness of his long deer's legs, the heavy-maned swell of his neck, the enormity of his ears that pick up whispers at a radar range. Perhaps it is his perverseness, his consummate genius for doing the wrong thing always, to confound his pursuer, such as being in the hills when he should be at the licks, or being by the river when he should be in the hills, or being by the licks when he should be by the river. A djinn gradually crawls into the body of the man who hunts him, to where he is devilishly possessed by kudu and is incapable of transferring his attention to anything else. The kudu is just under your hand, and yet he always manages to escape you. Sometimes he escapes you even if you kill him.

There is nearly always a sardonic touch to the story of a kudu. You always seem to get him at the last hour of the last day, with the rains sweeping down from the south, the money and the time running out, and personal patience whetted to an unbelievable edge of irritability. The frustration mounts and mounts and finally achieves an outlandish proportion, to where the whole camp pins its entire attention on the late-evening arrival of the hunting car. If there are horns in it the camp rejoices. If there are no horns the boys set out the whisky and move as quietly as possible, not laughing, and talking in whispers. Nobody asks you how it went that day. Everybody knows.

I heard of a rich old man who was not shooting his own stuff, and he eventually got a kudu. A big bull had knocked his horns on a tree and had ruptured a capillary. The hunters picked up the blood spoor, jumped the bull, and trailed him over the serried hills of Kandoa Irangi for about ten miles. They finally came up on the bull, weak from loss of blood and staggering on his feet. The professional shot him neatly and mercifully, and the bloated old buzzard who short-ordered the beast has him looking proud and noble on the walls of his lodge today. I claim that this debases the animal.

Harry told me that he and Bob Maytag hunted themselves into a constant fever for two weeks after kudu, just missing every time, almost getting but never quite achieving. Their time had run out, too, and they decided to make one last hunt while the boys were breaking camp. They put up a big bull, who confounded all rules of kudu conduct by walking leisurely across their bow, giving Maytag half a dozen whacks at him. They had tracked him in their stocking feet, and when the bull took off after being hit hard a couple of times, they raced him a mile over mountains, accumulating horrid stone bruises and a really notable collection of thorns in feet during the chase. They piled back into camp, bleeding worse than the animal, with the back seat full of kudu, which is about like trying to load a dead mule into a wheelbarrow. When they got there the camp had been broken and the lorry was piled high with gear. It had been that close.

There are all sorts of ways to hunt kudu. If you are hunting them in the mountains, you drive along the edge of the foothills and scan the cliffsides minutely with high-powered binoculars. Or else you find yourself a high point of vantage and sit there all day, endlessly sweeping the slopes with your

glasses until a faint flick of ear or a flash of sun on white belly
or gray flank exposes the animal. Then the work starts, the
tough, mean climbing, out-of-breath-and-pain-in-the-stomach
climbing, the long and difficult tracking, with the animal
always a good five miles ahead of you, until suddenly he
whimsically decides to stop to feed and you come up on him
and kill him if you can hit him. And a lot of people who can
hit everything else go mad when they finally come to close
association with kudu, fire into the air, throw the gun away,
and sit quietly on the ground to sob.

If you hunt him at the salt licks you are there before dawn
and you wait and wait and wait and fight the tsetses and the
mosquitoes, and maybe he comes, but then again maybe he
doesn't. If he comes maybe something else comes and spooks
him. If he comes at all it is almost certain that something will
happen to run him off.

Hunting him by the river was a new aspect of the business,
because apart from an infrequent trip to drink the kudu is not
a low-ground animal, and this finding him in profusion in the
flats was a thing neither Selby nor I had been exposed to. We
decided to hunt him by guess and by God, as we would hunt
anything else less exotic, and see how it turned out.

I do not remember how the days ran chronologically. We
hunted the Little Ruaha for a week. We hunted up the river
and down the river. Always we saw kudu. One day when we
were out a big bull ran right through the middle of the camp.
We hunted native gardens and we hunted the low hills. We
hunted the swamps and we hunted the thornbush plains. We
went to the 'Ndrobo's secret country and torturously traversed
huge flat grasslands where always the local bee robbers had
seen *mingi sana doumi* the day before.

We hunted from before dawn until black night. We cut
roads through thorn and rearranged Jessica's vitals on rocky

terrain that a tank couldn't have handled. Every day we saw kudu—big bulls, little bulls, young bulls, old bulls, and enough cows to start a ranch. Always something happened.

Once we made a very careful stalk, with the wind just so, on a marvelous animal with a rack that would have been at least fifty-eight inches, a full foot better than any exceedingly desirable bull. He was feeding with his harem of seven cows on the brown slopes of some gently rising hills. He had been down to the river's edge to drink or to eat the mysterious leaves or whatever he was supposed to be doing down there by the river. We saw him about eight o'clock in the morning, the grass still dew-wet, the leaves tremulous in the morning breeze, the sun hesitant and just warm enough, and the air as piercingly clear as a blast of pure oxygen in a doctor's tent.

We hunted him perfectly. We stalked him a mile or more, slowly, cautiously, not cracking the sticks, not stumbling over the stones, not talking, not even breathing loudly. We went over hills and into valleys and finally, the wind stiff into our faces, we came up to the brow of a hill that was crowned by a craggy battlement of stones. I was in wonderful shape by now after six weeks of exercise. I wasn't breathing hard, except maybe a little from excitement. I knew all I was going to do was rest that big .375 on a rock and lay the aiming post square on his shoulder and that would be the story. We would admire this monster and Harry would tell the boys to *taka* headskin. We would cut out his filet and the boys would rob him of his fat and of his hams. We would skin him carefully to make a sports coat for Virginia of his lovely blue-gray, white-barred hide, and we would go home and get drunk.

I crawled to the battlement of stones and rose cautiously, inch by inch. I slid the rifle through a parapet in the rocks and looked down the barrel at seven cows. For no reason at all the *doumi* was not there with his wives. He had fed off, not frightened, not because he was hungry, but only because he was of a mood to wander that morning. I saw him, two thousand yards away, fiddling aimlessly around a hilltop, looking for a crap game or a buddy to swap a lie with. The cows were completely unaware of us, we had stalked them so carefully. They fed for ten minutes at thirty yards, while their faithless lord meandered around the young mountains.

We spoored this fellow all day, or nearly all day. We tracked him slowly and meticulously, with all the skills that Harry and the blacks knew, and sometimes we got as close as four or five hundred yards from him. Then in the late afternoon the wind veered sharply and we heard him bark. When we got up to where he'd barked we saw the deep wounds his hoofs had made when he jumped. There would be no more of this fellow this day. Or any other.

That was a day among the days. Another day among the days was losing a big bull in the impassable elephant swamps, where we'd finally bayed him after six hours of vicious, wicked, awful walking. He barked. He crashed. He went away. He went away like the big bunch we jumped in the deserted ruined garden. He went away like the troupe Harry spotted from his hill and which could go only the one way. They went the other way. They went the same way the big bunch went on the 'Ndrobo's guaranteed plains, to which we cut our way painfully with *pangas* when Jessica couldn't butt the thorn trees down any more.

The paradise of game was still there, but we didn't see it any longer. We were no longer amused at the caperings of the impala or the cavortings of the baboons, the squeals of the elephants or the cackle of the guineas. The peak point of the day, the coming-home, bath-taking, drink-making, food-eating, bed-going part of the day, was soured and flawed by frustration. Harry was short and surly with the blacks. Virginia was intuitively intelligent enough not to speak to either of us. We would sit morosely in front of the fire and brood.

Meat was short in the camp. We would not fire a gun even for food. When the last impala and the guineas gave out we ate from cans and scarcely tasted what we ate. The quest of Cap'n Ahab for Moby Dick arose into my mind again, and I could begin to understand even more clearly than after the abortive effort for the rhino how a man may become obsessed with pursuit until it rides him like a witch on a broom. This was a beautiful camp, but it was not a happy camp.

On the fifth morning we had made a stab at one more bull in the low hills and lost him when the wind did a ring-around-the-rosy on us. We were driving morosely down toward the river, along the edge of the big donga, to give it a final sweep before we rode home for the lunch we didn't have any appetite for.

We were testing the edge of the donga for a place where the jeep might cross it without capsizing when Jessica stalled and Kidogo clamped my neck with his horny hand and Harry pointed straight ahead. There he was.

The sun was still low and rosy from the dawn, red and gold behind this kudu. He stood there, not scenting us, but seeing us, not frightened yet, not quite ready to jump. The sun was behind him and it splintered off his horns. His head was thrown back and his chin was pointed out. We could see only to the first curl, but he was as big as a bull elephant, and the massive roll of his horns as they came out of his skull made them look as thick as logs.

Harry raked him with the glasses and nodded. He checked him with naked eyes and nodded. He gave him the glasses some more and bobbed his head even more vehemently. He spoke very quietly.

"Get out and wallop him," Harry said. "Slip around the

edge of the donga to the right, and if you can make that tree while he's still looking at us he's your baby."

I slid out the door and wormed on my belly behind the jeep and then Indian-crawled for a light year until I made the tree. When I raised up behind the low thorn and poked the gun over a branch he was still there. Through the scope he looked as big as a bull moose. I still couldn't see anything beyond the first tremendous curl of horn, but they were as huge in the scope as mooring hawsers for a liner.

I hadn't been able to pick his body out of the gray bush he was standing in on the other side of the donga, but now I could see him clearly through the scope and it was a very mean shot. He was standing tail-end to. His foreshoulder was slightly out of alignment and his neck was crooked around so that while his head faced me all I had to shoot at was either his rear end or a thin wedge of shoulder blade. I settled for the shoulder blade and held just behind it, hoping the bullet would slip in and take the heart, or at least bust the other shoulder as it went through him diagonally. The post was steady on the fore end of his rib cage, and the trigger got squeezed and the big Winchester roared and the striking bullet made that soggy sound. I knew he was dead before I pulled, because you can feel it and you always know it and the rest is anticlimax.

The big bull never jumped. He pitched. He pitched over backward and fell out of sight in one of the little sandy inlets that ran along the edge of the donga. He was going to be there when I got there. He wasn't apt to be going anywhere. Not with that magnum through his heart and out the other side, smack on the shoulder blade.

The blacks and Harry came down on me like a festival of ravens. They were yelling, and the blacks were jumping in that jerky, spastic, uncontrollable leap that forms the basis of all their tribal dances. They screamed in their various dialects and hit me on the shoulders with clenched fists. Harry was swiping at me with his hat and yelling as loud as the boys were yelling. I was yelling, too, and jumping up and down in almost the same spastic leaps that the 'Ndrobo was practicing, that Kidogo was doing, that even the stolid Adam and the sophisticated Chabani were doing.

Then we started to run, slipping and sliding down the steep sandy sides of the donga, wanting to get close to him and see him and stroke him and measure him and marvel at him, to skin out his head lovingly and take his hide tenderly and then to carry his memory back to camp so we could sit and drink to him and talk about him over and over again, while the boys ate his fine rich flesh and told about how the *bwana* had done it right and carefully when the moment to do it came, saying *"Eeeehhh"* to each other and bragging about their part of it.

For that thirty seconds I was the richest man in the world, as we ran, hearts thudding, breath gasping, to see our kudu, the cumulation of our joint effort.

We pounded up the other side of the donga, and there he lay, dead on his side, with his horns obscured by his twisted neck, the neat hole where the bullet went in exactly as I aimed it. Blue-gray on top, as clean and beautiful and neat and sweet and lovely as any animal ever will be, immortal now and past the possibility of rinderpest or hyenas or poisoned arrows or native blunderbusses. He was big. My God but he was big. Big as a horse and as dainty as a dik-dik.

Harry lunged for his head, twisted the neck, and almost screamed. We all saw it at once. He was a huge bull, all right. His horns had five inches of clear ivory tip. The roll from the forehead and the front curl were even more massive than they had looked through the scope. These horns would go forty-eight inches at least, a damned fine length of horn for any kudu. I wasn't greedy. All I wanted was a good representative head.

The only thing was this: There was only *one* spiral to the horns instead of the great double spiral that makes a kudu a kudu. With his head thrown back against the sun, we had shot a three-year-old bull. The second curl was just starting. In two years he would have been sixty inches of magnificence. I had deprived him of the right to become worth collecting, the right to breed his wondrous possibilities into countless other calves who someday might be as magnificent as their father had had the chance to be before I robbed him of it by accident. I had cheated him and I had cheated me. I had done everything right except the one most important thing, the absolute certainty that this bull was of shootable qualification. I am afraid I cried a little. I cried for me and I cried for the bull and mostly I cried for the spoilage of perfection—of the ruination of the day and the trip and the location.

I do not know how to explain this, either. It was as if you had worked all your life to find gold, had found it, and suddenly it was transformed overnight into clay. It was as if you had courted a woman long and patiently, wooed her, won her, and she turned out to be the village dirty joke, a beautiful idiot with a nymphomaniac's sense of values.

We had shot at the symbol of the kudu, the symbol manifest in the splendor of his horns. We had shot at the symbol and captured it whole, in pride, and then had it turn into shame.

"Do you want the headskin?" Harry said quietly. "It's no trophy, of course. A one-curl kudu is like a tuskless elephant or a maneless lion or a hornless rhino. It's not worth anything to you unless you just like to kill things, and if you like to kill things you might just as well shoot cows or wildebeest or giraffes."

"Cut the head off and throw it to the hyenas," I said. "I don't want to be reminded of this ever again. I was so god-damned *proud* for thirty seconds. I thought this was all finished and I hadn't butched it, and now it isn't even started except for the lousy taste in my heart and in my mouth. I'd give ten of my own years to put him back as he was, standing high on that bank, waiting to grow that other curl, waiting to be worth immortalizing. The hell with him. Skin the poor bastard out and let the boys take his meat. But cut his head off first. I don't mind him dead so much if he's just a lovely hide for Virginia's coat and a lot of fresh meat for the boys. But don't expect me to eat any of him. I'd feel like a bloody cannibal."

He wasn't so bad with his head off. Now he was just a carcass. *Nyama.* The boys took his tenderloin and the two hindquarters and his liver, heart, and the stomach fat, and they skinned him carefully for Virginia's coat. We stuck the dripping hide, wrapped around the hindquarters, into the back of the jeep and headed for camp. Nobody said anything, but Selby drove like an embittered demon, fighting the Rover and punishing her for his mistake and for my mistake.

The camp was waiting for us, because we were in early. Juma and Katunga and Virginia had run down from the camp up to the edge of the sandy plateau, and when they saw the slim legs sticking up from the back seat and the bit of gray hide showing above the side rails, they let out whoops and started a war dance. The other boys came down too, yelling, but when they saw our faces they all shut up. Kidogo said something in Swahili. The boys' faces lengthened.

"*Eeeehhh,*" they said in sadness, and walked away.

"Lousy luck," I said to Virginia. "Shot an immature bull by mistake. Make you a nice coat, though."

"I don't want any nice coat," she said. "I'm awfully, dreadfully sorry."

"Skip it," Harry said. "There's more about, and if the old boy handles it the same way, he'll have no trouble. It was a lovely shot. A perfect shot for the circumstance. He shot it very well, really. Let's all have a spot of gin, what?"

"It's ready," Jinny said quietly. "I mixed up a batch of martinis when I heard Jessica coming down the river."

We had lunch and we did not hunt kudu any more that day. I took the shotgun and went out after the guinea fowl, to make them suffer for my sins. I didn't care how much noise I made now. That night we had a lot more drinks and Juma came in proudly bearing a wonderful-smelling dish of broiled kudu tenderloin. I didn't eat any of it. I ate a can of beans. I wasn't very hungry.

We gave it another three days on the Little Ruaha. We hunted upriver as far as we could drive Jessica, and we hunted down-river. We saw *mingi sana* waterbuck and crocodiles and located three leopards. We avoided the elephants and marveled at the impala. We saw plenty of kudu cows and plenty of young bulls, but the real bulls, the big bulls, were someplace else.

"Maybe in the hills back toward Iringa," Harry said. "Maybe in the licks that one-eyed Somali is so high on. We've worn this place out. Riding up and down it for a week would've spooked every decent bull for some time. It's my guess we're not here for the real right time when the bulls leave the cows and congregate in bachelor mobs.

"Bowman was here in September. It's my guess that whatever herb they're after doesn't leaf out until then. Then I think the cows hide out in the hills and the old men get together and go a little loco in the coco about that time. Frank said that they seemed a little goofy—that you could ride right up to them. We know there's kudu here—God knows we've seen enough. But every mature bull we've seen has had a harem with him, and a bull around his family is twice as scary as when he's off with the boys."

I had regained a little perspective since shooting the young one-curl bull and had reassumed some good nature, if not

charm. The humor of grown men grimly hunting an extra
curl to a horn began to crop out. You would have thought we
were looking for a lost lode or a mythological diamond pipe.

"Let's move back across the Great Ruaha to the *campi* by
the village," I said. "We can hunt the road back up toward
Iringa. That salt lick's kicking about somewhere off the Iringa
road, Abdullah the Charm Boy said. If they're not at the lick,
those hills are high enough to hide an army of 'em. Kidogo
said that when he and Bowman came in they saw quite a lot
of good bulls along the road."

"Right," Harry said. "I think we can give Jessica a rest and
use the lorry for this operation. It'll give Chege something to
do. He's been sitting on his fanny for the last week and courting the local demoiselles, and he'll be getting soft. We can
stand up in the back of that damned Annie and see a lot better
on both sides than we can from the jeep. It's a good ten feet of
extra elevation."

We packed up in echelons. I had some more writing to do,
so I went with the first load. I was sorry to leave the Little
Ruaha, the place of great promise that didn't pay off. We
hadn't hurt it any. Apart from the one kudu and a few fowl
for the pot, we had left the quiet and the trust of the animals
intact. I hadn't even shot any sand grouse, although that
little sand bar was rugged with them. We left it as we found
it, serene and beautiful and unspoiled.

We felt pretty good driving back to the other camp. Virginia was singing a song that went: "I killed a *kanga* in the
donga with a *panga, olé!*" which didn't make a whole lot of
sense but had a nice lilt to it and meant that she had slain a
guinea fowl in a dry arroyo with a big knife. I expect we were
all pretty silly at times.

I remembered our nice old man and shot him a big, tough,
ugly-horned impala ram just as we came up to his compound,

and he seemed properly grateful. We paid off our Wa-Arusha 'Ndrobo and sent him off into the bush again, looking only a little less miserable than before. We came up to the high cutbank, and I waded the freezing river again for the last time, staggering and slipping and sliding, and went to the main camp and set up the typewriter. Virginia corralled Juma and got busy turning her hair from black to white again, with a sizable gathering of the local maids gazing fascinated at the operation. There was more and more ham coming out in Juma as he gained in proficiency as a hairdresser. Old Juma already had half a dozen wives staked out in little teashops and other commercial ventures, just to keep them away from the Kikuyu cabdrivers when he was out in the bush. I could already see a new shop in the making, with a sign saying: "*Monsieur Juma. Coiffeuses élégantes.*"

While I was writing we had a visitor. It was Abdullah. Abdullah, the one-eyed dude. He was bareheaded this time. His hair was oiled with a perfume you could smell clean back to Dodoma. He was sweating some and the oil was running down his forehead. He was wearing sandals and a skirt and a Norfolk jacket and a bigger dagger. His fat stooge was now playing gunbearer. He was bearing a single-barreled shotgun guaranteed to blow up within the next week. They had been hunting, Abdullah said, making me a present. The present was a big, vicious, ugly Muscovy duck. Another stooge, a young boy stooge, had it on a leash. This was the ugliest duck I ever saw. He was even uglier than Abdullah, and when the Anointed One suggested that we have him for supper, Jinny muttered that if it came to a hard choice she personally would rather eat Abdullah. He figured to be both younger and tenderer. We gave the duck to the cook, with a short prayer that it would escape.

We were up reasonably early the next day and piled into

the back of the truck. We hunted the high rocky road all morning and saw nothing except a few scraggly guinea fowl. Abdullah the Mighty Hunter was with us, with two gun-bearers for one gun, a bottle of tea, and a sack of hard candy. Abdullah had on his big-game clothes now—a pith helmet, a silk shirt, gabardine shorts, and fancy embroidered sandals. Today's ceremonial sword had a tassel on it. Abdullah was a talker. He never quit. He told us about his children and his wives and his girl friends and his boy friends. He told us all about kudu. He showed us the way to the salt lick, about ten miles out of camp. It was a good lick. It had some animal droppings and a few kudu hoofmarks and some rhino tracks and one curled kudu horn from a good bull, since the horn was over fifty inches. We blinded and waited until after black dark, but nothing came to muzzle at the salty ooze that bubbled greenly up from the soft, white, rock-studded sand.

We were up there in the black dawn the next day, too, and nothing came until about ten, when Harry saw a small herd feeding down from the hills in our general direction. Harry was high on a hilltop, while I was low at the edge of the lick. It seemed we would have some luck at last. The band of kudu was within five or six hundred yards and feeding stead-ily when some transient honey hunters decided the time had come to burn off the plain. They set fire to the grasses, and that was the end of that.

Harry came scowling down from the hill, and on the way home, heading down the steep clay road, we jumped two youngsters who whipped across the road ahead of us and then paused, barked, and dashed across the road again. We were watching the juveniles without getting down from the truck when the biggest, oldest, heaviest-horned, longest-horned grandfather of all kudu burst from the bush, cantered down the road ahead of us, stopped in the middle of the road to let us look at him, and then hopped blithely off the road to stand not twenty feet from it in a patch of low bush. This was a kudu. This was a real kudu.

As he had run along, his horns swept back and passed his rump. Kidogo muttered to Harry: "Bigger than Bwana Bowman's."

A shootable mature kudu bull is forty-five or forty-six inches long in the horns. A good kudu is forty-eight. A fine kudu is fifty. A miraculous kudu is anything over fifty. Bowman's kudu was fifty-nine inches, a giant, a Primo Carnera, a freak. And this kudu, this kudu now standing, waiting, ears cocked in the bush, was bigger than Bowman's. He would go sixty or sixty-one. This was the Goliath of the kudu family. And he was right there, a couple hundred yards down the road, waiting to be collected. God was smiling again.

Harry and I soared over the side of the truck. We crouched and sneaked down the side of the road. Then God laughed right out loud. This kudu, this ancestor of all kudu, had chosen the only baobab tree within five miles to duck behind. We could hear him move in the bush. But between us and him, wherever he moved, he always kept a naobab tree about as big as a railroad roundhouse. No baobab, one kudu in the bag, one record in the books, one head for the wall, and away we go, singing and scattering flowers. One baobab in the way, no kudu, no head for the wall, no record for the books.

There wasn't anything for us to do but dash around the tree and try to belt him on the fly. We crept round it, and he had chosen his bush well. He was in it, but you couldn't see him in it. Then he caught our scent and saw us and he barked like a great Dane and went through the heavy thorn like a herd of elephants. We never saw him. We just heard him, those horns clattering as they tore holes in the intermeshed thorn.

"We haven't lost him yet," Harry said. "There's a cut there between the hills. He'll go out one end or the other. We'll take the high end of the pass and send the boys round to the other end to beat him. He almost has to come out our way, because he'll be heading for the cloud country. We'll have to hurry, though."

We hopped back in the truck. It deposited us at the top of a high hill. Harry spoke rapidly to Kidogo, and the truck departed for the other end of the draw. We fought our way over three or four hills and valleys and finally wound up in a commanding position at the high end of the draw. We sat down on rocks and lit cigarettes. The wind carried the smoke directly over our heads. We were even getting a break from the wind.

We waited and chatted in low voices, marveling at the size of this old grandfather and not daring to hope he'd come past us, although there really wasn't any other way for him to come. The hell there wasn't. In an hour the boys showed up, having beaten clear through and up the draw. Kidogo and Adam had seen him. Grandpa had gone straight up over the top. He didn't need draws or coulees to run in. This was a real alpine-type kudu. He saw a mountain and he just ran straight up the side of it, shook his scornful tail, and aimed for Rhodesia. We hunted him for the rest of the week. We never saw him again.

There were others. There was the good bull that Harry took a bang at from a range of no more than a hundred yards as the kudu stood proudly in a clump of bush, his chest and neck and head making a queer, camouflaged extension of the thorn. You could hear the bullet hit with a whack like a beater on a carpet. The bull went over. Or seemed to go over, just as my youngster had toppled. We shrieked again and ran to where he had stood. *Hapana doumi.* He was not there. We looked for blood, sure that he was hard hit and that we could track him easily. *Hapana damu.* No blood. No tracks, either, except the scars where he had jumped. The scars were there. A fresh pile of dung was there. Some hairs from his hide were caught in the thorn. He had been there. We had seen him there. We had heard the gun go off and heard the bullet strike, but there was no kudu and no blood and no tracks. *Hapana.* Three hours of hard work, six people tracking, six experts peering and spooring and sniffing, and no nothing at all. *Hapana kapisa.*

"I'm licked," Harry said. "I am not the best shot in the world, but I can hit a running lion or a charging leopard and I can shoot a Tommy at four or five hundred yards with no scope. I am dead on the chest of a bull kudu standing at eighty or ninety yards and I hear the bullet smack and see the bull go over, and when I get up to where he was there isn't any bull and there isn't any blood and there aren't any tracks leading out. Where the hell did he go? To heaven?"

"The angels came and took him away," I said. "He is riding up in heaven on a thornbush cloud. How the hell do I know what happened to him? You're the expert. At least we *find* the ones I shoot, immature bulls or not. They are on the ground when we come up to them. Are you sure you're a real professional hunter? After all, you got us lost at Ikoma and——"

"All right, all right," Harry said. "Let's go back to camp and eat that bloody duck of Abdullah's as penance. I can't think of a harder penance, can you?"

"Not even in a joke," I said. "Let's go report another futile expedition to the *memsaab.* I haven't seen her to speak to in about a week."

Ali had tenderized Abdullah's offering through incantation, prayer, and about two days of steady boiling. It was very tender and surprisingly good, but tempered by the fact that Abdullah came to call in his party clothes. Mohammedan or not, he seemed to expect an invitation to drinks, which was not offered. Harry is not the kind of Englishman who has the locals in to tea. Especially if the locals are Somalis.

Of course we hunted the road some more. We hunted the licks some more. Some 'Ndrobo came in one day with lofty stories of a fabulous lick they knew, where the *tendalla* were so *mingi sana* that only a bow and arrow was considered a sporting weapon. After a long and tough trek afoot we wound up at their fabled lick. It was the same old tired lick we had been patronizing for a week, and driving up to within a quarter mile of it. Some 'Ndrobo.

"They'd starve to death in a butcher shop," Selby said contemptuously.

We saw a lot more kudu, some good, some medium, some poor. We never got another shot. There was the one last, good, big bull we located, but he played baobab-around-the-rosy with us as his cousin had done, using the only other baobab in the locality as his operating base.

On the fifteenth day we said the hell with it and packed up. We weren't having any fun any more, the kind of fun we had had earlier. It had become a grim game, a monotonous business of riding the roads and climbing the hills, watching and waiting and always being bored and disappointed. The camp talk had degenerated into a one-track business of kudu, kudu, kudu, what we'd done wrong and what the kudu had done to thwart us. Virginia said that as companions we rated somewhere between deaf mutes and professional athletes.

"If I ever hear the word 'kudu' again I intend to scream and not stop screaming for a full day," she said.

We paid a call on Abdullah, who was got up in a red fez and a bolero jacket and jodphurs, with a purple-and-gold sash and something very heavy and fancy in the way of bangles. He had changed his scent and his pomade, and his hair was very artistically done. He had changed his earrings too. He seemed sorry to see us go, because he still had hopes of being asked to dinner.

We drove the jeep into Iringa, ahead of the lorry, and went to the little hotel to wait for the truck to labor and wheeze up the hills behind us. They had real scotch whisky at the bar and flush toilets. Virginia was so carried away by the bar and the flush toilets that she got rather uproariously loaded on no more than half a dozen scotches. She said later that it wasn't the whisky. It was the reaction from too much kudu. Kudu poisoning, she called it.

When the boys came up they were jabbering. I knew what they were saying without understanding it.

"They say they jumped the biggest kudu bull they've ever seen," Harry says. "On the road behind us. Chege says he was bigger than the huge old boy we lost behind the baobab. How about it? Make you angry?"

"I couldn't care less," I said. "Let's have the bartender throw another double at us and then let's go back down to Kiteti and shoot us an oryx before we go home. I'm all caught up on kudu."

"You know," Harry said, "if you ever write this I have a title for you. It's *Earned but Not Collected.*"

"It's a good title," I said. "I'll try to remember it."

Chapter 14

SOME PEOPLE say I look a little like Ernest Hemingway used to look when he was younger. At least I have a mustache. At least I read the man when I was much less aged and learned a lot thereby. I also followed his habits. He liked Cuba. So did I. We used to drink together, before the war, in different parts of the Floridita Café, which Constante runs off the square in Havana. I never spoke to Hemingway, who would be sitting behind the potted palm in the corner of the café, peering like a nearsighted professor over his glasses and reading the *Diario*, drinking the best daiquiris in the world, and looking very wise and schoolmasterish.

I liked the *cangrejos moros* that the maestro liked, and I

liked all the food next door at the Zaragozana, and I liked his
good friends around the town. I liked how he wrote and
what he had done and the things he was interested in. I liked
it that he had been to Africa, where I had not been. I liked it
that he had seen bulls that I had not seen, and that he had
married women I had not married. Also that he had divorced
women I had not enjoyed the opportunity of divorcing.

But I was very young and full of pride. I was too proud to
walk twenty feet to talk to Papa. I was too proud to ask Constante to introduce me. I couldn't go over to this man and say
that I was a writer too. Not especially since I toiled for the
same firm that had paid Papa's way through Paris when he
was learning to work with a typewriter. I was very possibly
making more money at that time than he was making when
he was learning how it felt to be young in Paris.

But you cannot just walk up to Ernest Hemingway and say,
"*Que tal*, Papa, I am a writer too," or "I am a *turista* who admires your stuff." So for two weeks I sat and looked at the
gran maestro and wished something would happen so we
could have a drink together, because there were so many
things I wanted to ask him. Nothing happened.

The time passed and a war came and I got mixed up in the
gunnery end of that one and made several experiments into
fear. I became an authority on fear, real fear and imagined
fear. We were hit once by a German and again by lightning.
We dodged mines and got bombed and watched friends dis-
integrate. That was real fear. A worse fear was seeing a naval
battle at night—a battle that did *not* actually happen—and
seeing a German E-boat run through the ranks of a convoy
while being bombed by a plane, and learning that although
everybody saw it there wasn't any E-boat there and no plane
was bombing the E-boat that wasn't actually there anyhow.

Then the war was over and I began to write again and I

went back to the Africa I knew now and loved and went to Spain and Mexico and saw bullfights. I shot quail and drank whisky and went back to Australia to see if the women were still pretty, and they were. I shot Nauru deer in the high hills of Kiawe Nui on Molokai and pheasants in Connecticut and ducks in Louisiana. I busted a general out of·Italy and chased a hoodlum out of Havana and imagined myself to be a hell of a fellow, always in the Hemingway pattern.

One day I looked around and realized that I was in Tanganyika, shooting lions with the same basic string of blacks that Hemingway had used fifteen years before. I had a handsome white hunter, just like the late Francis Macomber had a handsome white hunter, and a pretty wife I hoped wasn't going to shoot me in the head for convenience. I hoped I wasn't going to acquire gangrene or get chewed up, either. I am not Gregory Peck.

This day I was crawling after buffalo, which I did not really want to do. I am bitterly afraid of buffalo, the big, rope-muscled wild ox with horns like steel girders and a disposition to curdle milk. I had walked through a swamp that was full of water and snakes and rhinos. I had crawled and stumbled over two young mountains to reach a herd of buffalo that I didn't really want to associate with. I had already shot a buffalo and figured that was one thing I wouldn't have to do any more of. But Selby has a mad affection for the *mbogo*, a sort of perverse love and a completely unmanageable fascination for the big beasts. We had come back to the high plains under the Rift escarpment by Kiteti, back from the fruitless kudu expedition, back for one more try at rhino. And there was no rhino. But on the steep side of one of the hills reaching up to the escarpment there was a sprinkling of tiny black worms.

Adam, the Wakamba gunbearer, pointed. "*Mbogo*," he said,

and I could already feel my stomach start to knot. It was the same feeling I used to get when the lookout on the bow would reach for the phones and ring the bridge. "Periscope," he would say. "Periscope bearing so-and-so many degrees off the starboard bow," as if he were pleased at having done me a favor.

Harry looked at the buffalo through the glasses.

"There's a damned good bull in that herd," he said. "Better than the one you've got by six inches at least. I think we'd best go and collect him."

I didn't say anything. I just prayed inside me and hoped we would not have to crawl too far in order to scare me to death. I don't know what there is about buffalo that frightens me so. Lions and leopards and rhinos excite me but don't frighten me. But that buff is so big and mean and ugly and hard to stop, and vindictive and cruel and surly and ornery. He looks like he hates you personally. He looks like you owe him money. He looks like he is hunting you. I had looked at a couple of thousand of him by now, at close ranges, and I had killed one of him, and I was scareder than ever. He makes me sick in the stomach, and he makes my hands sweat, and he dries out my throat and my lips.

These buff were a herd of about two hundred, feeding up the edge of the hills below the escarpment and following a vague trail that meandered up the side and led eventually straight over the top. They were about two miles away, and it was walking all the way, walking when you could and crawling when you couldn't, and slipping on the loose stones and fighting through the wait-a-bit thorn, puffing and blowing and sweating and cursing in the hot sun in the middle of the day. And finally wiggling along on your belly, pushing the big gun ahead of you, sweat cascading and burning into your eyes, with your belly constricted into a tight hard kernel and your hands full of thorns and your heart two-blocked into your throat. And then the final, special Selby technique of leaping to your feet and dashing with a whoop into the middle of the herd, running at the bull, and depending on that thirty-second bewilderment to hold the buffalo stiff, like cattle, before you shot and hoped you hit him good so you wouldn't have to follow him into that awful thick bush he was certain to head for. And wait for you in it.

We crossed the mountains and were in the crawling, wiggling stage now. We had a good wind and the buff were just a few hundred yards ahead, looking blue-black and clean, as mountain buffalo are, instead of scabby and scaly and mud-splotched like the lowland fellows, or rusty red and scrubby like the herd that hung around Majimoto at Manyara. There were two good bulls—the old herd chieftain with a fine sweep of deeply rutted, heavy horns, and a younger gentleman, almost as good, who would be pushing the old boy out of the mob one of these days. Harry and I presumed to save him the trouble of a fight.

You judge a buffalo by the configuration and curl of horn as well as by the distance between his horn tips, and also by the depth of the horn boss as it rides his forehead, and by the degree of close-fitting joining of the two segments of boss as it comes together like a part in the middle of an Italian hoofer's head. Our bloke was very much all right on all counts. The boss covered his skull like a helmet, and the dividing line was as tight as a piece of string. The horns were shaped very well, not crooking in too much, and worn down evenly at the tips. He would be forty-eight inches or better, and forty-eight inches between those tips is a lot of buffalo. My first fellow was only forty-three and a bit, and he was impressive enough for me.

We were in the herd now, creeping on our bellies and pulling ourselves forward by digging elbows into sharp rocks. The buffalo were grazing unconcernedly all around us. The herd bull was lying down, resting, and there were a couple of cows obscuring him. It is a difficult sensation to describe, to be surrounded by two hundred animals weighing from eighteen hundred to twenty-five hundred pounds each, animals as testy and capricious of temper as stud fighting bulls, capable of killing you just as dead accidentally in a stampede as on purpose in a charge.

A buffalo close up is not handsome. His body is bulky, short-legged, and too long for symmetry. He smells of mud and dung and old milk. His patchy hide is scabby and full of flat ticks. Bits of his own excrement cling to him. Dirty moss grows on his horns, which are massive enough to bust everything up inside you if he even hits you a slight swipe with the flat, and sharp enough to put a hole in you big enough to hide a baseball bat in, and dirty enough to infect an army. He has the big bull's cloven hoofs, for he is a true unaltered ox and the progenitor of the Spanish fighting bull, and he delights to dance on your carcass until there is nothing much around but spatters of blood and tatters of flesh. Even his tongue is a weapon. It is as rough and harsh as a wood rasp. If you climb a tree or an anthill on the *mbogo* he will crane his ugly neck and lick the meat off you for as far up as he can reach. His tongue erodes your flesh as easily as a child licks the point off an ice-cream cone.

As I crawled along just behind Selby, with Adam and Kidogo following me, I was thinking these things. I knew a lot about buffalo by now. I knew how fast they are, despite their apparently lumbering gallop, how swiftly they can turn, how they stop cold on a dime, and how they go through bush at a spurt—bush that an elephant wouldn't recommend. I knew how much lead they would soak and keep coming, especially after being wounded. You may kill him easily with one bullet, but if you don't, the next fourteen .470s serve mostly as a minor irritant. And you cannot run away from a wounded buffalo. You have to stand and take him as he is, shooting at his nostrils as he comes at you with his head high and his horns swept back, his neck stretched and his cold eyes unblinking at you. You shoot for the nose and hope it gets into the brain, because if you shoot too high the bullets bounce off his massive horn boss like rubber balls off walls in a New York stick-ball game. And if he keeps on coming, like the one that got up on Bob Maytag a few months before, he comes with a hole under one eye and a hole under the other, and then somebody like Selby had best have one serious slug left to shoot him at four or five feet and catch him when he falls. When this one fell with his eye finally shot out they picked fifteen 500-grain bullets out of his carcass, all of them enough to kill him separately, but the first fourteen unable to kill him collectively.

A leopard will possibly claw up more people and is faster and tougher to hit when he lies back on your trail and begins to stalk you, but you can change his charge with a shotgun blast and he dies very easily, as all cats with thin hides and delicate bones and soft flesh die. You can change an elephant's mind, too, by shooting him in the face, and you can change a rhino's mind by shooting him anywhere that he's biggest. But the reason my friend *Mbogo* is generally rated as the toughest piece of all the African furniture is that he is a single-minded type. You got to kill him to discourage him. He scents very good and sees very far and hears marvelously. He keeps the egrets around to eat his ticks off him but not because he needs them for anything but ticks and society. The rhino and his tickbird sentries are another matter. The *faro* uses birds for eyes, and the ticks come in as a bonus for the bird-dog job they do for the rhino. The buff really fancies the snowy egrets because their white plumage looks nice and decorative on his black back. They are the only pretty thing about him.

God, as I was crawling and creeping and cursing and sweating, how I remembered all the buffalo I had met and the first one I had shot. Maybe the reason I was so sensitive about buff was that I took two stampedes and a dozen stalks before I finally shot one, and I had been in three more stampedes since. *This bloody Selby,* I said. *Him and his fascination for this awful animal. Him and his get-up-and-run-yelling technique of making the last fifty yards at a gallop, standing and shooting in the middle of the herd while the animals snort and explode past you, not wanting to run over you but not caring if they do run over you.* They wall their eyes with mad panic and stream past you, each one bigger than a pair of Brahman bulls, each one with two inches of skin thickness to cover the steel cables that make his muscles an armor plating, each one with enough obscene vitality to run for five miles shot through the heart.

As I crept along on my belly I remembered Mbogo Moja, the first one. We had stalked across a swamp and I was bitterly out of breath, the stomach muscles jumping and a piercing pain in the chest and a great tremble in the fingers that wasn't a fear-shake but a nervous reaction to fatigue. We walked as far as we could walk, with the long withes of grass tripping you at every step, and then here suddenly was an old bull and his *askari*—an expelled herd bull, driven off from the cows by his son, with a neophyte to run his errands for him and learn all his wisdom so that someday he could go back and kick the bejesus out of the reigning bull who had driven Papa off from his wives and his family security.

So we crawled this one, too, like you creep geese in Louisiana, stopping and freezing occasionally when the *askari* raised his head to stare at you with a colder stare than any actress ever wasted on an enemy.

This *askari* was mightily nervous. He felt that everything wasn't happy. He kept feeding away, edging off to the nastiest patch of thornbush in Tanganyika, with the starting of the Serengeti reserve on the other side of the swamp. If the one we shot got hurt and went across he would not only be sick and angry and venomous in his sickness, but he would also be illegal.

We crept to a bush and froze behind it, and there were the animals, fifty yards away and moving steadily out of range. Harry had his hand palm down behind him, and suddenly he lifted it in a curling beckon. I crawled, still blowing, up to his shoulder. He turned his head slightly and whispered.

"We're not going to get any closer," he said. "That *askari* is nervous and leading the old boy away. You better bust him now, although he's too far off for my pleasure. Try to take him just where his neck comes down into his chest."

Selby, when he is working with dangerous animals, always wears two stalks of extra bullets sticking like cigarettes from his right hand. Harry had said: *Do what I do.* I had two stalks of extra bullets sticking out between the second and third fingers of *my* right hand. At this time it had not occurred to me that Selby was left-handed.

I got up on one knee and sighted low into the old bull's chest, and the heavy Westley-Richards settled handily in balance and I squeezed off the trigger, and then the bull was gone and I was on the ground, my nose full of cordite fumes and my head full of chimes. Away off somewhere a gun exploded, and then there came a mournful bellow as morose as a hunting horn, a cow's horn, lonesome-sounding in the Carolina woods when a Negro cropper is lost and blowing hard on the horn to keep himself from being frightened blond until he finds the dirt road again.

Selby was standing now, spraddle-legged, with his hands on his hips and looking down at me.

"For Christ sake," he said, jerking his head toward the wood. "*One* of you ought to get up."

From this I assumed the buffalo was down too. It appeared that *right-handed* shooters are not supposed to store their spare ammunition in their shooting hand. In the effort to emulate Selby it never occurred to me that the guy was natural southpaw, and that bullets contained in a shooting hand would ride back against the second trigger and touch off the other barrel simultaneously, loosing 150 grains of cordite against your face.

"You all right?" Harry asked. "What happened?"

"Both barrels," I said. "At once. Dropped me. Did I hit him?"

"You knocked him tail over tin cup," Harry said. "He turned completely over. Then he got up and departed."

"I thought I heard somebody else shoot," I said. "Away over yonder."

"Me," Selby said. "This bugger was flat out for the bush. I'd not taken the time to check his blood pressure, you know. I didn't know how good you hit him. I thought I'd best break his back before he got stuck into that patch of bush. Very nasty in there. Actually I shouldn't have bothered. Hear that bellow? He's dying now. You'll find you got his heart. They don't bellow from a spine shot. Hope you don't mind, old boy, but once in a while a little collaboration saves all hands a lot of trouble. I know how to pull a sick one out of the bush. But it's just that I don't fancy it as a recreation."

We walked up to the buffalo. He was dying, bellowing,

making mournful sounds, and trying to drag himself toward us.

"Slip one bullet into the gun," Harry said. "I still don't trust that sear. Take him just behind the horns in the back of the head. You know what I always keep saying. The dead ones kill us."

I slid a single bullet into the right-hand barrel of the .470 and squinted carefully at the back of this boy's neck, where the muscle roll humped out like the back of the neck on a retired prize fighter. I was gun-shy. I pulled instead of squeezing, but the bullet went in and poor old *Mbogo* stretched his neck forward to its full length. Blood crept out of his nostrils and he was dead. Dead and ugly. Uglier dead than alive, and four times as ferocious.

My God, but he was immense. He was muddy from rolling, and the ticks were working on his scaly hide and it was a hot day and the flies were coming down. Maybe he was only forty-three inside the horns, but to me he looked like a hell of a lot of bull lying there in the yellow grass, his ugly face pointed straight out and the long striated lines of his horns and his ax-edged hoofs and the solid butting weight of his heavy casque of boss making him look like a contrived machine of destruction.

"Frightful brutes, aren't they?" Selby said. "We'll just take his marrow from a couple of legs. Tommy Shevlin says it tastes like *pâté de foie gras*. Rest of him too tough to eat. Except the tongue's wonderful. Boys'll take his belly fat, and we can make a tobacco pouch out of his scrotum. 'Less you want his hoofs for ash trays, we've had him. Except the horns are lovely. Not big but beautiful. I'm interested to see what you did to him with the first shot. I think you'll find you wrecked him, but I couldn't know that before you touched off the second fusillade, could I?"

Adam and Kidogo unsheathed a *panga* and a sharp skinning knife and started the post-mortem. They took out a rib section, which they would eat themselves, and they removed the heart and the kidneys and the liver. They snipped the fat from around his intestines, and we finally burrowed into his chest cavity in the interests of science.

This *mbogo* had accepted a .470 bullet, five hundred grains of hard-nose bullet powered by seventy-five grains of cordite. He had taken it through the jugular and into the heart, where it smashed all the major arteries and crushed the whole top of the heart. It had ranged backward through him and destroyed the lungs. When we opened him up about ten gallons of black lung blood gushed out. Yet he had gotten up off the ground with this terrible wound and taken off as blithely for the bush as if we had pinked him in the fanny with a .22.

"Nobody ever believes it," Harry said. "Sometimes I don't. But these creatures are damned near indestructible. Look there at the mess you made with that bloody cannon. And remember that he was two hundred yards away and rolling off like a steam engine when I popped his spine for him and put him down. He'd have gone half a mile and still had enough gas left to scare us green when he came from a piece of bush not big enough to hide a hare."

"I don't ever want to shoot another one," I said. "This is all the *mbogo* I need this day, or any other. Like the *memsaab* says: '*Hapana taka piga mbogo lio.*' Nor any other day. Any man with one buffalo doesn't need another. It's like what David Green says. A man with a Rumanian for a friend doesn't need an enemy. David's a Rumanian."

"You'll shoot another," Harry said. "You will always hunt buff. It's a disease. You've killed a lion and you don't care whether you ever take another. But you will hunt buffalo until you are dead, because there is something about them that makes intelligent people into complete idiots. Like me. They are the only beast in Africa that can make my stomach turn like it rolls over when you've had too much grog and don't know whether the bed will stay there for you. You'll hunt more *mbogo*, all right. Kidogo! *Taka headskin kwa bwana.*"

That was a long time ago as we measure time in Africa. That was practically in another century. There was another lion and a leopard and a cheetah and all sorts of the common stuff and some rhino we didn't get and some kudu that we butched and a lot of travel in between it. There was a stampede in between it. Like yesterday.

We were driving back to the camp in the latish afternoon, with the oryx and the cheetah done now and out of the way. Where the road dips low and the hills begin to slide down away from the escarpment there is a big swamp, a long, wide flat, full of high reeds, with the hills moving up on the other side into a tiptilted half bowl of land. This was just a few miles away from Kiteti, where the camp was pitched and where the hippo grunted in the front yard. This was two turns in the road and one baobab tree away from camp and a *bathi* and one of Dr. Ruark's nutritious deliciouses, the bone-building gin.

The sun had slipped a little in the sky and the evening nip was coming into the air when Harry slowed the Rover to an easy stop. Across the marsh, only a quarter mile away, the big fat black worms were crawling down the hill.

"*Mbogo,*" Harry said. "My sainted aunt, *what* a head on the big fellow."

They were probably the same herd that I was working on this moment, and thinking about now, but out of focus a few miles and feeding very quietly down the side of the hill and into the swamp. I was bitter enough.

"I know," I said. "*Kwenda.* Let us go and collect it. Let us struggle through the marsh and go and collect it. By all means. *Pese pese.*"

"Right," Harry said. "I was just going to mention that possibly we should go and collect it. Haven't much time, though. Past five now. What we do we will have to do in a hurry. *Kwenda. Pese pese.*"

We fought through the high grasses, in some spots eight

and ten feet tall, and treacherously mucky underfoot. We slipped and sloshed and stumbled and fell and bogged. The mosquitoes were in very good form. By the time we'd got across the swamp the buff had all fed down off the slope and were in the grass. We scouted carefully around them. You could see where they fed by where the egrets fluttered, zooming up into the sky and returning to settle on the animals' backs. One time we got too close on the way across. An old bull, his horns worn down by use to fists, was feeding out from the main mob and I almost tripped over him. Again the wind was right and he never cared that we were there. Big knob-billed geese flew over us and honked. Teals dipped and whizzed around us. We hit the far shore finally, wet and bug-bitten, and stumbled along its rocky outcrop to a big thorn tree. Harry went up it like a monkey. He could see from there. He could see very well from there. He was up the tree a long time.

He came down.

"How are your legs feeling?" he said. "Are you up to a bit of a sprint?"

"As up as I'm ever apt to be," I said. "Where are we running and from whom?"

"Look," he said soberly. "I don't kid you much. There are two hundred buffalo out there in that high grass. They are feeding down toward the neck of the marsh. We have to get back the same way we came. It's wet in there and sticky. There are going to be about five hundred yards where we have to run. We have to run in order to get past two hundred buffalo. If the wind twists and they catch a scent of us they may stampede. Charge they won't. You know this. But in that high grass, if they all start running we won't be visible to them until they're already swarming over us. That's why I want to know if you're willing to chance a run for it."

"What happens if they do take off?" I asked Harry. "What do you do when two hundred buff come bearing down on you?"

"I would *try* to shoot one," Harry said. "I would try to shoot one so we could climb up on him so's the others could see us and run around us. It would call for a bit of lucky shooting to drop one so we could use him in a hurry. You've seen how hard they are to stop."

It was nearly six when we headed back through the marsh where the car was and camp was and booze was. Off to the right as we slipped through the reeds you could hear the buffalo chewing and snorting and grunting. You could see the egrets and hear them squawk. We were doing fine and were nearly out of the thigh-high water and into the muck when we walked right up on the back of an outgrazing bull buffalo. He let out a large bellow and took off, galloping awkwardly, out to stir up the animals and alert the town. You could hear the sudden loud, harsh rustle in the reeds when he alerted the town.

"Run," Selby said in the smallest and most distinct voice I ever heard a man use. "Run. That way."

We ran. We ran through the stinking ooze, tripping over the long grasses, hearts hitting hard in chests and breath gasping in rattles, and over to the right other things were running. Two hundred buffalo were running. They weren't scenting us because we were still downwind, but old Uncle Wilbur with the knobby horns had passed the word and two hundred buffalo were galloping like a spread formation on a football field. They ran and we ran. You couldn't see them run because the grass was twice as tall as they were, but you could hear them breaking it down as they pounded steadily through it.

We reached some reasonably high ground and some shorter

grass. As we hit it fifty buffalo, the right wing of the spread, passed just aft of us at full gallop, something under fifty feet behind us. I was completely winded. Harry was short of breath. We still had the black boys with us.

"Jesus loving God," Harry said.

I didn't say anything. Kidogo said something in Nandi. Adam said something in Wakamba.

"I'd not like to have to do that again," Harry said. "Bit of a near thing there at the end."

We walked toward the other shore. I was walking slowly. Harry was out in front by twenty feet. All of a sudden his cupped hand reached out and drew me up to him. This one I wasn't really anxious to believe.

The damned buffalo had run the length of the marsh and had turned in formation and charged again, this time straight into our scent. They were standing like a Roman battalion, feet firmly rooted, heads proudly high, and noses sniffing, no more than twenty yards in front of Selby. I came up behind him on the run.

"Him on the left, by the cow," Selby said. "That one. The good one. Not the first one. The second bull."

I was gasping like a boated fish when I threw the .470 up just as the entire battalion wheeled to run the other way. I went for the big fellow's rear end, having read somewhere that if you shot at the root of the tail you either broke his back or discommoded his kidneys. The gun said bang and the buff went away and there was no whunk after the sound of the shot. It was almost dark now.

"Thank the Lord," Selby said reverently.

"Thank the Lord what?" I said peevishly.

"Thank the Lord you didn't hit him," Selby said. "Or else we'd have to go and find him in the dark."

"This has been quite a day," I said.

"*Ndio, bwana,*" Kidogo said, although he had not been asked.

Virginia was waiting for us when we came into the camp in the soft black night, the fires going cheerfully and what seemed to be a gin bottle on the table.

"I don't know why you let me do these things," I said. "Why the hell don't you keep me home like any decent wife would if she loved her husband?"

Virginia looked at us, thorn-torn, wet to the waist, tsetse-bit, mosquito-chewed, suicidally tired, sunburned, and out of humor.

"Buffalo again," she said. "Idiots."

I was thinking about this as we crawled into the middle of the herd, the herd of buffalo I didn't want anything else to do with ever, ever again.

We had to pause for a long time behind a big thornbush, waiting for the herd bull to get up and for the cows to move away off from in front of him. I got some little breath back and summed the situation. A big fat tsetse was biting me on the bite another big fat tsetse had created as an art form earlier. The sweat was running down in solid sheets, the salt of it burning my eyes. Grass seeds were secreted in my socks and chewing on my ankles like bugs. I had more thorns in my crown than any man needs. This was costing me a minimum of a hundred dollars a day after transportation.

At this particular moment an old cow with an evil expression, a cow I had not seen, looked right over the bush I was hiding behind. She looked at me cynically and hostilely.

"Woof!" the old cow said. "Garrumph!"

I got up on my feet. I had the gun with me.

"God *damn* Ernest Hemingway," I said bitterly, and when the bull lurched up, crooked-kneed, I walloped him. The bull went down. He got up again. "God *damn* Ernest Heming-way," I said again. "This has gone far enough." I squeezed on the bull again, and the gun was jammed. Then I heard Harry shoot, and the bull went over. He got up. He took off. All the buffalo took off. It was sort of like crossing Park Avenue against a light. Animals went past us like taxicabs.

"We killed him all right," Selby said. "We turned him over twice. Why don't we have a cigarette and give him a little chance to get slightly sick before we go after him?"

The cigarette tasted brassy in my mouth. Harry was looking cheerful again. The boys were not. Nor was I. I had a hunch a compliment was coming. It came.

"Well," Harry said, "let's go and pull him out by the tail."

This was the compliment. This, the accolade. This was what I had been waiting for. When a dangerous animal is wounded, especially a buffalo, the professional generally sends the client back to the car, with a gunbearer to hold his hand, while the hunter goes into the thick bush and earns his pay by finishing off the angry animal the client has wounded. If the client is a very good and deserving client, the hunter may ask him politely if he'd like to go along and share the fun. If the client is a very, very good client, he gets a compliment.

"Let's go get him," Harry said, as if he assumed there was no question about it. I gave him a brilliant answer and hated myself for it.

"Okay," I said.

We checked the loads on the rifles and we dived into the bush. Adam and Kidogo were spooring ahead of us, crouched, sniffing like dogs on a scent. There were lots of places in the bush for the buffalo to be, grown-over dongas and patches of tangled impossibilities where any buffalo in his senses would stop and wait for killable people to come by. The bloody dung and the bright gouts of heart blood always led into a cul-desac and always led out again. This was a peculiar buffalo. He never stopped once to bleed and sulk and build his hatred into a fever. He moved. He was a traveling man.

I found out all about me on this little *shauri*. I found out more about me than I found out in three years of war. I found out that I was a very brave man, because a man as scared as I was, poking my way through that bush and spreading the underbrush ahead of me with a gun barrel while two black innocents worked as bird dogs and trusted me to finally face the issue of a bull buffalo bursting out of bush at under twenty yards—I found out just how far you can carry fear. I found out at what point just ordinary fear is overcome by the fear of fear, and where it changes into cold determination.

JU-88s, scream and all, never scared me like walking cautiously and slowly through this Tanganyikan bush, tracking, searching each clump of grass and blob of trees for twenty-five hundred pounds of vindictive force and evil plotting. Submarines and ghosts and footpads and buzz bombs never scared me like this—never scared me into a glandular panic in which myself walked outside myself and observed the other myself at work, cold and competent and functional out of pride of trust by two blacks and an English schoolboy.

We tracked this bull for three hours and over three miles of mountain and bush. Sometimes you would go for several hundred yards without a single holly berry of blood to tell you what you were chasing. We sometimes found a sudden spatter of the pinker lung blood. Then we would find nothing at all and would be forced to recast our steps, working backward on the trail until we picked up the old blood trail, and heading in a new direction. Harry and I walked this boy up to tangled retreats that he had to be in and wasn't in, but we had to sort him out of it as though he was in it.

For three hours my safety was off the gun and it was carried at half-port. For three hours I was mentally and psychologically girded to stand flat-footed and spraddle-legged and shoot this ton of fury until there wasn't anything else left to shoot him with. For three hours I was nerve-edged to a sort of super-perception, where every sound, every scent, every blade of grass, every rustle of breeze, every upturned stone and disturbed piece of earth meant something with a sick and angry buffalo on the end of it.

We found him dead.

I hated him for not being alive, for not charging, for not making me prove out loud what I had already proved inside me.

He was lying dead like a damned old cow in a pasture, under the shade of an acacia. The flies were already at him. He had taken my bullet and Harry's through the lower heart and he had gone the three miles in the three hours and he had not even contemplated standing to make a fight. He was an unworthy enemy and he had degraded me by working me up to this point of desperate courage and had then cheated me of the opportunity to prove my courage. He had cheated the two black boys of a chance to scuttle and sprawl in the sudden rush of fierceness, while their *bwanas* did with guns what white *bwanas* are supposed to do. Here he was, dead, carrion, a hunk of meat, a slow trickle dried on his nostrils, looking beautiful in the horn department and just as dead as the Democrats, for more years than the Democrats will be dead. The buzzards were coming down.

"*Hapana,*" Adam said, looking disgusted.

"*Ehhh,*" Kidogo said.

"Bloody fraud," Selby said. "Never knew one before who wouldn't at least entertain the idea of standing and fighting. This one didn't. Never even paused long enough for the blood to collect in a pool."

"God *damn* Ernest Hemingway *and* Francis Macomber,"
I said.

This was a big buff and a handsome buff, but the littler
one, the uglier one, is the one I got hanging on the wall.

Chapter 15

THE last days at Kiteti, after the buffalo, were an odd mixture of things. There was the business of the scopes all going out at once. I missed a bull oryx, as big as a house, three straight times, holding on his shoulder and never touching him.

"I can't be that bad by now," I said. "I was on that baby as solid as ever I was on anything. You saw me knock that hawk out of a tree with the same gun yesterday. He was two hundred if he was an inch. I think the scope's gone crook."

"We'll see," Harry said, and drove on, circling crabwise up the side of the tilted shallow hill that runs up to the Rift escarpment and then plunges sheerly down for thousands of feet to a flat valley. The blue of the sky was blinding, this day, the sun was a solid brass ball, and all over the country you could see the grass fires starting, darkening the sky early and lighting up the dusk with a rosy, far-seen glow. The time was all gone. We would be off and away tomorrow or the next day or the next, depending on luck.

We came onto a herd of Grants, slow-grazing, unafraid, new to the country, and just off a reserve somewhere. There was a fine herd ram.

"I say," Selby said. "Would you mind awfully if I shot this fellow? I've not much of a collection, but I'd like him in it."

"Fire away, Junior," I said. "I got all the Grants I'll ever need. Take the Remington and wallop him, as Harry Selby says to the clients."

The boys *toaed* the .30-'06 and Harry got out. He crept up on the Grant, getting to within thirty-five or forty yards and resting the rifle barrel on an anthill. He fired. There wasn't any bullet-hitting sound. The Grants took off, and Harry let them run. At about three hundred yards they stopped. Selby fired again, and the ram went over on his horns.

"*Kufa,*" the boys said in the car. We drove off to collect Selby, who had walked over to the Grant and was looking at the precise hole in the geometric center of the gazelle's shoulder.

"Bloody gun's a good foot high, maybe more," Harry said. "I held on this fellow at thirty yards and missed him clean. I held on the same spot at three hundred and clobbered him. Let's sight her in."

We sighted her in. She was fourteen inches high and a little left. No wonder I'd been blowing them past the oryx bull. I had been aiming high to get the spine if possible, because the oryx is awfully hard to kill, and had been slipping them over his back. We moved a couple of graticules, and now she was accurate again.

She wasn't accurate long. We knocked up another oryx, a fine one, in the low meadows where the Rift dwindles, and I held steady on this one from another anthill. He was standing broad to me, and the shot was alarmingly simple. The welcome whunk came after the boom. The oryx leaped and took off, running hard with his horns laid back.

"You shot his jaw off, for God's sake," Harry said. "What's the matter with you, anyhow?"

"The gun again," I said, and bitterly, because I hadn't wounded much and hate it. "Let's sight her."

"Can't be out again so soon."

"Sight the gun."

This time she was a foot and a half to the right and another foot high. This, the gun that had gone two months so accurately that the boys just said "*Nyama*"—meat—when the gun fired.

"Bloody gun is possessed of demons," Harry said. "Let's go put that poor *choroa* out of his misery."

We coursed the wounded animal and came up on him and I had two belts at him. I missed him cold. This time it was my fault. I was nervous and upset at wounding him and I didn't trust the gun any more and I was jerking. He ran and went over a high, stone-cobbled hill where Jessica couldn't follow, and crossed some mountains, and at dark we had to give him up. I felt like hell, sick and sorry and ashamed.

"Leopards'll have him in an hour," Harry said. "That's one consolation. Every cat in the community will be on that blood spoor. Quit feeling so bad. Everybody butches one now and then. You can't say we didn't try. And you can't blame yourself for the gun."

"These damned scopes," I said. "You can't trust them. But everything you shoot around here you shoot at some impossible distance, and most of us haven't got your eyes. I haven't, anyhow."

"Forget it," Harry said. "Let's go get some *chacula* and hit the sack."

"You're beginning to talk like a bloody Yank," I said.
"Evil associations," Harry said, grinning. *"Kwenda."*

We got a fine oryx the next morning. I had checked the
sights again, and when we jumped this big fellow running
hard up the side of the hill, I led him two lengths and a
shoulder high, aiming at where I thought he might be when
the bullet got there, and sure enough he was there. There was
that bone-hitting crack and he slowed to an amble. I belted
him again and down he went. He was sort of snarling in a
bovine fashion, and I had to bust him in the neck before we
could come up on him. They are one of the two or three
actually fierce antelopes if they're hurt, and will skewer you
with those sharp, straight, thin stickers they wear on their
heads. This was a fine oryx, one horn worn down a little from
digging, as they always are, but the best horn past thirty-one
inches, clean and black and sharp enough to go all the way
through anything it hit. He was buff-gray, lying there, a stripe
down his back, a black-and-white mosaic pattern on his legs,
his big stupid donkey face oddly striped with black and white.
They look bigger than they actually are, but they run five or
six hundred pounds and are as tough as a destroyer's skin.

The gun was in again, but she went out again that afternoon. This was the last full day, and I wanted Virginia to see
some of the lovely country she had missed. We were just
cruising, enjoying the fresh breeze and the blue sky and the
wonderful yellow plains against their backdrop of blue hill,
when Kidogo pointed and said:

"Kitambile."

There were two big cheetahs, both toms, in the middle of

the yellow plain. Thc bigger was sitting on an anthill, profiling six or eight feet off the ground. Against the fierce blue of the early-afternoon sky, sitting on a yellow anthill in a sea of yellow grasses, his hide white against the black spots, he was something.

"I'd say this is a definite bonus," Harry said. "A *shauri mungu* sent to repay you for the no rhino, the bad joke with the kudu, the way your gun's been acting up. Magnificent, isn't he? You can remember him like this. It's a sight very few people get to see. Get out and——"

"Wallop him," I said.

There wasn't anything to it. I got out, Harry tooled the Rover away, and I found another anthill. This was an eight-foot cheetah, about half dog, half cat, with a round cat's face, a long cat's tail, a spotted cat's hide, long dog's legs, and a dog's non-retractile claws. I put the scope's post on his shoulder at sixty yards, squeezed off, and missed him as clean as anybody ever missed anything. He went straight up in the air about six feet, turned a somersault, and hit the deck, running. I don't know if you ever saw a cheetah run, but when I slung another one at him on the gallop, I was just kidding myself. A cheetah flat out can catch anything that runs, and there are people who say that in a hurry he will be doing about seventy-five miles an hour. This lad was long gone.

The other lad wasn't. He got up, stretched, walked a short distance away, and lay down in the grass. I could see his round head and hard, clear cat's eyes and the outline of his body as he lay. This time I held the damned gun low, pointing at the ground in front of him. I shot, and he jerked and stayed there. I aimed at the ground and I broke his back, so high up that another inch would have missed him clean. Now this bloody machine was shooting *two* feet high. I unscrewed the telescopic sight and threw it away. Then I walked up on the big cat, who was snarling and crawling toward me, and put him quietly to sleep. He was beautiful and would look just fine with the lions and the lovely, lovely leopard, but what I had now was not just a hide and mask but a complete capsuling of a country and a day, with the heat of the sun and the cool of the breeze and the friendship of the boys and all I loved of Africa in it. This was as good a way to end it as any, not shooting any more, with the oryx neat and the cheetah neat and the damned traitorous scope thrown away to rust in the long yellow grasses.

The next morning the boys were knocking the camp apart. "Let's go look at it for a couple of hours," I said. "I'm not content to leave it alone. I'm like a woman in a war who follows you to the airport or the railroad station and wants to keep on saying good-by—stretching the agony and fattening off the misery until the last bitter second."

"Okay," Harry said. "We'll take the .470 in case we just happen to see a rhino, and the .375. You really ought to shoot another zebra or so for those hides your friends wanted, and the boys can use a little fresh meat for the trip home. Pity about that fat cow you wanted to buy them for a farewell feast. But Juma spent the whole day trying to buy one. You know these Masai. They'd rather sell their mother than a cow."

We rode over the hills, rode for the last time, looking for the last time at all the landmarks we knew so well now—the cobbled hills there, the green knobbly hills there, the long blue slopes there, the baobab here where the road crooks just before you turn in toward Kiteti, the rhino hill yonder, the lonely village of musky anthills, the broad yellow plain, the swamp where the buffalo were, the high hill where the other buffalo were, the sheer drop of the escarpment, the green strip of lush grass with the giraffes always standing solemn and ludicrous nearby, the little scrubby orchards of thorn, the fleets of ostriches running and pacing like trotting horses at Roosevelt Raceway in New York, the buzzards wheeling, the dew fresh on the drying grass, the flowers beginning to wither, the sand-grouse specks in the sky, the doves looping and moaning lugubriously, the brilliant flight of the jays, the guineas running, the francolin scratching like chickens in the low grass between the ruts the car made, the weaver birds swarming like bees and dipping and rolling like a tornado. This was what I wanted to remember of it more than what I'd shot, but the shooting was important, because the presence of the animals in my home would bring it back as fresh and sharp as the air of this last morning, this last, sad morning.

"*Punda,*" Harry said, pointing at a herd of zebra. "Best take one, anyhow, for the meat."

There was a big stallion loping along at the end of his herd. I scrambled out of the jeep with the .375 and stuck one up his broad fat fanny as he went away. It was a long shot, but I was shooting with open iron sights and I wasn't surprised to hear it hit and see him lurch and break into a furious gallop I knew this shot. It had gone in him and all the way forward through him and it had taken his heart. He would run five hundred yards and would be dead when we got up to him.

He ran the prescribed distance and folded as if somebody had skulled him with a hammer. We drove up to him and he lifted his head. Adam jumped out to sanctify him for the eating with his knife, to *hallal* him for Mohammed. Adam cut his throat.

Throat cut, heart-shot, this zebra was dead and sanctified and ready to be skinned and eaten. But somebody forgot to tell him he was dead and approved of by Allah. He got up and threw Adam twenty feet. He reared on his hind legs and

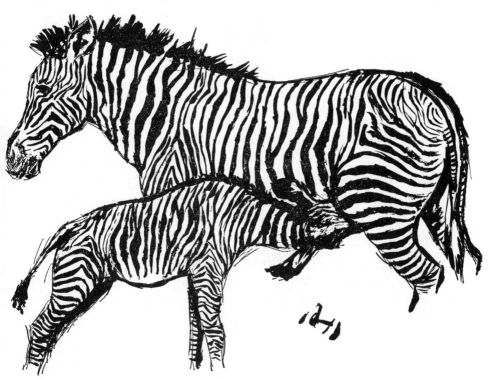

charged Selby and me. Harry was leaning against the open door of the jeep. I was leaning against the fender.

He was awful to see—bloody, fierce, making a stallion's angry fighting squeal with his mouth distended and those huge yellow teeth, which can snap off an arm, bared in an equine snarl and his mouth looking bigger and wider and fuller of teeth than any lion's. He was flailing the air with razor forefeet, each hoof capable of splitting your skull right down to your Adam's apple. And he had Selby trapped against the jeep, wedged against the door. He was biting at Selby's face and striking at him with hoofs, and Selby was yelling and shrinking backward into the jeep and trying to fend this monster off with one hand.

I ran round the front of the car and dived through the

back seat, diving horizontally like we used to dive in bar fights when I was young and full of orneriness in Hamburg and Antwerp and the tough sailor towns of the depression. On the way through the back seat I scooped up the .375 from the rack and pumped a bullet into the chamber as I dived. I stuck the barrel of the gun into the zebra's mouth and pulled the trigger, and the back of his head came off. This time he was *really kufa.* He fell forward on top of Selby, pushing Harry under the wheel of the jeep. There was Selby, wedged into his own car by a dead zebra, sitting there, looking ruffled and hurt-feelinged, with a lapful of dead *punda* whose gory head was laid lovingly on Selby's shoulder.

"Somebody get this goddamned creature off of me," Selby roared, his dignity shattered. And then we began to laugh.

The boys hurled themselves onto the ground and screamed with laughter. They ached with laughter. I fell down on the ground and began to hiccup with uncontrollable mirth. Finally Harry, still with a lapful of zebra, began to laugh, and the zebra's head moved up and down so it seemed he was laughing too.

The first hysteria played out a little, and the boys began to skin out the dead animal after dragging it out of the jeep and off the Bwana Haraka's lap. But one would say something to another, and then Harry would say something and the skinning would stop. The knives would be dropped and the entire pantomime of the semi-catastrophe would be re-acted, and everyone would fall on the ground and scream. It took an hour to skin out the zebra It usually takes fifteen minutes.

"Fancy," Harry said finally, the tears still streaming down his face and his sides hurting, "fancy the flap in the Queen's bar in Nairobi when the word spreads that old Selby, after all these years, had been done in by a bloody zebra. My family'd never live it down."

"It's sort of like being gored to death by a Tommy," I said.

"Or beaten to death by a dove," Harry said.

"Or nibbled to death by moths," I said.

"Or tickled to death with a feather duster," Harry said. "But suddenly you think: You're just as dead if a zebra bites you as you are if an elephant steps on you. Anything they've got here can kill you, from a snake to a thorn to lousy zebra. That's why this job is so interesting. It's the unexpected does you in."

There were some guinea fowl running down the track on the way in. Sentimentally, Kidogo had packed the shotty-gun 'Mkubwa for his friend, the Bwana Ndege, the Master of Birds. The Bird Master got out and chased the guineas and they flew, finally, and the Master of Birds missed with both barrels. All the boys fell out of the car again. We laughed all the way home—which as of that very moment was no longer home.

We headed down for Arusha to register the trophies, and in Babati they told us that Harry's friend, Tony Dyer, had been frightfully beaten up by a buff. We stopped in Arusha, the little Greeky-Englishy Arusha, registered the trophies with a fat Indian *babu* in the Game Department, and took the good fast road back to Nairobi. Nobody talked much. Virginia tried singing. She tried her parody about how skinned her knees, how tired her et cetera. She tried the *kanga*-in-the-donga-with-the-*panga* song. She even tried the hymn we had written in honor of the missionaries who seemed to have the finest hunting equipment in the world, fancy shooting cars, expensive rifles, fine scopes and cameras, and who seemed to spend more time on safari than they did in alleviating the plight of the poor natives. This one was called *"Taka* Headskin for the Lord" and was very funny. Nobody laughed.

"Shut up," I said. "I am a very sad man."

We stopped once near an anthill, which Virginia loved, and three giraffes, which she loved, walked up curiously to watch us. I looked at Virginia, and she was crying quietly.

All the way to Nairobi I kept feeling something familiar. I remembered suddenly: This was the way I felt when the Japs quit and the war was over and I was headed home. All the excitement and the dangerous security of the war were finished. Now it would be work and civilian frustration and complication again. All the neatness was gone with the war, all the feeling of complete fatalism was gone. Now the future was in my hands again. The Navy and fate were no longer responsible. If I got on a plane and it crashed and killed me I couldn't blame the Navy or fate. My *shauri mungu*—my God's work—was all over. That is how I felt as the jeep pressed on in the dust toward Nairobi, with old Annie Lorry, tractable for once, lumbering and creaking on behind us.

We hit Nairobi and found my friends, Tommy and Durie Shevlin, just back from an unsuccessful safari in Rhodesia or someplace, and Tony Dyer was there, limping around on crutches. Little Maureen at Ker and Downey's was just as pretty to look at, and there was a flock of other pleasant folk about. Old Zim, the taxidermist, oohed and ahed over the trophies, which were really quite fine and something to be proud of. Virginia bought a couple of leopard skins for some bags and shoes and a stole, and everybody drank a good deal too much. Harry's pretty airline hostesses were all over the place, and there was a party every night and one drunken South African Airlines pilot that I nearly had to slug but didn't.

None of it was any good. I was glad to leave. There was a part of me, of us, back there on a hill in Tanganyika, in a swamp in Tanganyika, in a tent and on a river and by a mountain in Tanganyika. There was a part of me out there that would stay out there until I came back to ransom that part of me. It would never live in a city again, that part of me, nor be content, the other part, to be in a city. There are no tiny-gleaming campfires in a city.

We got on the plane one day and pointed back to Paris and New York and work and cocktail parties and penthouses and expensive, fashionable saloons. Our first stop was in Addis Ababa. The natives were just as ugly, and there were even more flies than I remembered. I was sure New York would be worse.

END

December 5, 1952
At sea—en route to Nairobi, Kenya Colony
British East Africa